Daughters Of Destiny

A TREASURY OF HISTORICAL NARRATIVES,
LESSONS, AND POETRY
FOR DAUGHTERS YOUNG AND OLD

Compiled and Edited by Noelle Goforth

Dedicated to the virtuous women who have invested in my life.

To their daughters—the hope of the future.

And especially to my dear mother for her faithful example of service and self-sacrifice to her husband and children.

Contents

Introduction...7

CHAPTER 1

Daughters of Virtue

Beautiful Womanhood 11
Piety in the Truest Sense 12
Daughter's Duty to Parents 12
The Brother's Confidant 13
The Selfless Heart 13
Faithful Unto Death 15
What Our Country Needs 18

CHAPTER 2

Daughters of Home

The Cheery Home 21
Kind Words at Home 21
Smiles in the Home 22
Home Government 23
Home Religion and Family Prayers 24
Home 25
Home Sweet Home 25
Reveries in the Old Kitchen 26
Make Someone Happy 28
A Happy Home Defined 28
The Happy Home 29
The Happiest Home 29
Are All the Children In? 30

CHAPTER 3

Daughters of Strength

By Blazing Firelight .... Mrs. Shute 33
Alert at Her Post .... Mrs. Mack 36
Guardian of the Mohawk Valley ... Nancy Van Alstine 39

Mother of the Allegany Settlement ....Mrs. Jameson 44
The Flight For Life...Elizabeth Zane 49
Tried By Fire ....Mrs. Dalton 52
The Kentucky Amazon Woman ....Mrs. Merrill................. 62
The Suspicious Indian...Mrs. Parker................... 64
The Indian Girl Who Unlocked the Northwest.....Sacajawea 66
Mothers of the West.. 70

CHAPTER 4

Daughters of Service

Missionary to the Oneidas ....Jemima Kirkland.......... 75
The Devoted Missionary Wife.................................Ann H. Judson 77
The First Woman to Cross the Rockies ....Narcissa Whitman........ 86
Braving the Wilds of Oregon ....Mrs. White.................. 89
The Great "Ma" of Africa.......................................Mary Slessor................ 92
Your Mission.. 99

CHAPTER 5

Daughters of Royalty

Scotland's Angelic Queen ....Queen Margaret.......... 103
The Princess Who Dared ....Edith of Scotland....... 108
The Crown of Life ....Lady Jane Grey.......... 115
Princess of the Forest..Pocahontas.................. 124
Heir of Splendor..Queen Victoria 129

CHAPTER 6

Daughters of Stature

The Worthy Wife of Luther ....Catherine Von Bora .. 135
The Mother of Reformers...Susanna Wesley 146
Mother of the Father of Our Country...................Mary Washington 154
America's Most Gracious First Lady ....Dolly Madison 162

CHAPTER 7

Daughters of Liberty

The First Flag of Liberty...Betsy Ross................... 173
The Spy Who Saved the American Army .... Lydia Darrah 176

Guided By a Southern Girl .... Emma Sansom 177
The Daring Messenger .... Emily Geiger 180
The Heroine of Monmouth .... Molly Hays 181
Angel of the Battlefield .... Clara Barton 186

CHAPTER 8
Daughters of Lyrics

Nearer, My God, to Thee .... Sarah F. Adams 193
The Swedish Nightingale .... Jenny Lind 195
Blind and Content .... Francis Jane Crosby 201
Author of Elsie Dinsmore .... Martha Finley 208

CHAPTER 9
Daughters of Purpose

For the Want of a Bible .... Mary Jones 213
The Stormy Night Rescue .... Grace Darling 215
The Life-saver of Lime Rock Lighthouse .... Ida Lewis 218
Tragedy Turned to Triumph .... Anne Hughes 220
Heroism on the Darkest Day .... Mary McCann 223

CHAPTER 10
Daughters of Vision

They Call Her Blessed 227
Mother's Empire 233
The Controlled Mother ....:.. 234
A Mother's Opportunity 235
Care and Affection 236
They Who Mold the Men of Story 238
The Hand That Rules the World 239
Mothers the World Needs 240
True Loveliness 241
Mother's Elbows on My Bed 242
My Mother's Hands 244
I'd Rather 245
Mother 246
Mother! Mother! 247
Mother's Sacrifice 248
Benediction 249

Introduction

"For I know the plans I have for you, declares the LORD, plans to prosper you, and not to harm you, plans to give you hope and a future."
—Jeremiah 29:11

God has created everything on earth for a reason. He has a purpose for all of mankind. He knows our future—our destiny. He has established it. What a joy it is to know that everything is in the hands of the Creator of the universe. "How calmly may we commit our lives to the hands of Him who bears up the world."

You may be wondering what kind of a destiny God has in store for you. *Daughters of Destiny* sketches the lives of many noble women of the past and their heroic deeds that are worthy of being remembered. Though these daughters are no more, their testimonies still live on.

In examining the destiny of these women, we see one common thread woven throughout the pages of time. Created from Adam's rib, woman was meant from the beginning, to be by man's side; to be his loving companion; to encourage his heart—woman was destined to serve.

You may never reach the pages of recorded history; may never become famous; may never achieve great heights. But what is greatness? Jesus said, if we want to be great in God's kingdom, we must be a servant. Jesus came to earth to serve. He knelt down in humility and washed His disciples' feet. He laid down His very life for sinners. Self-sacrifice is the ultimate example of service.

Though young or old, man or woman, married or not, service is the destiny of mankind! It is not always the big things that prepare a person for life's purpose. David served his father in the sheep pasture before he became king and he defeated a lion and a bear before he defeated Goliath! True greatness begins in little things. A simple quote by Janet Erskine Stuart says it best: "Humility and service are the only expression and measure of greatness."

Are we willing to follow and obey the destiny of God's calling? Are we willing to serve in any and every capacity the Lord assigns us? Whatever comes our way, may we say, like the Virgin Mary, "behold the handmaid [servant] of the Lord; be it unto me according to Thy word."

As you read these pages, may you be blessed by the example of those women who have gone before us. **Daughters of Destiny** will give a glimpse into the lives of historic daughters who made themselves available to serve in ordinary daily life routines, little knowing that they were fulfilling a destiny of God's own purpose. May you become a daughter of destiny in service to our Lord and Savior, Jesus Christ.

"Let your light so shine before men, that they may see your good works [acts of service], and glorify your Father which is in heaven." —Matthew 5:16

CHAPTER ONE

Daughters of Virtue

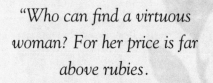

"Who can find a virtuous
woman? For her price is far
above rubies.

The heart of her husband
doth safely trust in her,
so that he shall have no
need of spoil.

She will do him good and not
harm all the days of her life."

Proverbs 31:10-12

Beautiful Womanhood

What is womanhood? Is there any more important question for young women to consider than this? It should be the highest ambition of every young woman to strive toward possessing a heart of true womanhood. Earth presents no higher object of attainment. To be a woman, in the truest and highest sense of the word, is to be the best thing beneath the skies. To be a woman is something more than to live eighteen or twenty years; something more than to grow to the physical stature of women; something more than to wear flounces, exhibit dry-goods, sport jewelry, catch the gaze of lewd-eyed men; something more than to be a beauty, a wife, or a mother. Put all these qualifications together and they do but little toward making a true woman.

Beauty and style are not the surest passports to womanhood—some of the noblest examples of womanhood in the world, have looked quite plain in outward appearance. A woman's worth is to be estimated by the real goodness of her heart, the greatness of her soul, and the purity and sweetness of her character; and a woman with a kindly disposition and well-balanced temper, is both lovely and attractive, even if her face is plain and her figure imperfect; she makes the best of wives and the truest of mothers. She has a higher purpose in living than the beautiful, yet vain and supercilious woman, who has no higher ambition than to flaunt her finery on the street, or to gratify her inordinate vanity by extracting flattery and praise from society, whose compliments are as hollow as they are insincere.

No gift from heaven is so general and so widely abused by woman as the gift of beauty. In many cases, it makes her thoughtless, giddy, vain, proud, frivolous, selfish, low and mean. I think I have seen more girls spoiled by beauty than by any other one thing. "She is beautiful, and she knows it," is as much as to say she is spoiled. A beautiful girl is very likely to believe she was made to be looked at. And believing and acting thus, she soon becomes good for nothing else, and when she comes to be a middle-aged woman she is that weakest, most sickening of all human things—a faded beauty. Outward beauty is shallow—only skin-deep; fleeting—only reigning for a season. But inward beauty will last forever.

If you desire to be admired and beloved, be an example of beautiful womanhood and cultivate the virtues of the heart. Wealth may surround you with its blandishments, and beauty, learning, or talents, may give you admirers, but love and kindness alone can captivate the heart. Whether you live in a cottage or a palace, these graces can surround you with perpetual sunshine, making you, and all those around you, happy.

Seek then, fair daughters, the possession of that inward grace, whose essence shall fragrance and vitalize the affections, adorn the countenance, make sweet the voice, and impart a hallowed beauty throughout your very being.

Piety In The Truest Sense

Piety is a word of Latin origin, and, among the old Romans who first used it, meant: that spirit of dutiful and generous love with which children do the will and seek the interests of their parents. The happiness of true-hearted children consists in seeking how they can best please and honor father and mother: what they do is not dictated by the fear of punishment or the hope of reward or the prospect of gain or self-gratification, but with the hope or certainty of delighting or pleasing or helping the dear authors of their being.

Daughters in many families are so noble-minded, that they are content to labor untiringly for their parents. They place their whole delight in doing all they can to lighten the burden of father and mother, and to make the home bright and pleasant for brothers and sisters, without seeking or expecting one word of praise and acknowledgment. This is the best description of filial piety.

Only transfer to God's service that same unselfish and generous disposition. Ask yourself how much you can do to please Him, to glorify Him, to make yourself worthy of Him, to make Him known, and have Him loved and served by others. Then you will have an idea of what piety toward God is.

The daughter accustomed to keeping God before her eyes, in all her ways, cannot help being pious in the truest sense: nothing can prevent her from seeking, in all that she does, the ultimate pleasure of Christ.

Daughter's Duty To Parents

The daughter is to honor both her father and mother. She is to seek ways to please her father and to serve him. But, she should learn that next to her duty to God, comes duty to helping mother serve the household—and thus prepare for the future.

An old proverb says that the son is son till he is married, but the daughter is daughter forever. Though the daughter leaves the parental roof when she gets

married, she is still followed by kindly regards. A good daughter is the steady light of her parent's house. Her father's memory is forever connected with that of his happy fireside. She is his morning sunlight—his evening star.

The Brother's Confidant

A good sister's love always holds a cherished place in the grateful memory of the brother! Many men have found a sister's love their ready and cheering resource. His confidence is set in her counsel and he is satisfied with the assurance that it will be uprightly and considerately given. How intimate is the friendship of such sisters! What a reliance for warning, excitement, and sympathy has each secured in each! How many are the brothers to whom, when thrown into circumstances of temptation, the thought of a sister's love has been a constant, holy presence, rebuking every wayward thought!

The relation of brothers and sisters forms another important element in the happy influences of home. A boisterous or a selfish boy may try to domineer over the weaker or more dependent girl, but generally the latter exerts a softening, sweetening charm. The brother animates and heartens; the sister mollifies, tames, refines. The vine-tree and its sustaining elm are the emblems of such a relation—and by such agencies our "sons may become like plants grown up in their youth, and our daughters like cornerstones polished after the similitude of a temple."

Sisters scarcely know the influence they have over their brothers. A young man once testified that the greatest proof to the truth of Christian religion was his sister's life.

The Selfless Heart

"WHAT DO WE LIVE FOR, IF IT IS NOT TO MAKE LIFE LESS DIFFICULT FOR EACH OTHER."

GEORGE ELIOT

Woman's entire existence, in order to be a source of happiness to others as well as to herself, must be one of self-sacrifice. The first step in this royal pathway to all goodness and greatness, is to forget self. Self, with its miserable little cares and affections, is the root of all the wretchedness we cause to others, and all the misery we endure ourselves. Every effort we make to forget self, to leave self behind us, and to devote ourselves to the labor of making every person with whom we live with, happy, is rewarded by inner satisfaction and joy. The first step to becoming unselfish is to forget one's own comfort in order to seek that of others; the next, is to forget one's own pains and suffering, in order to alleviate those of others.

What we need most, are benevolent wives, mothers, and sisters in the dwellings of our over-burdened laborers. We need women for whom the roof above them and the four walls which enclose their dear ones are the only world they care to know. We need women who set their hearts on making their homes pleasant, sunny, and fragrant for the husband. He who works from dawn till dusk for the little home and the wife and babes, looks forward to the warm welcome that awaits him when the long day is over; of the bright smile and the loving words that will be sure to greet him when he crosses the threshold of his own little Eden; of the cheerful fire in winter and the humble meal made so delicious by the love that prepares it and the sweet words that season it. This rest, security, and peace will encourage the overflowing heart of the husband and father and brother to think and to say that there is no spot of earth so dear and so blessed as the little sanctuary built up and adorned and made full of song by a true woman's heart.

O woman, if you only knew how much you have it in your ability, with Christ's unfailing assistance, to make true men of your chosen husband and sons, as well as true women of the little girls who will someday fill your apron.

The matrimonial union has its model in the union of Christ with his Church. His great love for her is the type of the great and self-devoting love which husband and wife should ever have for each other. Did you ever reflect, that when you put your hand in your husband's hand before the Church—giving him your heart and your life till death—that God has promised to be ever by the side of those who believe and trust in Him. Such grace enables you to love your husband more and more daily, with a deeper and a holier love, taking up his cross courageously, and cheering him to labor and to suffer, because you both know that God is ever with you.

No matter how poor the woman's home is or how hard her husband's lot, the true, selfless woman will cheer his heart, and so lighten his burden. May the quote of Shakespeare be constantly on her tongue:

"My heart is ever at your service."

Faithful Unto Death

The first duty of the wife is to study to be, in every way she can, the companion, the help mate, and the friend of her husband. All the happiness of both their lives, as well as the well-being of the whole family, depends on her earnest fulfillment of this threefold function.

One half of the unhappiness of married life comes from the fact that the wife is either unfitted or unwilling to be a true companion to her husband. This companionship requires that she should be suited by her qualities of mind and heart and temper to enter into her husband's thoughts and tastes and amusements, so as to make him find in her company and conversation a perfect contentment and delight.

Persons who are perfectly companionable never weary of each other,—indeed, they are never perfectly happy while away from each other. They enter into each other's thoughts, reflect the light in each other's mind, cultivate the same tastes, pursue the same ideals, and complete each other in original or acquired knowledge.

But there is more than that in the companionship of the true wife. She studies to make herself agreeable, delightful, and even indispensable to him who is her choice among all men.

There are wives who will study certain languages, sciences, arts, or accomplishments, in order to make themselves the companions of the men they love. Thus they are able to converse with them on the things they love most, or can bless the hours of home repose by music and song.

One young lady perseveringly applied herself to study the sign-language of the deaf-mutes in order to converse easily with her husband—a wealthy young merchant, thoroughly trained himself in the deaf and dumb institution of his native city. They were devoted to each other, and the young wife's earnestness in making herself companionable to her husband, must have brought many a blessing of virtue and bright hope on the home.

It must not be concluded from this, that a woman should thoroughly master either a language, a science, or an art. The word helpful, will furnish to every wife the true measure of the knowledge she may be prompted to acquire. Her husband has to know perfectly whatever he knows, because his success as a professional man or a business man depends on this thorough knowledge; his wife only aspires to please and to help her companion.

But there are other things beside this scientific, literary, or artistic knowledge, which may be more needful to a wife, if she would make herself the most delightful and necessary companion to her husband. She must study him—his needs, his moods, his weak as well as his strong points. She must know how to make him forget himself when he is moody and selfish, and bring out every joyous side of his nature when he is prone to sadness. God, who has united husband and wife in the duties and burdens of home-life, wills that they should complete each other. Man has bodily strength, because it is his duty to labor for the home and protect it; he has also certain mental and moral qualities which woman does not need, and which fit him for the battle of life and his continual struggle with the crowd. But she has, on her part, far more fortitude to bear and to forbear, to suffer silently and uncomplainingly while ministering with aching heart and head to the comfort, the cheerfulness, the happiness of all around her.

Do you not know that all men, even old men, even the proudest and coldest men, are only great children, who thirst for praise from a wife, a mother, or a sister? Man's heart is stirred through all its depths by one sweet word from her lips. Why O women, are you so stingy of a money which you can bestow without making yourselves the poorer, and which your dear ones prize above gold and gems?

Give generously, but discerningly, that which will only encourage those you love above all the world to strive tomorrow for still higher excellence, and look forward to still sweeter praise. Both husband and wife are necessary to each other. They ought to have but one heart and one mind in the pursuit of the happiness of their home and in the rearing children whom God sends them.

Where the wife labors conscientiously to be a true companion to her husband, there is little fear but she will also become a true, faithful, and constant friend. The reasons which will urge every right-minded and truehearted woman to be the most delightful and constant of companions and the most devoted of helpmates, must also inspire her with the resolution of being the most cherished of friends. She must not be jealous of the men for whom her husband entertains feelings of real friendship. On the contrary, she should show them every mark of regard, as if she were thereby the interpreter of his dearest wishes. Nothing pleases a man more than to see his old and true friends warmly acknowledged and treated with all honor and affection by the persons most dear to him.

But when companions fail him, and discouragement and difficulty block his way, it is the wife's calling to come to his aid—the husband's truest and most faithful friend.

"A man wished to make a pilgrimage to Cologne. He was a wealthy man, but not a wise one. He had an admirable wife, whose worth he knew not, and whose company he neglected for that of two neighbors, who played friends with him because he was rich and lavish of his money. As he was setting out on his pilgrimage, he asked his friends what he should bring them from Cologne. One answered that he would like a rich cloak, and the other begged him to buy a tunic of rare stuff. He next asked his wife what he should get for her, and she besought him to bring back sense and wisdom which might enable him to see and correct the evil of his ways.

He went among the merchants, bought the cloak and the tunic, but sought in vain for some one who would sell him sense and wisdom. They were not to be found in the market. As he returned crestfallen to his inn, the host inquired why he seemed downcast. When he learned the cause, he advised him on his return home to pretend to his friends that he had lost all his money and could give them neither cloak nor tunic. He returned home and followed this piece of advice, and both the false friends turned him out of doors, abusing him as a fool and a vagabond.

Not so his wife, however. He told her the story of his loss; but she, seeing that he was weary from the road and filled with sorrow and indignation because of this ill treatment, tenderly embraced him, consoled and refreshed him, assured him that God would send him heavenly treasures for the money he had lost. His eyes were opened to know what wealth he possessed in her true love and faithful friendship; and thus did he find sense and wisdom from having visited the city of Cologne."

WRITTEN IN THE MIDDLE AGES BY JOANNES, MAGNUM SPECULUM

"*Chivalry, to the original purity and power of which we owe the defense alike of faith, of law, and of love. . . assumes that in this rapturous obedience to the single love of his youth, is the sanctification of all man's strength, and the continuance of all his purposes. You cannot think that the buckling on of the knight's armor by his lady's hand was a mere caprice of romantic fashion. It is the type of an eternal truth—that the soul's armor is never well set to the heart unless a woman's hand has braced it; and it is only when she braces it loosely that the honor of manhood fails.*"—RUSKIN

Let every true wife daily brace more and more tightly round her husband's heart, the armor of the old principles which made our fathers invincible in their long battle against error and wrong. The honor of manhood will not fail among us, so long as every wife and mother aims at being the truest helpmate.

> "As unto the bow the cord is,
>
> So unto the man is woman:
>
> Though she bends him she obeys him;
>
> Though she draws him, yet she follows;
>
> Useless each without the other."
>
> *H.W. LONGFELLOW*

What Our Country Needs

What does our country need? Not armies standing

With sabres gleaming ready for the fight;

Not increased navies, skillful and commanding,

To bound the waters with an iron might;

Not haughty men with glutted purses trying

To purchase souls, and keep the power of place;

Not jeweled dolls with one another vying

For palms of beauty, elegance, and grace.

But we want women, strong of soul, yet lowly

With that rare meekness, born of gentleness;

Women whose lives are pure and clean and holy,

The women whom all little children bless;

Brave, earnest women, helpful to each other,

With finest scorn for all things low and mean;

Women who hold the names of wife and mother

Far nobler than the title of a queen.

UNKNOWN

CHAPTER TWO

Daughters
of
Home

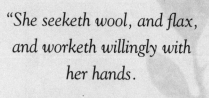

"She seeketh wool, and flax,
and worketh willingly with
her hands.

She is like the merchants'
ships; she bringeth her food
from afar.

She riseth while it is yet
night, and giveth meat to her
household, and a portion to
her maidens."

Proverbs 31:13-15

The Cheery Home

Thank God, O woman, for the quietude of your home, and that you are queen in it. Men come at eventide to the home; but all day long you are there, beautifying it, sanctifying it, adorning it, blessing it. Better be there than wear Victoria's crown. Better be there than carry the purse of a princess. It may be a very humble home. There may be no carpet on the floor. There may be no pictures on the wall. There may be no silks in the wardrobe; but, by your faith in God, and your cheerful demeanor, you may adorn that place with more splendor than the upholsterer's hand ever kindled.

The cheerful woman makes herself more attractive, the meal more presentable, and her whole house sparkle with fresh scents of her daily cleaning. Her whole house shines with the sweet music of her own delighted tones to welcome the laborer at evening. Ah! love has stores from which can be borrowed at little cost kind words and warm smiles and a thousand other things which go straight to the heart thirsting for the endearments, the joys, and the repose of home.

Young people who are employed outside of their home, feel an imperative need of the rest and comfort and love of their own fireside, when the end of the long day of toil has come. Blessed is the wife and mother who knows how to make the home bright and warm for all who enter!

Kind Words At Home

Speak kindly in the morning; it lightens the cares of the day, and makes the household and all other affairs move along more smoothly.

Speak kindly at night, for it may be that before the dawn some loved one may finish his or her space of life, and it will be too late to ask forgiveness.

Speak kindly at all times; it encourages the downcast, cheers the sorrowing, and very likely awakens the erring to earnest resolves to do better, with strength to keep them.

Kind words are balm to the soul. They oil up the entire machinery of life, and keep it in good running order.

Smiles In The Home

"WHEN YOU GIVE, GIVE WITH JOY, SMILING." *JOUBERT*

If people will only notice, they will be amazed to find how much a really enjoyable evening owes to smiles. But few consider what an important symbol of fine intellect and fine feeling they are. Yet all smiles, after childhood, are things of education. Coarse, brutal, cruel men may laugh, but they seldom smile. The richness, the blessing, the radiance, which fills the silence like a speech, is the smile of a full appreciative heart.

The face that grows finer as it listens, and then breaks into sunshine instead of words, has a subtle, charming influence, universally felt. Let your cheerfulness be felt for good wherever you are and let your smiles be scattered like sunbeams "on the just as well as on the unjust." Such a disposition will yield a rich reward, for its happy effects will come home to you and brighten your moments of thought. Cheerfulness makes the mind clear, gives tone to thought, and adds grace and beauty to the countenance. Joubert says, "When you give, give with joy, smiling."

Smiles are little things, cheap articles to be fraught with so many blessings, both to the giver and the receiver—pleasant little ripples to watch as we stand on the shore of every-day life. These are the higher and better responses of nature to the emotion of the soul. Let the children have the benefit of them—those little ones who need the sunshine of the heart to educate them, and would find a level for their buoyant nature in the cheerful, loving faces of those who need them. Let them not be kept from the middle-aged, who need the encouragement they bring. Give your smiles also to the aged. They come to them like the quiet rain of summer, making fresh and verdant the long, weary path of life. They look for them from you, who are rejoicing in the fullness of life.

Your face is to light up and brighten and beautify all things, and your heart is to be the source of that vital fire and strength. If your seat is hard to sit upon, stand up. If a rock rises up before you, roll it away, or climb over it. If you want money, earn it. It takes longer to skin an elephant than a mouse, but the skin is worth something. If you want confidence, prove yourself worthy of it. Do not be content with doing what another has done—surpass it. Deserve success, and it will come. The boy was not born a man. The sun does not rise like a rocket, or go down like a bullet fired from a gun; slowly and surely it makes its round, and never tires. It is as easy to be a lead horse as a wheel horse. If the job be long, the pay will be greater; if the task be hard, the more competent you must be to do it.

Encourage the bright spirit in your child; let its soul sing with all its strength while it may. The keen zest for enjoyment must be encouraged and directed. It is a blessed privilege for the mother to minister in every way she can to the delight and amusement of her dear ones. And one of the most beneficial industries of motherhood is to provide all manner of sport and recreation for her children at home, and to see to it that they feast their senses on garden and field and park and forest as often as possible.

But, most of all, set God before the mind of youth, then you will know how to make the spirit of your children joyous by teaching them that the life of heaven is joy without end. The beautiful things with which their Maker has surrounded them in, are only faint images of the beauties with which the infinite magnificence has decked out his and our eternal home.

But, O woman—whether you live in a palace or in a hovel—if your chief care be to have God ever live in your heart, His light within you will shed such unearthly beauty on all things. You will make your loved ones see a fairy palace in this world, in spite of your own poverty and your life of hard labor. So, keep that light ever full in your family's soul.

The chief aim in your sharing all joys and amusements with your dear ones should be to make them feel that your presence, your love is for them the source of all present happiness, and that they can come to your arms, to your heart at all hours.

Home Government

Home government is to watch anxiously for the first risings of sin, and to repress them; to counteract the earliest workings of selfishness; to repress the first beginnings of rebellion against rightful authority; to teach an implicit and unquestioning and cheerful obedience to the will of the parent. This earthly compliance is the best preparation for submitting to the laws of the great Ruler and Father in heaven.

Home government is to punish a fault because it is a fault, because it is sinful, and contrary to the command of God, without reference to whether it may or may not have been productive of immediate injury to the parent or others. It is to reprove with calmness and composure, and not with angry irritation,—in a few words fitly chosen, and not with a torrent of abuse. It is to punish as often as you threaten, and to threaten only when you intend and can remember to perform; to say what you mean, and infallibly do as you say.

It is to govern your family as in the sight of Him who gave you authority, and who will reward your strict fidelity with such blessings as he bestowed on Abraham.

Home Religion And Family Prayers

House may be full of persons who are very dear and kind to each other, full of affections hopes, and living interests; but if God is not there as the Ruler and Father of the house, the original and true idea of home will not be realized. Vacancy and need will still be at the heart of all. Good things will grow feebly and uncertainly, like flowers in winter, trying to peep out into sunshine, yet shrinking from the blast. Evil things will grow with strange persistency, not withstanding protests of the affections and efforts of the will. Mysterious gulfs will open at times where it was thought strong foundations had been laid. Little things will produce great distress. Great things, when attained, will shrink to littleness. Flickerings of uncertainty and fear will run along the days. Joys will not satisfy. Sorrow will surprise.

Family prayers is a custom held in honor wherever there is real Christian life, and it is the one thing which, more than any other, knits together the loose threads of a home and unites its various members before God. The short religious service in which parents, children, and friends daily join in praise and prayer, is at once an acknowledgment of dependence on the heavenly Father and a renewal of consecration to his work in the world. The Bible is read, the hymn is sung, the petition is offered. The sick and the absent are remembered, the tempted and the tried are commended to God, and, as the Israelites in the desert were attended by the pillar and the cloud, so in life's wilderness the family who inquire of the Lord are constantly overshadowed by his presence and love. Unless all has been done as a mere formality and without hearty assent, those who have gathered at the family altar leave it helped, soothed, strengthened, and armored, as they were not before they met there.

There are many interferences which are allowed to thrust aside the privilege of family prayer in homes where father and mother mean to have it daily. Whatever comes in the way ought to be set aside. If any among our readers recognize the need to have a daily open worship of God in their home, let them begin it at once. They must make the time, choose the place, and appoint the way. The actual time spent in worship may be a few minutes only. A brief service

which cannot tire the youngest child, in the morning when the day begins, and in the evening when its active labors close, is far more useful and edifying than a long service which fatigues attention.

It is possible to have a daily worship which shall be earnest, vivifying, tender and reverential, and yet a weariness to nobody. Only let the one who conducts it maintain the attitude of one who goes about earthly affairs with a soul looking beyond and above them to the rest that remaineth in heaven.

Home

'Tis whispered in the ear of God,

'Tis murmured through our tears;

'Tis linked with happy childhood days,

And blessed in riper years.

That hallowed word is ne'er forgot,

No matter where we roam,

The purest feelings of the heart,

Still cluster round our home.

Dear resting-place, where weary thought

May dream away its care,

Love's gentle star reveals her light,

And shines in beauty there.

FANNY CROSBY

Home, Sweet Home!

'Mid pleasures and palaces though we may roam,

Be it ever so humble, there's no place like home!

A charm from the skies seems to follow us there,

Which, seek through the world, is ne'er met with else where.

Home, home! Sweet home! There's no place like home!

An exile from home, splendor dazzles in vain;

O, give me my lowly thatched cottage again!

The birds singing gaily, that came at my call:

Give me these, and the peace of mind dearer than all.

Home, home! Sweet home! There's no place like home!

JOHN HOWARD PAYNE

Reveries Of The Old Kitchen

Far back in my musings my thoughts have been cast

To the cot where the hours of my childhood were passed;

I loved all its rooms to the pantry and hall,

But that blessed old kitchen was dearer than all.

Its chairs and its table none brighter could be,

And all its surroundings were sacred to me—

To the nail in the ceiling, the latch on the door,

And I love every crack on the old kitchen floor.

I remember the fire-place with mouth high and wide,

The old-fashioned oven that stood by its side,

Out of which, each Thanksgiving, came puddings and pies,

That fairly bewildered and dazzled my eyes.

And then, too, St. Nicholas, slyly and still,

Came down every Christmas our stockings to fill;
But the dearest of memories I've laid up in store,
Is the mother that trod on the old kitchen floor.

Day in and day out, from morning till night,
Her footsteps were busy, her heart always light,
For it seemed to me then, that she knew not a care,
The smile was so gentle her face used to wear;
I remember with pleasure what joy filled our eyes,
When she told us the stories that children so prize;
They were new every night, though we'd heard them before
From her lips, at the wheel, on the old kitchen floor.

I remember the window, where mornings I'd run
As soon as the daybreak, to watch for the sun;
And thought, when my head scarcely reached to the sill,
That it slept through the night in the trees on the hill,
And the small tract of ground that my eyes there could view
Was all of the world that my infancy knew;
Indeed, I cared not to know of it more,
For a world of itself was that old kitchen floor.

Tonight those old visions come back at their will,
But the wheel and its music forever are still;
The band is moth-eaten, the wheel laid away,
And the fingers that turned it lie mold'ring in clay;
The hearthstone, so sacred, is just as 'twas then,

And the voices of children ring out there again;

The sun through the window looks in as of yore,

But it sees strange feet on the old kitchen floor.

I ask not for honor, but this I would crave,

That when the lips speaking are closed in the grave,

My children would gather theirs round by their side,

And tell of the mother who long ago died:

'Twould be more enduring, far dearer to me,

Than inscription on granite or marble could be,

To have them tell often, as I did of yore,

Of the mother who trod on the old kitchen floor.

UNKNOWN

Make Someone Happy

"That is a good day in which you make someone happy. It is astonishing how little it takes to make one happy. Feel that the day is wasted in which you have not succeeded in this."

T. DE WITT TALMAGE

A Happy Home Defined

"Six things are requisite to create a happy home. Integrity must be the architect, and tidiness the upholsterer. It must be warmed by affection, and lightened up with cheerfulness, and industry must be the ventilator, renewing the atmosphere and bringing in fresh salubrity day by day; while over all, as a protecting canopy and glory, nothing will suffice except the blessings of God."

REV. DR. HAMILTON

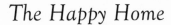

The Happy Home

Happy home! O, bright and cheerful hearth!

Look round with me, my lover, friend, and wife,

On these fair faces we have lit with life,

And in the perfect blessing of their birth,

Help me to live our thanks for so much heaven on earth.

MARTIN F. TUPPER

The Happiest Home

Where is the happiest home on earth?

'Tis not 'mid scenes of noisy mirth;

But where God's favor, sought aright,

Fills every breast with joy and light.

The richest home? It is not found

Where wealth and splendor most abound;

But wheresoe'er, in hall or cot,

Men live contented with their lot.

The fairest home? It is not placed

In scenes with outward beauty graced;

But where kind words and smiles impart

A constant sunshine to the heart.

On such a home of peace and love

God showers his blessing from above;

And angels, watching o'er it, cry,

"Lo! this is like our home on high!"

M. A. S. M.

Are All The Children In?

The darkness falls, the wind is high,

Dense black clouds fill the western sky;

The storm will soon begin.

The thunders roar, the lightnings flash,

I hear the great round rain-drops dash—

Are all the children in?

They're coming softly to my side;

Their forms within my arms I hide—

No other arms as sure.

The storm may rage with fury wild,

With trusting faith each little child

With mother feels secure.

But future days are drawing near—

They'll go from this warm shelter here,

Out in the world's wild din.

The rain will fall, the cold winds blow;

I'll sit alone and long to know,

Are all the children in.

MRS. S. T. PERRY

CHAPTER THREE

Daughters of Strength

"She considereth a field, and buyeth it: with the fruit of her hands she planteth a vineyard.

She girdeth her loins with strength, and strengtheneth her arms.

She perceiveth that her mer-chandise is good: her candle goeth not out by night.

She layeth her hands to the spindle, and her hands hold the distaff."

Proverbs 31:16-19

By Blazing Firelight

MRS. SHUTE

The life of the pioneer woman was hard, and its scope was narrow, but that scope was filled to its utmost bound with the nobility of duty and bravery. Here was no timid shrinking from a harmless mouse, no fainting at a tiny spider, no real or pretended fright at the attack of a flock of geese, but an eye that gazed unflinchingly on danger, and a heroic courage that did not falter at the thought of death.

Instead of fainting at the sight of blood, these women could act when the need came, and bind up the wounds of husband, father or lover. Here was the field where, instead of shuddering at the rifle's sound, a woman's hand should dextrously load, and if the worst came, she should be able to surely aim and fire the unerring weapon of the frontier.

How truly the border heroine played her part in the awful drama of the early settlement of the West. How uncomplainingly she endured hardships. How bravely she suffered the pains and horrors of captivity, and how nobly she submitted to the decrees of her lot when often, in a single night, she was made homeless, husbandless and childless.

Though dreary their lives, and familiar with peril rather than pleasure, their souls were noble, their hearts steadfast, and their actions irreproachable. They may have been unlettered, and untaught in frivolous accomplishments, but truly feminine they were for all that. Themselves the daughters of heroes, they perpetuated a race of courageous men and true-hearted women.

In the spring of 1676, James Shute, with his wife and two small children, set out from Dorchester for the purpose of settling themselves on a tract of land in the southern part of what is now New Hampshire, but which then was an unbroken forest. The piece of land where they intended to make their home was a meadow on the banks of the Connecticut River.

Taking their household goods and farming tools in an oxcart drawn by four oxen and driving two cows before them, they reached their destination after a toilsome journey of ten days. The summer was spent in building their cabin, and outhouses, planting and tending the crop of Indian corn which was to be their winter's food, and in cutting the coarse meadow-grass for hay.

Late in October they found themselves destitute of many articles which were of prime necessity. Accordingly, the husband started on foot for a small trading-post on the Connecticut River, about ten miles distant, at which point he expected to find some barge to take him to Springfield, thirty-eight miles further south. By nightfall Shute had reached the river, and before sunrise the next morning was floating down the stream on an Indian trader's skiff.

Within two days he made his purchases, and hiring a skiff, rowed slowly up the river against the sluggish current on his return. In twelve hours he reached the trading-post. It was now late in the evening. The sky had been lowering all day, and by dusk it began to snow. Disregarding the admonitions of the traders, he left his goods under their care and struck out boldly through the forest over the trail by which he came, trusting to be able to find his way, as the moon had risen, and the clouds seemed to be breaking. The trail lay along the stream on which his farm was situated, and four hours at an easy gait he thought would bring him home.

The snow, when he started from the river, was already nearly a foot deep, and before he had proceeded a mile on his way, the storm redoubled in violence, and the snow fell faster and faster. At midnight he had only made five miles; and the snow was two feet deep. It had been agreed between his wife and himself that on the evening of this day on which he told her he should return, he would kindle a fire on a knoll about two miles from his cabin as a beacon to assure his wife of his safety and announce his approach. After trying in vain to kindle a fire by the aid of flint and steel, he prayed fervently to God, and resuming his journey, struggled slowly on through the storm.

Suddenly he saw a glare in the sky.

During his absence, his wife had tended the cattle, milked the cows, cut the firewood, and fed the children. When night came she barricaded the door. Saying a prayer, she folded her little ones in her arms and lay down to rest. Three days had passed since she saw her husband disappear through the clearing into the dense undergrowth which fringed the bank of the stream. When the appointed evening came, she seated herself at the narrow window, or, more properly, opening in the logs of which the cabin was built, and watched for the beacon which her husband was to kindle. She looked through the falling snow but could see no light. Little drifts sifted through the chinks in the roof upon the bed where her children lay asleep; the night grew darker, and now and then the howling of the wolves could be heard from the woods to the north.

Seven o'clock struck—eight—nine—by the old Dutch clock which ticked in the corner. Then her woman's instinct told her that her husband must have started and been overtaken by the storm. If she could reach the knoll and kindle the fire, it would light him on his way. She quickly collected a small bundle of dry wood in her apron and taking flint, steel, and kindle, started for the knoll. In an hour, after a toilsome march, floundering through the snow, she reached the spot. A large pile of dry wood had already been collected by her husband and was ready for lighting, and in a few moments the heroic woman was warming her shivering limbs before a fire which blazed far up through the crackling branches and lighted the forest around it.

For more than two hours the devoted woman watched beside the fire, straining her eyes into the gloom and catching every sound. Wading through the snow, she brought branches and logs to replenish the flames. At last her patience was rewarded: she heard a cry, to which she responded. It was the voice of her husband which she heard shouting. In a few moments, he came up staggering through the drifts, and fell exhausted before the fire. The snow soon ceased to fall, and after resting till morning, the rescued pioneer and his brave wife returned in safety to their cabin.

Alert At Her Post

MRS. MACK

During the French and Indian War, and while the northern border was being desolated by savage raids, a hardy settler named Mack, with his wife and two children, occupied a cabin and clearing in the forest a few miles south of Lake Pleasant, in Hamilton County, New York. For some months after the breaking out of the war the Mack family had not been bothered, probably due to their shielded surroundings. Encouraged by this immunity from attack, and placing unbounded confidence in the vigilance and courage of his wife, Mr. Mack, when summoned to accompany Sir William Johnson's forces on one of their military expeditions, obeyed the call and prepared to join his fellow-borderers. Mrs. Mack cheerfully and patriotically acquiesced in her husband's resolution, assuring him that during his absence she would protect their home and children or perish in the attempt.

The cabin was a fortress, such as befitted the exposed situation in which it lay, and was supplied by Mr. Mack before his departure with provisions and ammunition sufficient to stand a siege. It was furnished on each side with a loop-hole through which a gun could be fixed or a survey could be made in every direction.

Yielding to the dictates of prudence and desirous of redeeming the pledge which she had made to her husband, Mrs. Mack stayed within doors most of the time for some days after her husband had bade her farewell, keeping a vigilant look-out on every side for the prowling foe. No sound but the voices of nature disturbed the stillness of the forest. Everything around spoke of peace and repose. Lulled into security by these appearances and urged by the necessities of her outdoor duties, she gradually relaxed her vigilance until she pursued the labors of the farm with as much regularity as she would have done if her husband had been at home.

One day while plucking ears of corn for roasting, she caught a glimpse of a moccasin and a brawny limb fringed with leggings, projecting behind a clump of bushes not twenty paces from her. Repressing the shriek which rose to her lips, she quietly and leisurely strolled back to the house with her basket of ears. Once she thought she heard the stealthy tread of the savage behind her and was about to break into a run; but a moment's reflection convinced her that her fears were groundless. She steadily pursued her course till she reached the cabin. With a vast weight of fear taken from her mind she now turned and cast a rapid glance towards the bushes where the foe lay in ambush. Nothing was visible there, and having closed and barred the door she peered through each of the four loop-holes of her fortress, but saw nothing to alarm her.

It seemed to her probable that it was only a single prowling savage who was seeking an opportunity to plunder the cabin. Accordingly with a loaded gun by her side, she sat down before the loop-hole which commanded the spot where the savage lay concealed and watched for further developments. For two hours all was still and she began to imagine that he had left his hiding place, when she noticed a rustling in the bushes and soon after descried the savage crawling on his belly and disappearing in the cornfield. Night found her still watching, and as soon as her children had been lulled to sleep, she returned to her post and straining her eyes into the darkness, listened for the faintest sound that might give note of the approach of the enemy. It was near midnight when overcome with fatigue she leaned against the log wall and fell asleep with her gun in her hand.

She was conscious, even in her slumbers, of someone watching her. Awakening with a start, she saw for an instant a pair of snaky eyes looking directly into hers through the loop-hole. They were gone before she was fairly awake, and she tried to convince herself that she had been dreaming. Not a sound was audible, and after taking an observation from each of the loop-holes, she became persuaded that the fierce eyes that seemed to have been watching her was the figment of a brain disturbed by anxiety and vigils.

Once more sleep overcame her and again she was awakened by a rattling sound followed by heavy breathing. The noise seemed to proceed from the chimney to which she had scarcely began to direct her attention, when a large body fell with a thud into the ashes of the fire-place, and a deep guttural "ugh" was uttered by an Indian who rose and peered around the room.

The first flickering light which follows the blackness of midnight, gave him a glimpse of the heroic woman who stood with her piece cocked and leveled directly at his breast. Waving his tomahawk, he rushed towards her yelling so as to disconcert her aim. But the brave woman with unshaken nerves pulled the trigger, and the savage fell, dead upon the floor. Almost simultaneously with the report of the gun, a triumphant warwhoop was sounded outside the cabin, and peering through the aperture in the direction from which it proceeded she saw three savages rushing toward the door. Rapidly loading her piece, she took her position at the loop-hole that commanded the entrance to the cabin, and taking aim, shot one savage dead, the ball passing completely through his body and wounding another who stood in range. The third made a hasty retreat, leaving his wounded comrade who crawled into the cornfield and there died.

After the occurrence of these events we may well suppose that the life of Mrs. Mack was one of constant vigilance. For some days and nights she stood sentinel over her little ones, and then in her dread lest the Indians should return and take vengeance upon her and her children for the slaughter of their companions, she concluded the wisest course would be to take refuge in the nearest fort thirty miles distant. Accordingly the following week she made all her preparations and carrying her gun started for the fort with her children.

Before they had proceeded a mile on their course she had the misfortune to drop her powder-horn in a stream: this compelled her to return to the cabin for ammunition. Hiding her children in a dense copse and telling them to preserve silence during her absence, she hastened back, filled her powder-horn and returned rapidly upon her trail.

But what was her agony on discovering that her children were missing from the place where she left them! A brief scrutiny of the ground showed her the tracks of moccasins, and following them she soon ascertained that her children had been carried away by two Indians. Like the tigress robbed of her young, she followed the trail swiftly but cautiously and soon came upon the savages, whose speed had been slowed by the children. Stealing behind them she shot one of them and clubbing her gun rushed at the other with such fierceness that he turned and fled.

Pursuing her way to the fort, with her reclaimed children, she met her husband returning home from the war. The family then retraced their steps and reached their home, the scene of Mrs. Mack's heroic exploit.

Guardian of The Mohawk Valley

Nancy Van Alstine

The traveler of today, passing up the Mohawk Valley will be struck by its fertility, beauty, and above all by the air of quiet repose that broods over it. One hundred years ago how different the scene! It was then the battle-ground where the fierce Indians waged an incessant warfare with the frontier settlers. The people who then inhabited that region were a mixture of adventurous New Englanders and Dutchmen, with a prevalence of the latter, who were a brave, steadfast, hardy race.

Womanly tact and presence of mind was often as serviceable amid those scenes of danger and carnage, as valor in combat. When woman combined these traits with courage and firmness she became the "guardian angel" of the settlement. Such preeminently was the title deserved by Mrs. Van Alstine, the "Patriot mother of the Mohawk Valley."

All the early part of her long life, (for she counted nearly a century of years before she died,) was passed on the New York frontier, during the most trying period of our colonial history. Here, dwelling in the midst of alarms, she reared her fifteen children. Here more than once she saved the lives of her husband and family, and by her ready wit, her daring courage, and her open-handed generosity shielded the settlement from harm.

Born near Canajoharie, about the year 1733, and married to Martin J. Van Alstine, at the age of eighteen, she settled with her husband in the valley of the Mohawk, where the newly wedded pair occupied the Van Alstine family mansion.

In the month of August, 1780, during the Revolutionary War, an army of Indians and Tories, led on by Brant, rushed into the Mohawk Valley. They devastated several settlements, and killed many of the inhabitants. During the two following months, Sir John Johnson made a descent and finished the work which Brant had begun. The two almost completely destroyed the settlements throughout the valley. It was during those trying times that Mrs. Van Alstine performed a portion of her exploits.

During these three months, and while the hostile forces were making their headquarters at Johnstown, the neighborhood in which Mrs. Van Alstine lived enjoyed a remarkable immunity from attack. Intelligence at length came that the enemy, having ravaged the surrounding country, was about to fall upon the little settlement. The inhabitants, who were mostly women and children, were almost beside themselves with terror.

Mrs. Van Alstine's coolness and intrepidity in this critical hour were quickly displayed. Calling her neighbors together, she tried to relieve their fears and urged them to remove with their belongings to an island owned by her husband, near the opposite side of the river. She believed that the savages would either not discover their hideout or would be in too great haste to cross the river and attack them.

Her suggestion was speedily adopted. In a few hours the seven families in the neighborhood were removed to the place of refuge. Mrs. Van Alstine was the last to cross. She assisted in placing their boat out of reach of the enemy. An hour after they had been all safely bestowed in their bushy retreat, the war-whoop was heard and the Indians made their appearance. Gazing from their hiding place the unfortunate women and children soon saw their loved homes in flames, Mr. Van Alstine's house alone being spared, owing to a friendship between Sir John Johnson and himself.

The voices and even the words of the Indian raiders could be distinctly heard on the island, and as Mrs. Van Alstine gazed at the mansion untouched by the flames she rejoiced that she would now be able to give shelter to the homeless families by whom she was surrounded. In the following year the Van Alstine mansion was raided by the Indians, and although the house was completely stripped of furniture and provisions and clothing, none of the family were killed or carried away as prisoners.

The Indians came upon them by surprise, entered the house without ceremony, and plundered and destroyed everything in their way. "Mrs. Van Alstine saw her most valued articles, brought from Holland, broken one after another, till the house was strewed with fragments. As they passed a large mirror without demolishing it, she hoped it might be saved. But presently two of the savages led in a colt from the stables and the glass being laid in the hall, compelled the animal to walk over it. The beds which they could not carry away they ripped open, shaking out the feathers and taking the ticks with them. They also took all the clothing. One young Indian, attracted by the brilliancy of a pair of inlaid buckles on the shoes of the aged grandmother seated in the corner, rudely snatched them from her feet, tore off the buckles, and flung the shoes in her face. Another took her shawl from her neck, threatening to kill her if resistance was offered."

The eldest daughter, seeing a young savage carrying off a basket containing a hat and cap her father had brought her from Philadelphia, and which she highly prized, followed him, snatched her basket, and after a struggle succeeded in pushing him down. She then fled to a pile of hemp and hid herself, throwing the basket into it as far as she could. The other Indians gathered round; as the young girl rose, they clapped their hands, shouting "Brave girl," while the Indian who had tried to take the basket skulked away to escape their derision. During the struggle Mrs. Van Alstine had called to her daughter to give up the contest; but she insisted that her basket should not be taken.

Winter was coming on, and the family suffered severely from the want of bedding, woolen clothes, cooking utensils, and numerous other articles which had been taken from them. Mrs. Van Alstine's arduous and constant labors could do but little toward providing for so many destitute persons. Their neighbors were in no condition to help them. The roads were almost impassable besides being infested with the Indians, and all their best horses had been driven away.

Mrs. Van Alstine suggested to her husband to organize an expedition, and attempt to recover their property from the Indian forts eighteen or twenty miles distant. But the plan seemed scarcely feasible at the time, and was therefore abandoned.

The cold soon became intense and their necessities more desperate than ever. Incapable of witnessing any longer the sufferings of those dependent upon her, Mrs. Van Alstine boldly determined to go herself to the Indian country and bring back the property. Firm against all the entreaties of her loved ones who sought to move her from her purpose, she left home with a horse and sleigh accompanied by her son, a youth of sixteen.

Pushing on over wretched roads and through the deep snow she arrived at her destination. The Indians were all absent on a hunting excursion. Only the women and children were left at home. On entering the principal house where she supposed the most valuable articles were, she was met by an old squaw in charge of the place and asked what she wanted. "Food," she replied; the squaw sullenly commenced preparing a meal and in doing so brought out a number of utensils that Mrs. Van Alstine recognized as her own. While the squaw's back was turned she took possession of the articles and removed them to her sleigh. When the custodian of the plunder discovered that it was being reclaimed, she was about to interfere forcibly with the bold intruders and take the property into her possession. But Mrs. Van Alstine showed her a paper which she averred was an order signed by "Yankee Peter," a man of great influence among the savages. She succeeded in convincing the squaw that the property was removed by his authority.

She next proceeded to the stables and cut the halters of the horses belonging to her husband. The animals recognized their mistress with loud neighs and bounded homeward at full speed. The mother and son then drove rapidly back to their house. Reaching home late in the evening they passed a sleepless night, dreading an instant pursuit and a night attack from the infuriated savages.

The Indians came soon after daylight in full war-costume armed with rifles and tomahawks. Mrs. Van Alstine begged her husband not to show himself but to leave the matter in her hands. The Indians took their course to the stables when they were met by the daring woman alone and asked what they wanted. "Our horses," replied the marauder. "They are ours," she said boldly, "and we mean to keep them."

The chief approached in a threatening manner, and drawing her away pulled out the plug that fastened the door of the stable, but she immediately snatched it from his hand, and pushing him away resumed her position in front of the door. Presenting his rifle, he threatened her with instant death if she did not immediately move. Opening her neck-handkerchief she told him to shoot if he dared.

Awed by her boldness, or fearing punishment from their allies in case they killed her, the Indians retired from the premises. They afterwards related their adventure to one of the settlers, and said that were fifty such women as she in the settlement, the Indians never would have molested the inhabitants of the Mohawk Valley.

On many subsequent occasions Mrs. Van Alstine exhibited the heroic qualities of her nature. Twice by her prudence, courage, and address, she saved the lives of her husband and family. Her influence in settling difficulties with the savages was acknowledged throughout the region, and but for her it may well be doubted whether the little settlement in which she lived would have been able to sustain itself, surrounded as it was by deadly foes.

Her influence was felt in another and higher way. She was a Christian woman, and her husband's house was opened for religious worship every Sunday when the weather would permit. She was able to persuade many of the Indians to attend, and as she had acquired their language she was wont to interpret to them the word of God and what was said by the minister. Many times their hearts were touched, and the tears rolled down their swarthy faces, while she dwelt on the wondrous story of our Redeemer's life and death, and explained how the white man and the red man alike could be saved by the grace of the Lord Jesus Christ. In after years the savages blessed her as their benefactress.

Nearly a hundred summers have passed since the occurrence of the events we have been describing. The war-whoop of the cruel Mohawk sounds no more from the forest-ambush, nor in the clearing. Calm and peaceful in the sunshine lies the grave where the patriot mother is sleeping; but still in the memory of the sons and daughters of the region she once blessed, lives the courage, the firmness, and the goodness of Nancy Van Alstine, the guardian of The Mohawk Valley.

Mother Of The Alleghany Settlement

MRS. JAMESON

Mrs. Jameson was the child of wealthy parents, and had been reared in luxury in the city of New York. Soon after peace was declared, she was married to Edward Jameson, a brave soldier in the American Revolution, who had nothing but his stout arms and intrepid heart to battle with the difficulties of life.

The first two years of her married life had been spent on a farm in Westchester County, New York, where she had acquired some knowledge of farming and woodcraft, by assisting her husband in his labors or by accompanying him while hunting and fishing. She was strong and healthy; strengthened by exercise in the open air, and her face was tinged by the kisses of the sun.

Gathering together the remains of what was once a large fortune, the couple purchased the usual outfit of the emigrants of that period and set out to seek their fortunes in the West. All went well with them until they reached the Alleghany River, which they undertook to cross on a raft. It was the month of May. The river had been swollen by rains, and when they reached the middle of the stream, the part of the raft on which Mr. Jameson sat became detached, the logs separated, and he sank to rise no more. The other section of the raft, containing Mrs. Jameson, her babe of eight months, and a chest of clothing and household gear, floated down-stream at the mercy of the rapid current.

Bracing herself against the shock, Mrs. Jameson managed to paddle to the side of the river from which she had just before started. She was landed nearly a mile below the point where the cattle and the oxcart had been left, which her husband expected to carry over the river on the raft later. The desolate mother succeeded in tying up the remains of the raft to the shore. Clasping her babe to her bosom, she followed the bank of the river till she reached the oxen and cart, which she drove down to the place where she landed. By great exertions, Mrs. Jameson succeeded in hauling the chest upon the bank. Her strength was now exhausted, and, lying down in the bottom of the cart, she gave way to grief and despair.

Her situation may be easily imagined: alone in the forest, thirty miles from the nearest settlement, her husband torn from her in a moment, and her babe smiling as though he would console his mother for her terrible loss. In her sad condition, self-preservation would have been too feeble a motive to impel her to make any further effort to save herself; but maternal love—the strongest instinct in a woman's heart—gave her the will to persevere.

The spot where she found herself was a dense forest, stretching back to a rocky ledge on the east, and terminated on the north by a meadow nearly bare of trees. Along the banks of the river was a thick line of high bushes and saplings, which served as a screen against the observations of savages passing up and down the river in their canoes. The track which the Jamesons had followed was about midway between the northern and southern routes generally pursued by emigrants, and it was quite unlikely that others would cross the river at that point. The dense jungle that skirted the river bank was an impediment in the way of reaching the settlements lower down, and there was danger of being lost in the woods if the unfortunate woman should start alone.

"On this spot," she said, "I must remain till some one comes to my help."

Slowly recovering from the terrible anguish of her loss, she went in search of food and shelter. The woods were swarming with game, both large and small, from the deer to the rabbit, and from the wild turkey to the quail. The brooks were alive with trout. The meadow was well suited for Indian corn; wheat, rye, or potatoes. The forest was full of trees of every description. Her study was to utilize all these raw materials.

A rude hut, built of boughs interlaced, and covered thickly with leaves and dry swamp grass, was her first work. This was her kitchen. The cart, which was covered with canvas, was her sleeping-room. A shotgun, which she had learned the use of, enabled her to keep herself supplied with game. She examined her store of provisions, consisting of pork, flour, and Indian meal, and made an estimate that they would last eight months, with prudent use. At first she tied up the oxen, but afterwards tied the horns to one of their fore feet, and let them roam. The two cows having calved soon after, she kept near at hand by making a pen for the calves, who by their bleating called their mothers from the pastures on the banks of the river. In the meadow she planted half an acre of corn and potatoes, which soon promised an amazing crop.

Thus two months passed away. In her solitary and sad condition she was cheered by the daily hope that white settlers would cross her track or see her as they passed up and down the river. She often thought of trying to reach a settlement, but dreaded the dangers and difficulties of the way. Like the doe which hides her fawn in the secret covert, this young mother deemed herself and her babe safer in this solitude than in trying unknown perils, even with the chance of falling in with friends. She therefore contented herself with her lot, and when the toils of the day were over, she would sit on the bank and watch for voyagers on the river.

Once she heard voices in the night on the river, and going to the bank she strained her eyes to gaze through the darkness and catch sight of the voyagers. She dared not hail them for fear they might be Indians. Soon the voices grew fainter in the distance, and she heard them no more. Again, while sitting in a clump of bushes on the bank one day, she saw with horror six canoes with Indians, apparently directing their course to the spot where she sat. They were hideously streaked with war-paint, and came so near that she could see the scalping knives in their girdles. Turning their course as they approached the eastern shore they silently paddled down stream, scanning the banks sharply as they floated past. Fortunately they saw nothing to attract their attention. The cart and hut were concealed by the dense bushes, and there was no fire burning.

Fearing molestation from the Indians, she now moved her camp a hundred rods back, near a rocky ledge, from the base of which flowed a spring of pure water. Here, by rolling stones in a circle, she made an enclosure for her cattle at night, and within in it built a log cabin of rather frail construction. Another two weeks was consumed in these labors, and it was now the middle of August.

At night she was at first much alarmed by the howling of wolves, who came sniffing round the cart where she slept. Once a large grey wolf put its paws upon the cart and poked its nose under the canvas covering, but a smart blow on the snout drove it yelping away. None of the cattle were attacked, owing to the bold blow showed to these midnight intruders. The wolf is one of the most cowardly of wild beasts, and will rarely attack a human being, or even an ox, unless pressed by hunger, and in the winter. Often she caught glimpses of huge black bears in the swamps, while she was in pursuit of wild turkeys or other game; but these creatures never attacked her.

One hot day in August she was gathering berries on the rocky ledge beside which her house was situated. When seeing a clump of bushes heavily loaded with the finest blackberries, she laid her babe upon the ground and soon filled her basket with the luscious fruit. As she descended she saw her babe sitting upright and gazing with fixed eyeballs at some object near by. What it was she could not clearly make out, on account of an intervening shrub. Hastening down, a sight met her eyes that froze her blood. An enormous rattlesnake was coiled within three feet of her child, and with its head erect and its forked tongue vibrating, its burning eyes were fixed upon those of the child, which sat motionless as a statue, apparently fascinated by the deadly gaze of the serpent.

Seizing a stick of dry wood, she dealt the reptile a blow, but the stick being decayed and brittle, inflicted little injury on the serpent. The huge reptile gradually and slowly uncoiled its body and steadily fixed its malignant eyes on its new victim. Mrs. Jameson could only cry, being unable to move, "Oh God, preserve me! Save me, Heavenly Father!"

We continue the story in Mrs. Jameson's own words, "The snake now began to writhe its body down a fissure in the rock, keeping its head elevated more than a foot from the ground. Its rattle made very little noise. Every moment it darted out its forked tongue, its eyes became reddish and inflamed, and it moved rather quicker than at first. It was now within two yards of me. By some means I had dissipated the charm, and, roused by a sense of my awful danger, determined to stand on the defensive. To run away from it, I knew would be impracticable, as the snake would instantly dart its whole body after me. I therefore resolutely stood up, and put a strong glove on my right hand, which I happened to have with me. I stretched out my arm. The snake approached slowly and cautiously towards me, darting out its tongue still more frequently. I could now only recommend myself fervently to the protection of Heaven. The snake, when about a yard distant, made a violent spring. I quickly caught it in my right hand, directly under its head; it lashed its body on the ground, at the same time rattling loudly. I watched an opportunity, and suddenly holding the animal's head, while for a moment it drew in its forked tongue, with my left hand I, by a violent contraction of all the muscles in my hand, contrived to close up effectually its jaws!

"Much was now done, but much more was to be done. I had avoided much danger, but I was still in very perilous circumstances. If I moved my right hand from its neck for a moment, the snake, by avoiding suffocation, could easily muster sufficient power to force its head out of my hand; and if I withdrew my hand from its jaws, I should be fatally in the power of its most dreaded fangs. I retained, therefore, my hold with both my hands; I drew its body between my feet in order to aid the compression and hasten suffocation. Suddenly, the snake, which had remained quiet for a few moments, brought up its tail, hit me violently on the head, and then darted its body several times very tightly around my waist. Now was the very acme of my danger.

Thinking, therefore, that I had sufficient power over its body, I removed my right hand from its neck, and in an instant drew my hunting-knife. The snake, writhing furiously again, darted at me; but, striking its body with the edge of the knife, I made a deep cut, and before it could recover its coil, I caught it again by the neck; bending its head on my knee, and again recommending myself fervently to Heaven, I cut its head from its body, throwing the head to a great distance. The blood spouted violently in my face. The snake compressed its body still tighter, and I thought I should be suffocated on the spot, and laid myself down. The snake again rattled its tail and lashed my feet with it. Gradually, however, the creature relaxed its hold, its coils fell slack around me, and untwisting it and throwing it from me as far as I was able, I sank down, and swooned upon the bank.

"When consciousness returned, the scene appeared like a terrible dream, till I saw the dead body of my reptile foe amid my babe crying violently and nestling in my bosom. The ledge near which my cabin was built was infested with rattlesnakes, and the one I had slain seemed to be the patriarch of a numerous family. From that day I vowed vengeance against the whole tribe of reptiles. These creatures were in the habit of coming down to the spring to drink, and I sometimes killed four or five in a day. Before the summer was over I made an end of the whole family."

In September, two households of emigrants floating down the river on a flatboat, caught sight of Mrs. Jameson as she made a signal to them from the bank, and coming to land were pleased with the country, and were persuaded to settle there. The little community was now swelled to fifteen, including four women and six children. The thriving colony received accessions from the East, and, surviving all casualties, grew at last into a populous town. Mrs. Jameson was married again to a stalwart backwoodsman and became the mother of a large family. She was always known as the "Mother of the Alleghany Settlement."

The Flight For Life

ELIZABETH ZANE

On September 11th, 1782, a party of fifty British soldiers, known as the "Queen's Rangers," along with three hundred Indians, laid siege on Fort Henry. The whole body of Indians and British were under the command of the infamous Simon Girty. Fort Henry was the stronghold of defense for the nearby settlers in the small capitol of West Virginia.

It was a long and tedious battle. The fort was so strongly guarded that the redskins at first made little impression upon it, but one by one the inmates dropped away, until only eighteen men remained. Still, they were not daunted by the terrible odds.

Almost overcome by fatigue, they kept constant watch for the enemy which surrounded the fort. Few were allowed to leave the gates, for the attempt meant probable death. It became necessary, however, to have reinforcements, and messengers were safely dispatched to neighboring villages. The sun was just sinking, when Girty endeavored to persuade the inhabitants of the garrison to surrender.

"We know you Girty, for a dirty dog, too cowardly to be honest, and so filthy a beast that you felt yourself only fit to live amongst savages. Your promises are plentiful, but you are such a liar that, if you tried, you couldn't tell the truth. If you want us, you will have to do some better fighting than you and your sneaking Indians have ever yet done. We only hope that you will hang around our walls until our messenger brings up reinforcements, and we will exterminate you."

"Yes," replied Girty, "but I've got your messenger safe. He won't bring up any help for you."

"Have you really?" asked Sullivan. "What sort of a man was he—how did he look?"

"Oh, he's a fine, active fellow, young and good looking."

"That's a lie!" put in Sullivan. "He was an old, gray-headed man."

At this Girty retired, and in a short time led up his forces to the attack. Thinking that they would have but a short time in which to reduce the fort, the mixed troops of Girty fought with more than their usual courage and determination.

At last the long night passed away, and with the daylight the Indian attack slackened. A new idea had seized the red men. At the wharf lay a barge loaded with cannon balls. These were under the charge of Mr. Sullivan, who was taking them from Fort Pitt to Louisville, when he stopped at Wheeling to aid the little garrison there. The savages determined to utilize these munitions of war, and went to work to make a cannon out of which to fire them. Selecting a large log, they split it open, scooped out a bore in it of the proper size, and then, placing the two pieces together, bound it with ropes, chains and iron bands.

Would it work? Of this its builders had not the slightest doubt, and pouring in several pounds of fine rifle powder, they rammed home several of the balls, and aimed the huge barrel at the fort. Proud of their invention, the Indians gathered in a dense mass around it, each anxious for the honor of touching it off, and all expecting to see the fort speedily demolished.

At last, the match was applied, and a terrific explosion was the result; pieces of chain, huge splinters, and mangled Indians flying through the air in all directions. When the viewers in Fort Henry saw the effect of this cannon, they only wished Girty's army had a dozen more.

Before they had the time to secure help for the fort, a new and bewildering trouble befell its garrison. To their horror, they found that the ammunition was giving out. If more was not somehow obtained, they must fall victims to their savage foes. As soon as they suspected that the white men were out of powder or shot they would advance and take the fort with little resistance, probably massacring and scalping the whole company.

Colonel Ebenezer Zane, the commander of the fort, was nearly worn out from the constant watch which he had been keeping. He peered out of the fort in the direction of his own home. There it was, still standing, and not more than sixty rods from the spot where he was taking his observations.

"We must have ammunition," he said to his friends, "or we are lost. There is a keg of powder in my house, but how can we get it?"

Courageous young men advanced and offered themselves for the hazardous service.

"It is a great risk," said the commander, "and there are so few of us left that we must conserve our strength. We cannot afford to lose more than one man."

The volunteers, never flinching, still stood ready.

"We cannot afford to lose even one man. A woman ought to go," spoke clearly a girl's voice at the side of the Colonel.

Every eye turned instantly to the speaker. Standing there, lovely to look upon, in the glory of her youth, yet with every line of her face and figure portraying courage and determination, was Miss Elizabeth Zane, the sister of the Colonel.

She had just come from a fashionable boarding school in Philadelphia, and had been visiting her brother, when the Indian outbreak occurred. She had fled with him to the fort. Strange, indeed, sounded the words of this refined young woman, amid the boom of the guns of this frontier fort in the wilderness.

"Please let me go," she insisted. "I know where the powder lies, so that it would take me less time than anyone else. And as I said before, you cannot spare even one man to take the risk."

For a time no one would hear of Elizabeth's pleas, but at last, with a heart full of misgiving, Colonel Zane finally swung open the gate. The young and beautiful girl bounded out into the lion's den, and swift as the wind sped for the solitary house.

It was hardly a moment before the door of the house swung open again, and Miss Zane emerged carrying the powder in her apron. Instantly, the whole proceeding was clear to the enemy. There was naturally but one conclusion: the powder was getting low or no one would have taken such a dangerous chance.

Instantly, rifles were leveled at the girl and hundreds of bullets whistled about her head. But swift as a deer, she sped on to the fort.

The men in the fort watched her breathlessly. As she came near to the gate, it opened to receive her and then closed again. Protected by the hand of God, she remained miraculously unscathed through the rain of fire and bullets. She laid the precious burden at the Colonel's feet, while a shout went up for the girl who was willing to sacrifice her life to save others.

Tried by Fire

MRS. DALTON

It was with reluctance that Mrs. Dalton consented to follow her husband into the wilderness. She had been reared in the ease and luxury of an eastern home, and possessed those strong local attachments which are characteristic of females of her temperament. Having at last consented, she showed the greatest firmness in carrying out a resolution which involved the loss of a happy home at the place of her nativity, and consigned her to a life of hardship and danger.

Her first experience in this life was in the wilds of northern New York. Her husband had purchased a small clearing and a log cabin in that region on the banks of the Black river. After a wearisome journey they reached their destination one cold rainy evening early in May.

Her first impressions must have been gloomy indeed. The black sky was pouring out rain; the forest was dark as Erebus. No fire blazed in the hearth of the new cabin, and the flickering light of a tallow candle made the darkness but the more visible. A coarse table and chairs made out of rough planks, were all the furniture the cabin could boast. There was no ladder to reach the loft which was to be her sleeping room. The rain beat in through the cracks in the door and through the window which was a mere opening without glass in the side of the cabin. The rain trickled through the roof and the wind blew keenly through a hundred seams and apertures in the log walls.

The night, the cold, the storm, the dark and cheerless abode, were too much to bear. The delicate young wife threw herself upon a settle and burst into a flood of tears. This was but a momentary weakness. Rising above the depression produced by the dreary scene, the woman's genius for creating comfort out of the slenderest materials and bringing sunshine into darkness, soon began to manifest itself.

We will not detail the ways by which that forlorn cabin was transformed into a comfortable home, nor how fared Mrs. Dalton the first rather uneventful year of her life in the woods. The second spring saw her a mother, and the following autumn she became again a homeless westward wanderer. Her husband had sold the cabin and clearing in New York, and having purchased an extensive tract of forest-land a few miles south of Georgian Bay in Upper Canada, decided to move thither.

The family with their household goods took sloop on Lake Ontario late in October, and sailed to Toronto; from this place on the 15th day of November, they proceeded across the peninsula in sleighs. Their party consisted of Mr. and Mrs. Dalton and their child, and John McMurray, their hired-hand, and his wife.

The first forty miles of their journey lay over a well-beaten road, and through a succession of clearings, which soon began to diminish until they reached a dense forest, which rose in solemn stillness around them and cast across their path a shadow which seemed to the imagination of Mrs. Dalton an omen of coming evil.

The sun had now set, but the party still drove on through the forest shadows; the moon having risen giving a new and strange beauty to the scenery. The infant had fallen asleep. A deep silence fell upon the party. Night was above them with her mysterious stars; the ancient forest stretched around them on every side; nature lay wrapped in a snowy winding sheet; the wind was rising and a drifting scud of clouds from the northeast passed across the moon, casting a still more strange and somber character to the scene. They drove up to the cabin in the clearing where they were to pass the night. It was occupied by an old black man and his wife, who had found a safe refuge from servitude in the Canadian woods.

Hardly had they and their horses been safely bestowed under shelter when the sky became entirely overcast. The wind rose to a gale, and a driving storm of snow and sleet filled the air. All night and the following day, the tempest raged without intermission. On the morning of the second day, the sun struggling through the clouds, looked down on the vast drifts of snow. Some of them were nearly twenty feet in depth, completely blocking their farther passage. They were confined to their present quarters for some days.

The babe fell ill, and grew worse so rapidly that Mr. Dalton determined to push through the snow-drifts on horseback to procure the services of a physician in the nearest settlement, which lay eight miles south of them. He started early in the morning, expecting to return in the afternoon. But afternoon and evening passed, and still Mr. Dalton did not return. His course was a difficult one through forest and thicket. When evening came, and night passed with its bitter cold, Mrs. Dalton's anxiety was increased to torture. Her only hope was that her husband had reached the settlement in safety, and had been induced to remain there till the following morning before returning.

Soon after the sun rose that morning, Mrs. Dalton and Mr. McMurray set out on horseback in search of the missing husband. Tracing his course through the snow for four miles, they at length caught sight of him standing up to his waist in a deep drift, beside his horse. His face was turned toward them. So lifelike and natural was his position that it was only when his wife grasped his cold rigid fingers that she knew the terrible truth. Her husband and the horse were statues of ice thus transformed by the deadly cold as they were endeavoring to force a passage through those immense drifts.

From the speechless, tearless trance of grief into which Mrs. Dalton was thrown by the shock of her awful loss, she was roused only by the recollection of the still critical condition of her child and the necessity that she should administer to its wants. Its recovery from illness a few days after, enabled the desolate widow to cast about her in grief and doubt, and decide what course she should pursue.

As her own marriage portion as well as the entire fortune of her late husband was embarked in the purchase of the forest tract, she concluded to continue her journey twenty miles farther to the point of her original destination, and there establish herself in the new house which had been provided for her in the almost unbroken wilderness.

After a few days a large amount of snow had thawed, enabling Mrs. Dalton and her companions, to reach their destination. It was a large and commodious cabin built of cedar logs in a spacious clearing by the former owner of the tract.

The cares and labors of pioneer-life are the best antidotes to the corrosion of sorrow and regret, and Mrs. Dalton soon found such a relief in the myriad toils and distractions which filled those wintry days. A thousand duties were to be discharged: a thousand wants to be provided for: night brought weariness and blessed oblivion: morning again supplied its daily tasks and labor grew to be happiness.

Midwinter was upon them with its bitter cold and drifting snows; but with abundant stores of food and fuel, Mrs. Dalton was thanking God nightly for his many mercies. She little dreamed that a new calamity impended over her household.

One bitter day in January the two women were left alone in the cabin, McMurray having gone a mile away to fell trees for sawing into boards. Mrs. McMurray had stuffed both the stoves full of light wood. The wind blowing steadily from the northwest produced a powerful draft, and in a few moments the roaring and crackling of the fire and the suffocating smell of burning soot attracted Mrs. Dalton's attention. To her dismay, both the stoves were red hot from the front plates to the topmost pipes which passed through the plank-ceiling and projected three feet above the roof. Through these pipes the flames were roaring as if through the chimney of a blast furnace.

A blanket snatched from the nearest bed, that stood in the kitchen, and plunged into a barrel of cold water was thrust into the stove, and a few shovels full of snow thrown upon it soon made all cool below. The two women immediately hastened to the loft and by dashing pails full of water upon the pipes, contrived to cool them down as high as the place where they passed through the roof. The wood work around the pipes showed a circle of glowing embers, the water was nearly exhausted and both the women running out of the house discovered that the roof which had been covered the day before by a heavy fall of snow, showed an area of several square feet from which the intense heat had melted the snow; the sparks falling upon the shingles had ignited them, and the rafters below were covered by a sheet of flame.

A ladder, which, for some months, had stood against the house, had been moved two days before to the barn which stood some thirty rods away. There seemed no possibility of reaching the fire. Moving out a large table and placing a chair upon it, Mrs. Dalton stood upon the chair and tried to throw water upon the roof, but only succeeded in expending the last dipper full of water that remained in the boiler, without reaching the fire.

Mrs. McMurray now abandoned herself to grief and despair, but Mrs. Dalton, still keeping her presence of mind, told her to run after her husband, and to the nearest house, which was a mile away, and bring help.

Mrs. McMurray, after a moment's remonstrance, on account of the depth of the snow, regained her courage, and, hastily putting on her husband's boots, started, shrieking "fire!" as she passed up the road, and disappeared at the head of the clearing.

Mrs. Dalton was now quite alone, with the house burning over her head. She gazed at the blazing roof, and, pausing for one moment, reflected what should first be done.

The house was built of cedar logs, and the suns and winds of four years had made it as dry as kindling; the breeze was blowing briskly and all the atmospheric conditions were favorable to its speedy destruction. The cold was intense, the thermometer registered eighteen degrees below zero. The unfortunate woman thus saw herself placed between two extremes of heat and cold, and apprehended as much danger from the one as from the other. The hopeless extent of the calamity promised to put the finishing stroke to her misfortune, and to throw her naked and houseless upon the world.

"What shall I first save?" was the question rapidly asked, and as quickly answered. Anything to serve for warmth and shelter—bedding, clothing, to protect herself and babe from that cruel cold! All this passed her mind like a flash, and the next moment she was working to save what she could of these essential articles from her burning house.

Springing to the loft where the embers were falling from the burning roof, she quickly threw the beds and bedding from the window, and emptying trunks and chests conveyed their contents out of reach of the flames and of the burning brands which the wind was whirling from the roof. The loft was like a furnace, and the heat soon drove her, dripping with perspiration, to the lower room, where, for twenty minutes, she strained every nerve to drag out the movables. Large pieces of burning pine began to fall through the boarded ceiling about the lower rooms, and as the babe had been placed under a large dresser in the kitchen, it now became absolutely necessary to remove it. But where?

The air was so bitter that nothing but the fierce excitement and rapid motion had preserved Mrs. Dalton's hands and feet from freezing. To expose the tender nursling to that direful cold was almost as cruel as leaving it to the mercy of the fire.

A mother's wit is not long at fault where the safety of her child is concerned. Emptying out all the clothes from a large drawer which she had dragged a safe distance from the house, she lined it with blankets and placed the child inside, covering it well over with bedding, and keeping it well wrapped up till help should arrive.

The roof was now burning like a brush heap; but aid was near at hand. As she passed out of the house for the last time, dragging a heavy chest of clothes, she looked once more despairingly up the clearing and saw a man running at full speed. It was McMurray. Her burdened heart uttered a deep thanksgiving, as another and another figure came bounding over the snow towards her burning house.

She was without bonnet or shawl, and with hands bare and exposed to the biting air, but in the intense anxiety to save all she could she did not feel the bitter cold. Her thoughts were so far from herself that she took no heed of the peril in which she stood from fire and frost. But now the reaction came. Her knees trembled under her, she grew giddy and faint, and dark shadows swam before her.

The three men sprang on the roof and called for water in vain; it had long been exhausted. "Snow! snow! Hand us up pails full of

snow!" they shouted.

It was bitter work filling the pails with frozen snow, but the two women (for Mrs. McMurray had now returned) scooped up pails full of snow with their bare hands and passed them to the men on the roof.

By spreading this on the roof, and on the floor of the loft, the violence of the fire was checked. The men then cast away the smoldering rafters and flung them in the snow-drifts.

The roof was gone, but the fire was at last subdued before it had destroyed the walls. Within one week from the time of the fire the neighboring settlers built a new roof for Mrs. Dalton in spite of the intense cold, and while it was building Mrs. Dalton and her household were sheltered at the nearest cabin.

The warm breath of spring brought with it some blissful days, as if to reconcile Mrs. Dalton to her life of solitude and toil. She soon learned the use of the rifle, the paddle, and the fishing rod. Blissful hours of leisure and freedom were passed upon the water of the lake, or in rambles through the arches of the forest. In these pleasures, enhanced by the needful toils of the household or the field, the summer sped away.

August came, and the little harvest of oats and corn were all safely housed. For some days the weather had been intensely hot. The sun was entirely obscured by a bluish haze, which seemed to render the unusual heat of the atmosphere more oppressive. Not a breath of air stirred the vast forest, and the waters of the lake took on a leaden hue.

Before the sun rose on the morning of the 12th, the heavens were covered with hard looking clouds of a deep blue-black color, fading away to white at their edges, and in form resembling the long, rolling waves of a heavy sea, but with the difference that the clouds were perfectly motionless, piled in long curved lines, one above the other.

As the day advanced the same blue haze obscured the sun, which frowned redly through his misty veil. At ten o'clock the heat was suffocating. The thermometer in the shade ranged after midday from ninety-six to ninety-eight degrees. The babe stretched itself upon the floor of the cabin, unable to jump about or play, the dog lay panting in the shade, the fowls half-buried themselves in the dust, with open beaks and outstretched wings. All nature seemed to droop beneath the scorching heat.

By mid-afternoon the heavens took on a sudden change. The clouds, that had before lain so still, were now in rapid motion, hurrying and chasing each other round the horizon. It was a strangely awful sight. Before a breath had been felt of the mighty blast that had already burst on the other side of the lake, branches of trees, leaves, and clouds of dust were whirled across the water, which rose in long, sharp furrows, fringed with foam, as if moved in their depths by some unseen but powerful agent.

The hurricane swept up the hill, crushing and overturning everything in its course. Mrs. Dalton, standing at the open door of her cabin, speechless and motionless, gazed at the tremendous spectacle. The babe crept to its mother's feet and appealed to her for protection. Mrs. McMurray, in helpless terror, had closed her eyes and ears to the storm, and sat upon a chest, muffled in a shawl.

The storm had not yet reached its acme. The roaring of the blast and the pealing of the thunder redoubled in violence. Turning her eyes to the southwest, Mrs. Dalton now saw, far down the valley, the tops of the huge trees twisted and bowed, as if by some unseen but terrible power. A monstrous cloud marked the course of this new hurricane. Nearer and nearer it came, with a menacing rumble, and swifter than a race-horse.

The cabin lay directly in its track. In a moment it would be upon them. Whither should they fly? One place of safety occurred on the instant to the unfortunate woman. Clasping her babe to her breast and clutching the gown of her companion, she ran to the trap-door which conducted to the cellar and raising it pushed Mrs. McMurray down the aperture and quickly following her, Mrs. Dalton closed the trap.

Not five seconds later the hurricane struck the cabin with such force that every plank, rafter, beam, and log was first dislocated and then caught up in the whirlwind and scattered over the forest in the wake of the storm. As the roar of the blast died away, the rain commenced pouring in torrents accompanied by vivid flashes of lightning and loud peals of thunder.

The air in the close shallow cellar, where the women were, soon grew suffocating, and as the fury of the tempest was spent, they took courage and pushed at the trap. But it stuck fast. Again they both applied their shoulders to it but only succeeded in raising it far enough to see that the trunk of an enormous tree lay directly across the door.

The cellar in which they were, was little more than a large pit, eight feet by six, and served as a receptacle for their winter's stores. As it lay directly in the center of the floor which was formed of large logs split in halves and their surfaces smoothed, there was no mode of egress except by digging underneath the floor as far as the walls of the cabin and so emerging. But this was a work of extreme difficulty, owing to the fact that the soil was full of the old roots of trees which had been cut down to make room for the cabin.

The first danger, however, was from suffocation; to meet this Mrs. Dalton and her companion pried open the door as far as the fallen trunk would allow, and kept it in position by means of a large chip which they found in the pit. This gave them sufficient air through a chink three inches in width.

They next looked about them for means of emergence. After trying in vain to dislodge one of the floor logs, they proceeded to dig a passage through the earth underneath the floor. Discouraged by the slowness of their progress in this undertaking, and drenched with the rain which poured in through the crevice in the door, they began to give themselves up for lost. Their only hope was that McMurray or some one of the neighbors would come to their relief.

The rain lasted only one hour; and the sun soon made its appearance. This was after six o'clock, as the prisoners judged from the shadows cast over the ruins of the cabin. The shades of evening fell and at last utter darkness; still no one came. No sound was borne to the ears of the women in their earthly dungeon save that of the rushing waters of the creek and the mournful howling of wolves who, like jackals, were prowling in the track of the tempest. Several of these animals, attracted by the infant's cries, came and put their noses at the door of the pit and finding that it held prey, paced the floor above it all night. But with the first light of morning they scampered away into the woods.

Meanwhile the women resumed their efforts to burrow their way out, taking turns in working all night. By daybreak the passage lacked only four feet of the point where an outlet could be had. Ere noon, if their strength held out, they would reach the open air.

But after four hours more of severe toil they met an unexpected obstacle: their progress was blocked by a huge boulder embedded in the soil. Weary with their protracted toil and loss of sleep, and faint from want of food, they desisted from further efforts and sat down upon the damp earth of that dungeon which now promised to be their tomb.

Sinking upon her knees Mrs. Dalton lifted her heart to God in prayer that he might save her babe, her faithful domestic and herself from the doom which threatened them. Hardly had she risen from her knees, when, as if a messenger had been sent in answer to her prayer, voices were heard and steps sounded upon the floor above them. The party had come from a neighboring settlement for the express purpose of relieving the sufferers from the recent storm. A few blows with an axe and the prisoners were free. Recognizing their preservation as a direct answer to prayer, and with deep gratitude both of the women fell on their knees and lifted up their hearts in humble thanksgiving to God who had saved them by an act of his providence from an awful death. When all hope was gone his hand was stretched forth, making his strength manifest in the weakness of those hapless women and that helpless babe.

Before the first of October a new cabin had been built for Mrs. Dalton by her generous neighbors, and the other ravages of the storm had been repaired.

On the 16th of October, two parties of hunters had rested one noon on opposite sides of Mrs. Dalton's clearing and carelessly dropped sparks from their pipes into the dried herbage. A long continued drought had parched the fields and woods until but a spark was needed to kindle a conflagration. Two hours after their departure, the flames, fanned by a gentle breeze, had formed a junction and encircled the cabin with a wall of fire. A dense canopy of smoke hung over the clearing, and as it lifted, tongues of flame could be seen licking the branches of the tall pines. Showers of sparks fell upon the roof. The atmosphere grew suffocating with the pitchy smoke and it became a choice of deaths, either that of choking or that of burning.

Only one avenue of escape was left open to the family. If they could reach the lake and embark in the canoe which lay moored near the shore they would be safe. They must pass through a single passage conducted to the water, and that was a burning lane lined with trees and bushes which were bursting into fiercer flames every moment as they gazed down it.

Nearer and nearer crept the fire, and hotter and hotter grew the choking air. There was no other choice. Mr. McMurray threw water on the gowns of his wife and Mrs. Dalton until they were drenched; then wrapping the baby in a blanket and enveloping their heads in shawls, the whole party abandoned their house to destruction, and ran the gauntlet of the flames. They passed the spot of ordeal in safety, reached the canoe and embarking pushed off into the lake. The women clasped their hands and looked up. Both were supplicating the Father of All that their home might be spared.

A rescue was coming from an unlooked for source. While Mrs. Dalton's face was uptuned to heaven in silent prayer, a large drop splashed upon her brow; another followed—the first glad heralds of a pouring rain which extinguished the fire just as it had begun to feed on that unlucky habitation.

After nearly an unbroken series of disasters and losses, we might well inquire whether the succeeding life of Mrs. Dalton was saddened and darkened by similar experiences. But, every cloud has a silver lining—the hardest and saddest lives have their hours of softness, their gleams of sunshine. If there was no pain in life, there would be no way to experience relief; if there was no work, pleasures would fall as common pennies upon the well trodden ground; and if there was no sorrow, there would be no reason to trust in the great Giver of life's joys.

We may truly say of Mrs. Dalton, that her latter days were more blessed than the beginning. She was happily married the following spring and lived a long life of prosperity and peace after her escape from the last great danger. She was fittingly rewarded for her courage, diligence, and perseverance in the untamed northern wilderness.

> *But Thou art making me, I thank Thee, sire.*
> *What Thou hast done and doest Thou knowes't well.*
> *And I will help Thee; gently in Thy fire*
> *I will lie burning; on Thy potter's wheel*
> *I will whirl patient, though my brain should reel.*
> *Thy grace shall be enough the grief to quell,*
> *And growing strength perfect through weakness dire.*

GEORGE MACDONALD

The Kentucky Amazon Woman

MRS. MERRILL

About twelve o'clock one night, during the summer of 1787, the Indians surrounded the house of John Merrill, in Nelson County, Kentucky. The faithful dog gave warning of their presence, and Mr. Merrill incautiously opened the door to look out. This was just such a chance as the savages wished, and firing a volley from their rifles, Merrill fell to the floor with a broken arm and thigh.

Calling hastily to his wife to close the door, the Indians were thus made aware of his crippled condition, and fearing no danger from the white woman, the door was no sooner closed than they began hacking at it with their tomahawks and soon effected a large breach.

They now prepared to force their way in, but here they met with unexpected opposition. Mrs. Merrill, who was a perfect Amazon, and who knew no fear, seized a keen axe standing near, and stood on guard.

At last one of the savages protruded his head and shoulders into the breach, when, with a powerful sweep of her heavy axe, the brave woman cleft his skull in twain, and then pulled him through the opening in the door.

Supposing that their comrade had effected a lodgment, and hearing no signs of a struggle, another Indian pressed forward, and met with the same fate.

In this manner four of the savages met their deaths, when the others, becoming suspicious, determined to try another entrance. Climbing to the roof, two of the marauders entered the broad chimney, leaving their last comrade on watch at the door. It was a trying moment, and only a ready wit and quick action could save the household. Leaving the door for a few seconds, Mrs. Merrill darted to the bed, took off the feather quilt, ripped it open and emptied it upon the fire.

Rushing back to the front door, she found that the Indian outside was making no attempt to enter. Just then there was a bright blaze, then a dense smoke and in a few seconds two almost suffocated savages fell into the fire-place. To dash forward, and cleave their shaven skulls, was the work of but a moment, and before they had recovered from their suffocation, the tawny murderers were ushered into eternity.

Not knowing how many more of them there might be, she again mounted guard at the door, and as the surviving savage put in his head, calling for his companions, she aimed a strong blow at him. Dodging just in time to

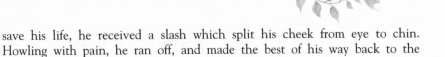

save his life, he received a slash which split his cheek from eye to chin. Howling with pain, he ran off, and made the best of his way back to the Indian town of Chillicothe.

A white man, who was a prisoner in Chillicothe at the time, said that the report of the Indian was to the effect that, after shooting a man in Kentucky, they attempted to enter the house, and were met by a white squaw, at least ten feet high, who had an immense tomahawk, with an edge two feet long, and who fought them with all the fury of a demon. The others had fought her bravely, and had perished. He alone, by his superior skill and courage, after dealing the terrible squaw some deadly blows with his tomahawk, was able to make his escape with the wound in his cheek.

The Suspicious Indian

MRS. PARKER

In 1812 there lived on the Illinois River, some two hundred miles above its mouth, a hardy old pioneer, commonly known as "Old Parker, the Squatter." The family consisted of a wife, two boys—one aged nineteen, the other fourteen—and a daughter, seventeen years old. As their only dependence for meat was upon the game procured, Parker and his oldest son were often gone for days at a time on hunting expeditions, the Illinois Indians at that period being all peaceable.

At the time of which we write, he and his oldest son had been gone three days in company with some Indians regarded as friendly. On this day, (the third after their departure), one of the Indians returned, entered the cabin, and sitting down began to smoke. This was not regarded as any thing odd. They supposed the savage had been discouraged by something which his superstition caused him to regard as an ill omen, and had turned back from the hunt.

After remaining silent for some time, the Indian at last spoke. "Old Parker die," said he. The family was now terribly aroused, and Mrs. Parker hurriedly asked what was the matter with her husband. To this the Indian answered, "Parker sick, tree fell on him—Parker die—You go see." To questions as to where her husband was, and whether he had sent for her, the Indian gave contradictory replies, that excited the suspicions of the woman, but she determined to send the remaining boy along with the savage to see if there was any truth in his report. Neither Indian nor boy returning that night, nor the next day, the suspicions of the woman were confirmed, and she determined to keep strict watch.

Accordingly, she secured the door with the strongest fastenings she could devise, and awaited the attack she felt sure would come. For arms she had the rifle of the youngest boy and an axe. Scarcely had the darkness of the night descended, when steps were heard approaching the cabin, and after knocking at the door, some one called out, "Mother—mother." The daughter started to unfasten the door, but holding her back, the mother, who fancied she detected an Indian accent in the voice, said, "Jake, where are the Indians?"

"Um gone," was the confident reply of the savage.

Mrs. Parker, now fully satisfied that her husband and sons had been foully murdered, was seized with an idea, that, if well carried out, would lessen the number of the traitors by one at least. "Put your ear to the key-hole, Jake, I've something I want to tell you, and don't want anyone to hear—the Indians may be skulking around." She had already cocked her boy's rifle, and when the head was laid against the door, she sent a bullet through it and lightly stepped to one side. The Indian fell dead, but his two comrades fired hastily through the door, and nothing but the prudent forethought of the woman, in stepping aside, saved her life.

Turning now to her daughter, she told her that one of the savages was dead, and that if they could kill another, the third one would fly. "I will load the rifle again, and when they break in the door, which they will do, if they hear no noise, I will fire on them, and if I shouldn't kill one, you must use your axe." The daughter promised that she would not fail, and just then the Indians again fired through the door. Not a movement inside. The Indians again reloaded, and fired two more shots, without hearing a sound.

Fully convinced that their random shots had killed the women, and eager for scalps and plunder, they obtained a heavy log, and after a few unsuccessful attempts, at last succeeded in breaking down the door. Dropping their battering-ram, they sprang into the breach, when the unerring aim of the heroic woman stretched another one dead upon the threshold. The third Indian, now thoroughly terrified, fired his gun at the women without effect, and turning quickly fled into the night.

"We must leave, before he can raise others to aid him," said the mother, and deserting their cabin, they entered a canoe, carrying the faithful rifle and the axe. For six days they drifted down the current of the river, and at last reached the French settlement of St. Louis, having in all that time had no other food than one duck and two blackbirds. These were eaten raw, as they had no way of making a fire.

A party of men started out from St. Louis to search for "Old Parker" and his sons, but no trace of them could be found, and indeed, they were never again heard of.

The Indian Girl Who Unlocked the Northwest

SACAJAWEA

In the early 1800's the tribe of Indians, known to history as the Shoshones, made their home a little west of the Rocky Mountains, known to the natives as the "Bitter Root Mountains." It was here that Sacajawea, and her little friends romped in the woods and played their childish games, with no thought of anything outside of their own lives. It was not always play-time even among those children. From infancy they were taught to labor with their hands, and their education in other respects was not neglected. At a surprisingly early age, they became skilled in the use of the bow, and they were sent into the forest to gather herbs and roots, for medicine and food.

One day, into this peaceful valley, without warning, the powerful Hidatsa Indians swept down into the unsuspecting Shoshone village, in full battle array. Devastation followed in their wake. Many of the Shoshones were killed and many were carried away into captivity. Among the captives was Sacajawea. She was carried, over the mountains, into the far east where there was little hope of twelve-year-old Sacajawea ever returning to her beloved tribe. But, naturally alert and observant, the little maid oriented herself with every inch of sod in which they tread.

Traded from one Indian to another, Sacajawea was finally bought by Toussaint Charbonneau, a French Canadian, who was an Indian interpreter. When she was fourteen he made her his wife and a year later she bore him a son, whom they named Jean Baptiste.

It was about this time that American explorers were looking toward the great, mysterious region in the Far West. They believed that it was a land of great wealth, and they longed to plant the American flag on its mountains. Many called the explorers foolhardy and said that it was a worthless jungle of forests and rocks and beasts; that it was not worth risking lives unnecessarily.

But there were two explorers—Lewis and Clark— who were willing to undertake it. Shortly after starting on their hazardous journey, they entered the little Indian village of Mandan. There they found Charbonneau, who could speak many Indian languages. Their eyes fell also upon the little Indian mother, Sacajawea. Charbonneau told them that his Indian wife knew the whole country, and was a natural guide. Sacajawea, in her native tongue, told them how she knew the trails; how she could take them through country, never before traveled by the feet of white men; and how she could show them the

beauties of the land of her birth.

Charbonneau and Sacajawea agreed to go with the American explorers. They were primary characters that God used to help to unlock the door to the westward expansion. And so they began the expedition—Charbonneau as the interpreter and Sacajawea as a guide. Sacajawea strapped her newborn babe to her back and carried him throughout the entire journey. She was the only woman in the party and she rendered vital service to the explorers.

Lewis wrote in his journals that Sacajawea was the expedition's: "only dependent for a friendly negotiation with the Snake [Shoshone] Indians on whom we depend for horses to assist us in our portage from the Missouri to the Columbia River."

Into the heart of the wilderness they plunged. When all signs of human life were left far behind them, and there were none to beckon them onward, then it was that the native instinct of this woman came to their assistance, and the great explorers were willing and thankful to throw themselves upon her guidance. At times sickness or starvation seemed imminent. Then Sacajawea would go into the woods, where in secret she gathered herbs to cure each ailment; or dug roots, from which she prepared savory dishes for their meals.

The men marveled at the courage and ingenuity of this faithful guide. Burdened though she was with the care of the young child, she never seemed to feel fatigue. No complaint ever escaped her lips. Patient, vibrant, and determined, she was a constant source of inspiration to the explorers. The baby laughed and cooed as the wonders of the world were revealed to it. With all its mother's fearlessness, it swung calmly on her faithful back while she climbed over jagged precipices and forded swiftly running rivers.

On May 14, 1805, Lewis and Clark had gone ashore to walk the banks of the Missouri River, leaving Charbonneau to steer the boat. A strong wind began to blow and dark clouds whirled towards them. Because of Charbonneau's inexperience, he turned the sail into the wind, causing the vessel to be turned on its side. Charbonneau terrified with fright, dropped to his knees and begged God for mercy. They would have overturned completely, but miraculously the boat corrected itself!

From where Lewis and Clark were, the current was too strong for them to swim to the boat. They anxiously shouted orders to the desperate seafarers, "cut the halyards, haul in the sail—."

Lewis wrote later that "almost every article [was] indispensably necessary to insure the success of the enterprise." Without some of these important items, the party would have been obliged to retrace its steps hundreds of miles, in order to replace them.

Calmest of all was Sacajawea. Even with her baby strapped to her back, Sacajawea immediately plunged onto the raging, water, risking her own life and that of the infant strapped to her. Clothing, bundles, and many valuable documents of the expedition were thus rescued. This is, indeed, the heroism that makes history. In gratitude for her great services, the explorers named the next river that they discovered after her.

Some months later, as they made their way across land, Sacajawea thought she remembered seeing certain scenes before. But it couldn't be. She had never traveled thus far—or had she? Could they be nearing her old home? At last they reached the spot, where years before, she had been taken captive. Here she soon found old friends, and to her unspeakable delight she discovered among them her own brother. Wrapped closely in his arms, she sobbed out all the sorrow which had been bound up in her heart for so many years. From him she learned that all of her family had died, except two of her brothers and a son of her eldest sister.

Sacajawea was at home again. Now and then songs of contentment reached the ears of the members of the great expedition. They might naturally have thought that now it would not be easy for the girl to attend them on their westward journey. But if they entertained this fear, they misjudged Sacajawea. She never flinched from her first intention, and cheerfully left her long-lost friends to plunge once more into the unbroken and unknown forests beyond the Rockies. The solitude was enough to shake a strong man's courage. Never a sound was to be heard except the dismal, distant howl of wild beasts and occasionally the war-cry of savages, but Sacajawea did not falter.

Thus they plodded overland, ever westward until the end of the journey drew near. They made a camp inland, leaving Sacajawea in its protection, and then pushed to the coast.

"It is the Pacific at last!" they cheered.

In their enthusiasm, the explorers forgot the brave Sacajawea. They talked of the Pacific in the camp, but did not allow her to go to the coast until she pleaded with them to let her gaze upon the waters, to behold which she had made the long journey. They brought her to a beautiful spot where she viewed the "great waters" and the "fish," as she called the whale. Her heart was contented.

It was an epoch-making journey, in which this worthy woman served

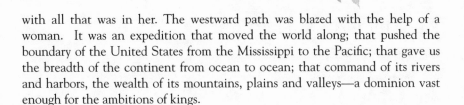

with all that was in her. The westward path was blazed with the help of a woman. It was an expedition that moved the world along; that pushed the boundary of the United States from the Mississippi to the Pacific; that gave us the breadth of the continent from ocean to ocean; that command of its rivers and harbors, the wealth of its mountains, plains and valleys—a dominion vast enough for the ambitions of kings.

The Mothers Of The West

The Mothers of our Forest-Land!

Stout-hearted dames were they;

With nerve to wield the battle-brand,

And join the border-fray.

Our rough land had no braver,

In its days of blood and strife—

Aye ready for severest toil,

Aye free to peril life.

The Mothers of our Forest-Land!

On old Kentucky's soil,

How shared they, with each dauntless band,

War's tempest and Life's toil!

They shrank not from the foeman—

They quailed not in the fight—

But cheered their husbands through the day,

And soothed them through the night.

The Mothers of our Forest-Land!

Their bosoms pillowed men!

And proud were they by such to stand,

In hammock, fort, or glen.

To load the sure old rifle—

To run the leaden ball—

To watch a battling husband's place,

And fill it should he fall.

The Mothers of our Forest-Land!

Such were their daily deeds.

Their monument!—where does it stand?

Their epitaph!—who reads?

No braver dames had Sparta,

No nobler matrons Rome—

Yet who here lauds or honors them,

E'en in their own green home!

The Mothers of our Forest-Land!

They sleep in unknown graves:

And had they borne and nursed a band

Of ingrates, or of slaves,

They had not been more neglected!

But their graves shall yet be found,

And their monuments dot here and there

The Dark and Bloody Ground.

WILLIAM D. GALLIGHER

CHAPTER FOUR

Daughters of Service

"She stretcheth out her
hand to the poor;
yea, she reacheth forth
her hands to the needy."

Proverbs 31:20

Missionary To The Oneidas

JEMIMA KIRKLAND

Prominent among the earlier pioneers in the missionary cause was Jemima Bingham. She came of a devout and God-fearing race, and was reared amid the religious privileges of her Connecticut home. She was a niece of Eleazur Wheelock, D. D., himself a successful laborer in the Indian missionary work. In 1769, she married the Rev. Samuel Kirkland, who had already commenced among the Oneida Indians those active and useful labors which only terminated with his life.

Entering with a sustained enthusiasm into the plans of her husband, she shortly after her marriage, accompanied him to his post of duty in the wilderness near Fort Stanwix—now Rome, New York. This was literally on the frontier, in the midst of a dense forest which extended for hundreds of miles in every direction, and was the abode of numerous Indian tribes, some of which were hostile to the white settlers.

Their forest-home was near the "Council House" of the Oneidas—in the heart of the forest. There, surrounded by the dusky sons of the wilderness, the devoted couple, alone and unaided, commenced their joint missionary labors. The gentle manners and the indomitable courage and energy of Mr. Kirkland, were nobly supplemented by the admirable qualities of his wife. With the sweetness, gentleness, simplicity, and delicacy so becoming to women under all circumstances, were blended in her character, energy that was unconquerable, courage that danger could not blench, and firmness that human power could not bend. Faithfully, too, in the midst of her missionary labors, did she discharge her duties as a mother. One of her sons rewarded her careful teaching by rising to eminence, and becoming President of Harvard College.

Prior to his marriage, Mr. Kirkland made his home and pursued his missionary labors at the "Council House." After his marriage to Jemima, he still continued to preach and teach at the "Council House," addressing the Indians in their own language, which both he and his wife had acquired. Mrs. Kirkland visited the wigwams and instructed the squaws and children, who in turn flocked to her house where she ministered to their bodily and spiritual wants.

The women and children of the tribe were her chosen pupils. Seated in circles on the greensward beneath the spreading arches of giant oaks and maples, they listened to her teachings, and learned from her lips the wondrous story of Christ, who gave up his life on the cross that all tribes and races of mankind might live through Him. Then she prayed for them in the musical tongue of the Oneidas, and the "sounding aisles of the dim woods rang" with the psalms and hymns which she had taught those dusky children of the forest.

The change wrought by these ministrations of Mr. and Mrs. Kirkland was miraculous. A peaceful and well-ordered community, whose citizens were red men, rose in the wilderness, and many souls were gathered into the fold of Christ.

During the years of her residence and labors among the Oneidas, she won many hearts by her kind deeds as a nurse and medical benefactor to the red men and their wives and children. She was thus presented to them as a bright exemplar of the doctrines which she taught. Both she and her husband gained a wide influence among the Indians of the region, many of whom they were afterwards and during the Revolutionary contest, able to win over to the patriot cause.

The Devoted Missionary Wife

ANN H. JUDSON

There is no greater exhibition of moral heroism in the world's history than that which the life of Mrs. Ann Hasseltine Judson affords. She was the first American woman who resolved to leave friends and country to carry the Gospel of Christ to the heathen in foreign climes. This resolve was made, not when the missionary cause had already enlisted the sympathies and benefactions of the whole Christian world, not when the feasibility of the great enterprise had been demonstrated by tens of thousands won to Christ in heathen lands, but when the work was new, and when the wisest and the best were doubtful of its resources and results. But if her early consecration to the cause was heroic, her subsequent devotion to it, amid scenes that might have caused the stoutest heart to faint, was still more glorious.

Ann Hasseltine was born in Bradford, Massachusetts, December 22, 1789. In her earlier years she was distinguished for great mental strength and activity, for practical sense and inexhaustible fertility of resource, as well as great energy of character. She was educated at Bradford Academy, and was distinguished for the ardor and intenseness of her application to intellectual pursuits. Her mind was well disciplined, and her acquisitions large. Something of the character of her mind may be inferred from the fact that, when awakened to a sense of her sinful and lost condition—though only seventeen years of age—Edwards on Redemption became her chosen companion, and by that she was "specially instructed, quickened, and strengthened." Her consecration to Christ was now complete. She says: "I have seasons when I feel I have given myself unreservedly to the Savior, to be disposed of as he sees fit for time and eternity." No wonder that her growth was rapid, and we soon find her rejoicing in full assurance. "I have seasons of feeling," says she, "that I do sit at the feet of my Savior, and that I do choose him for my Prophet, Priest, and King. At these seasons I have felt that if my soul was lost the whole plan of salvation must fail, so conscious am I of loving him, and giving myself to him in his appointed way."

When some one sought to subject her faith to the old Calvinistic test by asking her whether she was willing to be lost, her reply is worthy to be written in letters of gold: "I am not willing to be an enemy to God. With this submissive spirit I could not be unhappy, however He might dispose of me." The secret of her rapid growth in grace, and of the development, of a sturdy Christian character, is found in the fact that from the time of her conversion and spiritual consecration she became an active laborer in the vineyard of the Lord. It was well said of her that the zeal which made her a missionary abroad first made a missionary of her at home.

Her early friends testify that from the time of her conversion till she sailed for Burma she rarely spent half an hour in any company without introducing the subject of personal religion. On the Sabbath it was her custom to fix her mind upon some one of her friends, take their arm, and, as they walked home from Church, endeavor to stir them up to seek Christ. She visited her neighbors for a like object, after having as a teacher performed the labors of the day, till nearly every family had been blessed with her presence, and every individual earnestly and affectionately reasoned with upon the soul's great concern. What might not be hoped for from so promising an early Christian life?

In 1810 the celebrated memorial drawn up by Mr. Judson, and signed by himself and Samuel Nott, Samuel J. Mills, and Samuel Newell—proposing to devote themselves to the missionary cause in heathen lands—was laid before the General Association. This was the origin of the American Board of Commissioners for Foreign Missions. It is remarkable that Bradford was the place where this Association was held, and that during its session Mr. Judson for the first time saw Miss Hasseltine, who afterward became the partner of his early missionary toils.

In making to Miss Hasseltine the offer of marriage, Mr. Judson accompanied it with a declaration of his purpose to devote his life to the cause of Christ in heathen lands, and an invitation to share with him the responsibilities and perils of missionary life. It was an untried path, beset with difficulties and dangers, and it was not in her nature to enter it without a thorough consideration of any question which might suitably bear upon her decision. Mr. Judson, with an honorable manliness, in the very act of proposing to her and to her parents his participation in missionary life, portrayed every discouragement in its truest colors. The struggles through which her own mind passed in arriving at a decision she has faithfully recorded, and they furnish a beautiful tribute to her delicacy as a woman, and to her fortitude and devotion as a Christian.

Mr. Judson's offer was accepted, and thus were brought together two extraordinary characters, most remarkably suited to each other, and to the exalted sphere of Christian duty to which they were assigned. They were married at Bradford, February 5, 1812. Mr. Judson, Messrs. Newell, Nott, Hall, and Rice, were ordained the next day at Salem, and on the 19th of the same month Mr. and Mrs. Judson embarked for Calcutta.

The missionaries, it is well known, were expelled from the British possessions in India. The East India Company could better aggrandize its power and increase its wealth by protecting heathenism than by permitting

the introduction of Christianity. God's wrath may be long delayed, but the terrible Sepoy rebellion, so fresh in all our recollections, attests the certainty and fearfulness of his judgments. The little missionary band was broken, and its members scattered. After much suffering and many hair-breadth escapes, Mr. and Mrs. Judson landed on the Isle of France. Here they were watched as suspected persons, and could find no permanent stay. How desolate must have been their condition! Persecuted and hunted down—not by heathen but by professedly Christian power! Mrs. Judson wrote the following in her journal:

> O, when will my wanderings terminate? When shall I find some little spot that I can call my home in this world? Yet I rejoice in all Thy dealings, O, my heavenly Father, for Thou dost support me under every trial, and enable me to lean on Thee. Thou dost make me to feel the sweetness of deriving comfort from Thee when worldly comforts fall. Thou dost not suffer me to sink down in despondency, but enablest me to look forward with joy to a state of heavenly rest and happiness. Then shall I have to wander no more; the face of Jesus shall be unveiled, and I shall rest in the Arms of Love through all eternity.

After being beset with uncertainty, buffeted, imperiled, and tossed about, they landed, July, 1813, at Rangoon, in the great Burman empire. We have not space for the details of missionary life and labors that now followed. Three years were devoted mainly to the acquisition of the language. Mrs. Judson outstripped her husband in the acquisition of the colloquial, but he obtained a more thorough knowledge of the structure of the language. It was not till six years after they landed in Rangoon that they were able to rejoice over the first native convert to the Christian faith.

In 1821, the prostration of her health led Mrs. Judson to return to America on a visit. Here she was the object of distinguished attentions, and by her letters, her personal appeals, and by the publication of her History of the Burman Mission, she contributed largely to awaken an interest in the cause of foreign missions among the American Churches. With her health only partially restored, she rejoined her husband at Rangoon in the Autumn of 1823. Now opens a new and splendid chapter in her history—one that the Christian world will never forget. From the record made of it by Dr. Cutting, in the American Missionary Memorial, we gather an outline sketch, which is all our space will admit.

Mrs. Judson while in this country seemed to have observed almost prophetically the gloomy shadows of that crisis, but she was undismayed, and returned to her post with the true martyr spirit. During her absence the number of converts had been nearly doubled, and Mr. Judson had completed a translation of the New Testament, as well as an epitome of the Old. The arrival of Dr. Price soon after her departure, and the information at court of his skill as a physician, had occasioned a summons from Ava, which brought Mr. Judson and his new missionary associate into the presence of the king, and an order that the missionaries should remain at the capital, where land was given them on which to erect dwellings. These arrangements having been made, Mr. Judson descended the river to Rangoon, where he met Mrs. Judson, with whom he soon returned to Ava, leaving Mr. and Mrs. Wade with Mr. Hough to carry forward the work at the old station. For a while Mr. Judson proceeded with his missionary labors at the capital, but no time had elapsed for, the gathering of fruits before the sudden breaking out of war between the British East India Company and the Burmese Government brought upon the missionaries and other foreign residents of Ava perils, privations, and sufferings, such as language is hardly adequate to record.

For nearly two years no tidings came of their fate. Whether this lack of intelligence was a mere incident of the war, or whether they had at once fallen victims to the jealousy of an implacable despot, or were still surviving in chains and sorrow, were painful questions of which no solution could be gained. The deepest anxiety possessed the heads of American Christians during this long period, and when at length, tidings came of their safety, the joy and thanksgiving were universal. The record of their sufferings, unsurpassed by any narrative of fiction, was written by Mrs. Judson, and will remain through successive ages one of the most exciting chapters of missionary history. To abbreviate it, or to attempt a sketch in other language, may be permitted only under the sternest necessity, and the best success will poorly compare with the graphic original.

Mr. and Mrs. Judson received their first certain intelligence of the war as they were approaching Ava, and on their arrival found themselves regarded with some coldness by the king and court. On May 23rd, 1824, the fall of Rangoon was made known at Ava, and, though the proud monarch did not doubt his power to repel and punish the British, the necessity of large military preparations was admitted, and intense excitement prevailed at the palace. Golden chains were prepared in which to bring to Ava the captive Governor-General, and ladies and gentlemen of the court anticipated the service of English slaves as attendants! The soldiers embarked in high glee, ignorant of the irresistibleness of scientific warfare, and looking for an easy victory over

barbarians and cowards.

No sooner had the army embarked, than suspicions arose of the presence of spies, and three Englishmen residing at Ava were forthwith arrested and examined. In this examination it was found that the accounts of one of them showed considerable sums of money paid to Mr. Judson and Dr. Price, and, ignorant of the methods of transmitting funds practiced by Europeans and Americans, the Government found in this fact what it deemed evidence of their complicity with the English in the war.

On the 8th of June, Mr. Judson was suddenly arrested at his dwelling by a posse of officers, one of whom, known by his "spotted face," was an executioner. Throwing Mr. Judson upon the floor, they bound him with cords, answering the importunity of his wife on his behalf with threats to take her also. She offered the "spotted face" money to loosen the cords, but he spurned the gift, and dragged away his victim, pausing at a few rods' distance to tighten the instruments of torture. The faithful disciple, Moung Ing, followed, to trace the teacher's steps, and to procure, if possible, a mitigation of his sufferings. He returned with the intelligence that the order of the king had consigned Mr. Judson to the death-prison; he saw no more. Next Mrs. Judson found herself a prisoner in her own house, the magistrate of the place summoning her to the veranda for examination. Hastily destroying all letters and papers in her possession, lest they should disclose the fact that she and her husband had correspondents in England, and had taken notes of all occurrences which they had witnessed in the country, she submitted to the scrutiny of her inquisitor, who left her under the guard of ten ruffians, whom he charged to keep her safe. Night came, and darkness. Barring herself and her four little Burman girls in an inner room, she was ordered by the guards to open the doors and come out, or they would tear the house down. Partly however, by threats, and partly by bribes, she quieted them so far that they let her alone, carousing however, through all the night, and pouring forth the most diabolical language to which she had ever listened.

This dreadful night of personal danger and of painful apprehensions as to her husband's fate, was but the beginning of sorrows. The next morning Moung Ing brought to her the information that her husband and all the white foreigners were confined in the death-prison, with three pairs of iron fetters each, subsequently increased to five, and fastened to a pole to prevent their moving. She entreated the magistrate for leave to go to some member of the Government in behalf of her husband, and wrote a letter to her friend, the king's sister, but in vain. Night found her a prisoner still.

On the third day a message to the governor of the city, expressing her desire to appear before him with a present, resulted in an order for her release. Gifts wrung from the wretched woman secured the promise of an amelioration of her husband's sufferings, and permission to visit him in prison, and by the same means, all the prisoners were delivered from their suffocating confinement, and placed in an open shed within the prison inclosure. Hither she sent food and mats for them all, commencing those angelic ministries to the sufferers which have rendered her name immortal. Next, her hopes were raised by the prospect of a successful petition to the queen; then came the confiscation of Mr. Judson's effects, the most exact list of them being made by officers in attendance.

Fertile in resources, she secreted a considerable sum of money, alike indispensable to her support and to any successful intervention in behalf of her husband, and saved likewise, numerous articles which, during the long imprisonment, proved to be of inestimable value. Then followed the dashing of all her hopes by the refusal of the queen to interfere. Again she was refused admittance to her husband, and the sufferings of the prisoners were increased, and again relief to them was purchased by her judicious use of presents.

Month after month passed away, during which this incomparable woman employed her time in devising and executing measures for the comfort of the prisoners, and specially for the release of her husband, scarcely a day passing in which she did not visit some member of the Government or some branch of the royal family, with no other effect, however, than that she and the objects of her solicitude were kept from despair by the encouraging promises of the capricious court. No one dared to approach the despot on the throne in favor of a foreigner while the English were on their successful march toward Ava.

An incident connected with this imprisonment remained to the end of his life among Dr. Judson's most vivid recollections. Seven months of these privations and sufferings had passed away, during which Mrs. Judson had used her inexhaustible resources of talents and influence in ministering to the necessities of the prisoners, meeting extortion and oppression with gifts, and capricious and vexatious orders with extra fees, and conciliating the good-will of those in power by her intelligence and eloquent persuasion. In a letter to her husband, Mrs. Judson wrote:

> O, how many, many times, have I returned from that dreary prison at nine o'clock at night, [a distance of two miles] solitary, and worn-out with fatigue

and anxiety, and thrown myself in that same rocking-chair which you and Deacon L. provided for me in Boston, and endeavored to invent some new scheme for the release of the prisoners!

At this period occurred the birth of her daughter. Twenty days after that event she was again at the prison door, with the child in her arms, begging for admission. The prison was a rough building, like a New England barn of former days, without ceiling or lining of any kind, without windows, or even an aperture for air. There were in the prison about one hundred prisoners, mostly Burmese, many of them in the stocks or otherwise tortured. The group nearest the door was composed of ten foreigners, of whom two were Americans, three Englishmen, two Armenians, one Spaniard, and one Portuguese priest. Their clothing was reduced to shirts and trowsers. They wore five pairs of fetters each upon their ankles, and were further confined by a bamboo, as before mentioned, passing between their legs, and confined to the two outside men, so that they could sit or lie, each one at his pleasure, but could move only by a common effort. The wretched men were in this condition, when suddenly the door opened, and Mrs. Judson, clad in Burmese costume, which she had adopted for safety's sake, stood before her husband with their little child, unconscious of its parents' woes. Behind her stood the faithful Moung Ing, and by her side the diabolical "spotted face." She was not permitted to enter, and, as the father struggled to receive the precious gift, his companions in misery, impelled by an instant benevolence, seconded his wishes by a simultaneous movement toward the door. It is not strange that such a scene was impressed indelibly on the mind of every one present.

But new miseries were yet in store. The hot season had now come, and the close confinement of the prisoners was scarcely to be endured. New severities were practiced, and the unremitted exertions of Mrs. Judson failed to procure more than the slightest alleviations. Even the governor of the city, to whom she was indebted for many friendly offices, resisted her appeals till her husband was prostrated with a fever, when he ordered his removal to a bamboo hovel, a palace in comparison to the place he had left.

Three days afterward the governor sent for her in great haste, detaining her with inquiries about his watch, while her husband and all the other white prisoners were removed, she knew not whither. She ran in every direction, making inquiries in vain, till at length she learned from an old woman that they had gone toward Amarapoora, the old capital, distant six miles. "You can do nothing for your husband," said the governor, adding kindly and significantly, "take care of yourself." She was satisfied that there was danger, but she was not to be deterred from her purpose. She obtained a passport, and the next morning, with her child, the two Burmese children, and a Bengalee servant, set off for Amarapoora, first in a boat and then in a cart. Through the dreadful heat and dust she arrived at the government house, but the prisoners had just left for a village beyond Oung-pen-la. Arriving at that place, she found them in an old shattered building, scarcely protected from the sun, chained two and two, and almost dead from suffering and fatigue.

"Why have you come?" said Mr. Judson in gentle and sad reproof. "I hoped you would not follow, for you can not live here."

The jailer would not permit her to remain at the prison, but he gave her a shelter in one of the rooms of his own house, and there she spent the next six months of wretchedness. It was on the dreadful march to this prison, under the burning heat of a midday sun, that Mr. Judson's feet stained the sand with their blood, and that he was saved from perishing by the considerate kindness of the Bengalee servant of one of the prisoners, who tore his turban from his head, and, dividing it between his master and Mr. Judson, bound it around their feet, and then permitted Mr. Judson to lean upon him the rest of the way. When night came, the kindness of women furnished refreshments for the prisoners, and in the morning carts were provided to bear them the rest of the way to Oung-pen-la.

On their arrival at this place the prisoners supposed they were to be burned, and endeavored to prepare their minds for the event. But the repairs upon the building rekindled their hopes, and they soon found some alleviations of their condition. These alleviations were not of such character, however, as to remove their miseries. Oppression and extortion still remained the features of their prison discipline, and the tender mercies which they experienced were only the capricious indulgences of tyrants. Mrs. Judson, in turn, became now the helpless sufferer. Her health gave way; her poor child lost its accustomed nourishment, and the wretched father, permitted to go abroad from the prison by the force of presents to his keepers, bore the famishing and helpless babe from house to house about the village, begging food from mothers who had young children. But deliverance was at hand.

The English army made its triumphant march toward Ava, and the humbled king at length sent an embassage, desiring conditions of peace. The services of Mr. Judson were now important to him, and his release was ordered. The period of their sufferings had not yet expired, but they were cheered with brighter hopes, and in February, 1826, they were permitted to rest under the protection of the British flag, in the camp of General Sir Archibald Campbell,

who had demanded their release.

Descending the river to the territories granted by the Burman Government to the English, Mr. and Mrs. Judson commenced missionary operations at Amherst, a new town designed to be the British capital. Scarcely, however, were they fixed in this new abode when urgent overtures were made to Mr. Judson to accompany an embassy to Ava, to negotiate a new treaty. In the hope that an article providing for religious toleration might be incorporated, Mr. Judson yielded to the wishes of the commissioner, and parted with Mrs. Judson on the 5th of July—never to see her more on earth.

Her constitution, broken by the intense sufferings and cares of the long imprisonment, yielded to an attack of fever, and, after eighteen days' illness, she departed this life, October 24, 1826, in the thirty-seventh year of her age. Her husband returned to his desolate home in the deepest affliction, unable to gain any particular information as to the state of mind with which she approached death, saving only that she resigned her spirit to God who gave it with calm and trusting faith. Her funeral was attended by all the English residents, and the Assistant Superintendent, with thoughtful kindness, placed a small rough fence around her grave to protect it from incautious intrusion. Her child survived her just six months, "And then that little moaning one went to its mother's bosom, and slept sweet 'neath the cool branches of the hopia-tree."

Thus lived and died Ann H. Judson. Her life was short, but filled with stirring incidents and useful deeds. It is not strange that, living, she gained the love and admiration of the Christian world, nor that, dying, her name found its place at once among the heroines of history.

The First Woman To Cross The Rockies

NARCISSA WHITMAN

Dr. Marcus and Narcissa Whitman, and Mr. and Mrs. Spaulding, were among the earliest to respond to the appeal of setting up a mission in Oregon. In 1836 they crossed the continent, scaled the Rocky Mountains, and penetrated to the heart of the wild region which was to be the scene of their heroic labors and the blessings of civilization and religion.

Mrs. Whitman and Mrs. Spaulding were the first white women that ever crossed that mighty range which nature seems to have intended as a barrier against the aggressive westward march of Anglo-Saxon race. Strong indeed must have been the impelling motive which carried these two women over that rugged barrier! But these heroic Christian women abated not their zeal or efforts in the work to which they had put their hand.

For a period of eight years Dr. and Mrs. Whitman resided on the banks of the Walla-Walla River, doing all in their power to benefit the Indians. Such labors as theirs deserved a peaceful old age, and the enduring, gratitude of their tawny proteges. But, alas! that we have to record that such was not their lot!

The measles had broken out among the Indians and spread with frightful rapidity through the neighboring tribes. Dr. Whitman did all he could to stay its progress, but great numbers of them died. The Indians supposed that the doctor could have stopped the course of the disease if he had wished it, and accordingly concocted a plan to destroy him and his whole family. With this object in view about sixty of them armed themselves and came to his house.

The inmates, having no suspicion of any hostile intentions, were totally unprepared for resistance or flight. Dr. and Mrs. Whitman and their nephew—a youth of about seventeen or eighteen years of age—were sitting in the parlor in the afternoon, when Silaw-kite, the chief, and To-ma-kus, entered the room and addressing the doctor told him very coolly they had come to kill him. The doctor, not believing it possible that they could entertain any hostile intentions towards him, told them as much; but whilst in the act of speaking, To-ma-kus drew a tomahawk from under his robe and buried it into Dr. Whitman's head. The unfortunate man fell dead in his chair. Mrs. Whitman and the nephew fled up stairs and locked themselves into an upper room.

In the meantime Sil-aw-kite gave the war-whoop, as a signal to his party outside, to proceed in the work of destruction, which they did with the ferocity and yells of so many fiends. Mrs. Whitman, hearing the shrieks and groans of the dying, looked out of the window and was shot through the breast by a son of the chief, but was not mortally wounded. A party then rushed up stairs and dispatched the niece on the spot, dragged her down by the hair of her head and taking her to the front of the house, mutilated her in a shocking manner with their knives and tomahawks.

There was one man who had a wife bedridden. On the commencement of the affray he ran to her room, and, taking her up in his arms, carried her unperceived by the Indians to the thick bushes that skirted the river, and hurried on with his burden in the direction of Fort Walla-Walla. Having reached a distance of fifteen miles, he became so exhausted that, unable to carry her further, he concealed her in a thick clump of bushes on the margin of the river, and hastened to the Fort for assistance.

On his arrival, Mr. McBain immediately sent out men with him, and brought her in. She had fortunately suffered nothing more than fright. The number killed—including Dr. and Mrs. Whitman—amounted to fourteen. The other females and children were carried off by the Indians, and two of them were forthwith taken as wives by Sil-aw-kite's son and another. A man employed in the little mill, forming a part of the establishment, was spared to work the mill for the Indians. The day following the awful tragedy, a Catholic priest, who had not heard of the massacre, stopped on seeing the mangled corpses strewn round the house, and requested permission to bury them, which was readily granted.

When the priest left the place, he met Mr. Spaulding, a fellow missionary of the deceased, whose labors lay about a hundred miles off, at a place on the river Coldwater. He communicated to him the melancholy fate of his friends, and advised him to fly as fast as possible, or, in all probability, he would be another victim. He gave him a share of his provisions, and Mr. Spaulding hurried homeward, full of apprehensions for the safety of his own family; but, unfortunately, his horse escaped from him in the night, and after a six days' toilsome march on foot, having lost his way, he at length reached the banks of the river, but on the opposite side to his own home.

In the dead of the night, in a state of starvation, having eaten nothing for three days, everything seeming to be quiet about his own place, he cautiously embarked in a small canoe, and paddled across the river. But he had no sooner landed than an Indian seized him, and dragged him to his own house, where he found all his family prisoners, and the Indians in full possession. These Indians were not of the same tribe with those who had destroyed Dr. Whitman's family, nor had they at all participated in the outrage; but having heard of it, and fearing the white man would include them in their vengeance, they had seized on the family of Mr. Spaulding for the purpose of holding them as hostages for their own safety. The family were uninjured; and he was overjoyed to find things no worse.

Notwithstanding this awful tragedy the heroic women remained at their posts in the different missionary stations in the territory, and long afterwards pursued those useful labors which, by establishing pioneer-settlements in the wilderness, and by civilizing and christianizing the wild tribes, prepared the way for the army of emigrants which, is now converting that vast wilderness into a great and flourishing state.

Braving the Wilds of Oregon

MRS. WHITE

The same noble spirit which carried the Whitmans across our continent on their lofty errand, also inspired another band of gospel messengers to move in the same great enterprise.

Dr. White of New York, and his wife, were prominent in this latter movement. Their immediate company consisted of thirteen individuals, five of whom were women: Mrs. White, Mrs. Beers, Miss Downing, Miss Johnson, and Miss Pitman. These ladies were all admirably fitted both physically and mentally for the enterprise in which they had embarked.

Mrs. White was a lady in whom were blended quiet resolution, a high sense of duty, and great sensibility. When her husband informed her one cold night, in the winter of 1836, that there was a call for them from Oregon; that the Board of Missions advertised for a clergyman/physician, and as he could act in the capacity of doctor, he thought it might be well to respond thereto. She did not immediately answer; and looking up, he was surprised to find her weeping. This seemed to him singular, as her disposition was so unusually cheerful, and it was seldom there was a trace of tears to be found upon her cheek, especially, as he thought, for so trivial a cause. In some confusion and mortification, he begged her not to allow his words to cause her uneasiness. Still she wept in silence, till, after a pause of several moments, she struggled for composure, seated herself by his side, extended her hand for the paper, and twice looking over the notice, remarked that if he could so arrange his affairs as to render it consistent for him to go to Oregon, she would place no obstacle in his way, and would willingly accompany him.

Dr. White offered his services to the Board of Missions, they were accepted, and he was requested to be in readiness to sail in a few weeks, from Boston to Oregon. The thought that they were now to leave, probably for ever, their dear home and dearer friends, was a sad one. Mrs. White shed tears of regret though not of reluctance to go. She pictured to herself her mother's anguish, at what must be very like consigning her only daughter to the grave.

The anticipated separation from that mother, who had nursed her so tenderly and loved her with that tireless, changeless affection which the maternal heart only knows, filled her with sorrow. However, they were spared the painful scene they had feared, and obtained her consent with little difficulty. When they visited her for that purpose, she had just been reading for the first time the life of Mrs. Judson. The example of this excellent lady had so interested her that when the project was laid before her she listened with comparative calmness, and though somewhat astonished, was willing they should go where duty led them. This in some measure relieved Mrs. White, and with a lightened heart and more composure she set about the necessary preparations.

In a short time all was in readiness, the last farewell wept, rather than spoken, the last yearning look lingered on loved ones, and they were on their way to Oregon. On the day that their eldest son was one year old, they embarked from Boston. That their adieus were sorrowful may not be doubted, indeed this or any other word in our language is inadequate to describe the emotions of the party. As the pilot-boat dropped at the stern of the vessel, its occupants waved their handkerchiefs and simultaneously began singing a farewell "Missionary Hymn." The effect was electric; some rushed to the side in agony as though they would recall the departed ones and return with them to their native land. Others covered their faces, and tears streamed through their trembling fingers, and sobs shook the frames of even strong men. They thought not of formalities in that hour; it was not a shame for the men to weep. The forms of their friends fast lessened in the distance, and at last their boat looked like a speck on the wave. The sweet cadences of that beautiful song faintly rolling along to their hearing, like the sigh of an angel, were the last sounds that readied them from the home of civilization.

The voyage was a prolonged one. But the close relationship into which they were brought served to knit together the bonds of Christian fellowship, and inspire them with a oneness of purpose in carrying out their noble enterprise. Immediately on arriving at their field of labor they entered on their first work: that of establishing communities. In that almost unbroken wilderness, cabins were erected, the ground prepared for tillage, and steps were taken towards the building of a saw and grist-mill. The Indians were conciliated, and a mission-school for their instruction was established. The party received constant accessions to their numbers as the months rolled away, and opened communication with the other mission-colonies in the territory.

During the summer the ladies divided their labors; the school of Indians was taught by Miss Johnson; Miss Downing (now Mrs. Shepherd) attended to the cutting, making, and repairing of the clothing for the young Indians, as well as those for the children of the missionaries; Mrs. White and Miss Pitman (now Mrs. Jason Lee) superintended the domestic matters of the little colony.

In September, Mr. and Mrs. Leslie, three daughters, and Mr. Perkins the fiance of Miss Johnson, joined them. The family was now enlarged to sixty members. Dr. and Mrs. White removed into their new cabin—a mile distant.

Here ensued a repetition of trials, privations, and hardships, such as they had already endured in their former habitation.

Their cabin was a rude affair, scarcely more than a shanty, without a chimney, and with only roof enough to cover a bed; a few loose boards served for a floor; one side of the house was entirely unenclosed, and all their cooking had to be done in the open air, in the few utensils which they had at hand. But though they had many discomforts, nothing compared with another annoyance to which they were nightly subject. The territory where they lived was infested by black wolves of the fiercest species. Their situation was so lonely; and Doctor White's absences were so frequent, that Mrs. White was greatly terrified every night by the frightful howls of these ferocious marauders.

One night Doctor White left home to visit Mr. Shepherd, who was ill, and some of the sick mission children. Mrs. White, while awaiting his return, suddenly heard a burst of prolonged howling from the depths of the forest through which the Doctor would have to pass on his return homeward. The howls were continued with all the eagerness which showed that the brutes were close upon their prey. She flew to the yard, and in the greatest terror, besought the two hired men to fly to her husband's rescue.

They laughed at her fears, and endeavored to reason her into composure. But the horrid din continued. Through the wild chorus she fancied she heard a human voice faintly calling for help. Unable longer to restrain her excited feelings, she snatched up a long pair of cooper's compasses—the first weapon that offered itself—and plunged out into the woods, accompanied by the men, armed with rifles.

They ran swiftly, the howls guiding them in the proper course, and in a few moments they came to a large tree, round which a pack of hungry monsters had collected, and were baying in full chorus, jumping up and snapping their jaws at a man who was seated among the branches.

The cowardly brutes, catching sight of the party, sneaked off with howls of baffled rage, and were soon beyond hearing. The doctor descended from his retreat, quite panic-stricken at his narrow escape. He informed them that on first starting from the mission, he had picked up a club, to defend himself from the wolves, should they make their appearance. But when one of the animals came within six feet of him, and by its call, gathered others to the pursuit, his valiant resolutions vanished. He dropped his stick and plied his heels, with admirable dexterity, till the tree offered its friendly aid, when he hallooed for help with all the power of his lungs. Because of Mrs. White's intuition of the danger, and her speedy appearance upon the scene, Dr. White's term of usefulness in the Oregon mission would have been greatly abridged.

The Great "Ma" of Africa
Mary Slessor

"Oh, I wish I could help the bush children," sighed a little Scottish lassie one day after hearing her mother tell about the poor black boys and girls in faraway Africa. "I am going to be a missionary when I grow up, and go out there and teach those folks—God's ways."

"But you're only a girl," protested her elder brother haughtily. "I'm going to be the missionary from this house." Seeing the look of distress which his remarks had flung across his sister's countenance, the little fellow added in a generous tone, "It'll be perfectly all right for you to come and help me, though, if you're real good. I'll let you sit up in the pulpit right beside me."

The two youthful daydreamers were little Robert and Mary Slessor, children of a shoemaker who lived in Aberdeen, Scotland, about the middle of the nineteenth century. Their mother was a brave Christian woman, deeply interested in missionary work. She wished more than anything else that at least one of her children would someday carry the gospel story to people in a faraway land. When she heard the childish prattle of these two little ones, she smiled, and in her heart she prayed that if it pleased God, her little Robert might indeed become such a man as he now aspired to be. But God chose to call Robert to himself not long afterwards.

Now Mary became the eldest child in the family, and a very dependable child was she. There were few toys in the plain home, but Mary found more enjoyment playing with her baby brother and sisters as they came, one by one, than with make-believe doll babies. She could care for them and dress them and hush them to sleep like a little mother. Sometimes when the younger children did not need her care, she would play at teaching school. All alone in a corner of the room she would sit, talking to the imaginary children in her schoolroom. Her mother, overhearing her remarks, knew that Mary was still thinking about helping the bush children in faraway Africa.

Although Mary's mother was a sincere Christian, her father was not. He kept company with men who cared more for strong drink than they did for their own good. And as a result, he began to spend most of his earnings for drink. Often on Saturday nights he would come home with his pockets empty and with his mind crazed by whisky. Then he would be cruel to the family, and Mary would have to rush out of doors to hide until he would go to sleep.

In his better moods Mary's father was ashamed of his weakness, and he decided to move away from Aberdeen, leaving his old friends in the hope that he might get away from the temptation to indulge in drink. He left his shop in the city and moved his family to the busy, smoky town of Dundee, on the River Tay. Here there were many large mills and factories, and the streets climbed right over the tops of steep hills overlooking the countryside. Sometimes Mary would take the children for long walks, and they would climb the hilltops and gaze on the green fields lying along the river. Sometimes when the tide came in they would go down to the riverbank to breathe the fresh smell of the sea.

Sad to say, Mary's father did not leave his bad habits behind when he moved away from Aberdeen. Soon he was behaving himself as unmanfully as before, and his wife was compelled to go to work in one of the mills in order to earn money to buy food and clothes for the children. Now Mary was left to do the housework and care for the little ones. She did not mind these tasks, for always she had been her mother's cheerful helper. But she did mind the dark shadow which her father's conduct cast over their shabby home—she minded that very, very much.

By the time Mary was eleven years old her father had become a hopeless drunkard, and her mother could not always earn enough money to provide for the family needs. Mary also went to work in the mills. There was no law against child labor to forbid her taking a place among the other children who toiled long hours in factories. At first she was allowed to work only half a day. The other half she was sent to school at the factory, where the working girls were taught to read and write and count.

Mary was glad for the privilege of going to school. She was eager to learn how to read and write, but she did not like numbers. They seemed to dance before her eyes and get themselves all mixed up as she tried to work simple problems on the blackboard.

Although Mary found her arithmetic lessons hard to learn, she was clever with her fingers and soon knew all about weaving. Then her name was placed on the big pay roll at the factory and she became a wage earner. How pleased she felt when she ran home with her first week's earnings! She laid the money in her mother's lap and danced up and down in glee. To her surprise, she saw tears roll down her mother's faded cheeks, just as if it hurt her to take that money and use it.

A few years later Mary was working at a large machine and receiving a good wage. She was spending long, tiresome hours at her work, waking each morning when the factory whistles blew at five o'clock, and taking her place in the factory, ready to begin the day's work, at six. She would keep the machine going until six o'clock in the evening, having only two hours off for lunch periods during the day. In summer she often carried her lunch and ate it in the factory. Then she would go out for a walk in the park, to get away from the noise of buzzing machines and whirling belts.

Saturday afternoons and Sundays Mary did not work in the factory. She always found plenty to do at home to help her tired mother get ready for Sunday, and when Sunday came she was never too tired to take her brother and sisters to Sunday school. Through her mother's careful training she had formed the habit of attending Sunday school before she began to work at the factory, and because it was a good habit she always kept it up. She gave her heart to Jesus when she was quite young, and there came into her heart a great desire to learn more and more about His loving ways. She studied her Bible lessons very carefully, and the teacher always knew that Mary would be able to answer every question correctly.

As Mary grew older she thought often of her childhood's longing to become a missionary. This longing kept growing up, too! But she knew that now her mother hoped to educate her brother John for the ministry. "John will be our missionary, now that Robert has gone to heaven," she had often heard her mother say. Mary understood how much her mother needed her earnings at the factory, for she was the breadwinner for the family now. She worked on quietly and asked God to help her find some work to do for Him at home.

The church where Mary attended services was built over shops and looked down on streets and lanes which were filled at night with big boys and girls who had no Christian training. They were rude and wicked, and Mary longed to find some way to interest them in right conduct. She wanted to lead them to Jesus, but they refused to attend church and pretended to care nothing about God.

A mission was opened on a side street, and Mary believed that these young people might be persuaded to attend services there. So she asked the superintendent of the mission if she might have a class in his school. She looked so small and frail that the superintendent feared the work would be too hard for her. He knew the young people would be hard to reach and difficult to influence aright. But when he saw the eager longing in Mary's eyes to work for God he consented to let her begin there. Mary had no easy time trying to start her class.

The young people insisted that they did not want anybody to bother about them, and many refused to come. Some who attended were wild and noisy and almost unmanageable. Rowdy gangs would gather outside the building and throw stones and mud against the walls, trying to discourage the faithful Christian workers. Mary refused to be discouraged. Although she suffered unkind treatment from the rough crowd, she never acted frightened or angry. When they saw she was no coward, they quit bothering her and began to follow her to the mission and take their places in her class. They even grew fond of her and tried in their awkward manner to help her.

Feeling that she needed to know more about the young people in her class, Mary visited in their homes. She found that they lived in the slums, in wretched places, but she paid no attention to the untidiness and filth. She talked with their mothers, took the dirty babies on her knees, and acted so friendly and willing to help that soon she won her way into the hearts of these unfortunate people. They were ready to listen to her teachings, and some of them tried to do better.

During these years Mary's brother John grew tall and taller, but he was a frail lad. The doctor shook his head and said that John could not live much longer in the cold climate of Scotland. They sent him away to New Zealand, hoping the change would do him good, but soon after arriving there he died. Thus his mother's fond hopes of a missionary son were never fulfilled, and her disappointment was very bitter.

One day while Mary was grieving over the loss of her brother, whom she loved devotedly, the thought flashed into her mind that now, after all, she would have to be the missionary from that family. Both Robert and John were gone, and there were no more boys for her mother to offer to God. Now the missionary would have to be a daughter. The thought came again and again, "Perhaps you are the one whom God has chosen to carry the story of Jesus to the bush children in Africa."

Mary knew she was uneducated and that she could not stop her work to go to school. She knew too, that her mother depended very much on her, and she wondered how the family could get along if she should leave them. But she believed that if God really wanted her to go as a missionary He would help her find a way to overcome these difficulties. Then she began to study harder than ever. She would borrow good books, or buy them, and slip one into her pocket to take along when she went to work. Often she propped a book open on a corner of the loom, where she could read a few lines whenever she had a minute to spare. Thus by the greatest effort she added to her store of learning day by day.

But we must not think that Mary slighted her work. She was one of the cleverest weavers at the factory, and by working fast she found that she could increase her pay check. Then she laid aside more money each week in a savings account for the needs of the family if she should go away.

Thus the days, weeks, months, and years passed by while Mary was preparing to become a missionary. For fourteen years she toiled as a factory worker, working hard and waiting patiently for her call to a foreign land. Then one day the sad news came to Scotland that Dr. David Livingstone, the great missionary hero, had died in Africa. "Send another volunteer to take up the work he laid down," came the call from the mission fields in that faraway country. Mary felt in her heart that God wanted her to answer that call.

Mary's mother was glad to give this consecrated daughter to work for God in Africa. "You'll make a fine missionary," she said, smiling into Mary's wistful face, "and I'm sure God will be with you." Then it was easy for Mary to bid her loved ones good-by and sail away.

On August 5, 1876, Mary was on her way to Calabar, on the west coast of Africa—the land of her dreams. Efik is the principal language used in that part of the continent, and Mary's first task was to learn it. She studied hard, and in a short time was able to converse with the natives. This surprised her fellow teachers and pleased the natives. They said of her that she was "blessed with an Efik mouth." Then her old dream came true, for she began to teach black boys and girls in the day school.

Mary loved every one of the children and was disappointed because there were so few in her school. She found out that the African chiefs did not believe in educating children and that was the reason why only a few came to be taught. At first she laughed to see the children carry their slates on their heads and their pencils in their woolly hair. She found that some of them were mischievous, fun-loving children, just the same as the boys and girls in her own homeland. Sometimes she went out to the rude lodgings, called the yards, where they lived, and talked to their fathers and mothers about the love of Jesus.

At first Africa seemed like a wonderland to Mary, for its beautiful scenery thrilled her through and through. She had spent so many of her waking hours shut up within factory walls, that now her eyes feasted on the forest green and the gorgeous colorings. But when Mary saw the terrible condition of the ignorant, superstitious people who lived there she thought less of the beauty and more of the sorrow which surrounded her. She longed to do more to help the people find the way to God.

Mary spent several years at the first station in Calabar, getting acquainted with Africa's people and their need. Then she went to another station farther up the river where more work awaited her. She lived in a hut built of mud and slips of bamboo, with a roof of palm leaves. A "sure-enough" African house, it was. She wore old clothes and ate the food of the natives, which was cheap. In this way she saved up quite a bit of her salary, and that money she sent back to her widowed mother in Scotland. The natives respected her and were pleased to have her live among them. By and by they listened to her when she objected to their wicked customs, and some of them began to do better.

One of the evil practices of the Africans which grieved Mary's heart was the killing of twin babies. Her mother had told stories about this evil practice when Mary was only a child. Now she saw that the Africans were really afraid of twins. She resolved to show them how foolish their superstition was, so one day she took a twin baby that had been thrown away into the bush to die. A little black baby girl it was, and she named it Janie. The natives looked on in horror, and would not come near the child. They expected something dreadful to happen to Mary because she took the twin; but nothing happened. Whenever she heard of twin babies who had been thrown away she hurried out to find them. Many of them died before she could save them. Others she saved, and after a while her hut swarmed with little tots whom nobody else loved. They had a happy home with her and grew to love her dearly.

Mary often talked to the grownups about Jesus. They would gather in groups about her and listen very closely while she explained to them the words of God. They began to call her "the Ma who loves babies." Sometimes they called her Ma Akamba, which means "The Great Ma." By and by they respected her so much that even grown men and women began to mind her like children.

When the natives began to quit their evil ways and try to worship the true God, Mary sent for other missionaries to come to teach them. Then she gathered her few belongings together, packed them into boxes, and piled them into a boat on the river. Taking the children, she rowed upstream into another district where the story of Jesus had never been told. Here she built another African house and set up housekeeping, and little by little she won the respect and confidence and love of her new neighbors.

Over and over Mary endured the hardships of such beginnings, sometimes going into districts where she did not receive a welcome. "We do not want to change our ways; we do not want your teaching," the chiefs would say, frowning at her. Then her friends would plead for her not to go and risk her life among those dark-minded people. But Mary loved best the work of a pioneer missionary, and on and on she would go, carrying the gospel of Jesus.

She had such a strong influence over the natives that the British government appointed her consul of the district in which she lived. Dr. Livingstone had held this same government position while he toiled in Africa, but Mary was the first woman to be thus honored by Great Britain. She refused to wear a blue cap with a gold band to show that she was a British consul. "It is enough," she would say, "that the natives know and that they respect my decisions in court."

Mary spent thirty-four years of hard work as a missionary. Many of her friends in that dark land called her "The White Queen," but the natives called her by the more endearing term of "Our Mother." The boys and girls whom she saved from cruel death in the bush grew up into Christian men and women, to love and care for her when she became old. From her little mud hut she answered the death call, and went to rest in the beautiful place which Jesus made ready for her in his Father's house above.

Your Mission

Hark, the voice of Jesus crying,—
"Who will go and work today?
Fields are white and harvest waiting!
Who will bear the sheaves away?"
Loud and strong the Master calleth,
Rich reward he offers thee;
Who will answer gladly saying,
"Here am I; send me, send me!"

If you cannot cross the ocean,
And the heathen lands explore;
You can find the heathen nearer,
You can help them at your door.
If you cannot give your thousands,
You can give the widow's mite;
And the least you do for Jesus,
Will be precious in his sight.

If you cannot speak like angels;
If you cannot preach like Paul;
You can tell the love of Jesus,
You can say He died for all.
If you cannot rouse the wicked
With the judgment's dread alarms,
You can lead the little children
To the Saviour's waiting arms.

If you cannot be the watchman
Standing high on Zion's wall,
Pointing out the path to heaven,
Offering life and peace to all;
With your prayers and with your bounties
You can do what heaven demands;
You can be like faithful Aaron,
Holding up the prophet's hands.

If among the older people,
You may not be apt to teach;
"Feed my lambs," said Christ, our Shepherd,
"Place the food within their reach,"
And it may be that the children
You have led with trembling hand,
Will be found among your jewels
When you reach the better land.

Let none hear you idly saying,
"There is nothing I can do,"
While the souls of men are dying,
And the Master calls for you.
Take the task he gives you gladly;
Let his work your pleasure be;
Answer quickly when he calleth,
"Here am I; send me, send me!"

DANIEL MARCH, D. D.

CHAPTER FIVE

Daughters of Royalty

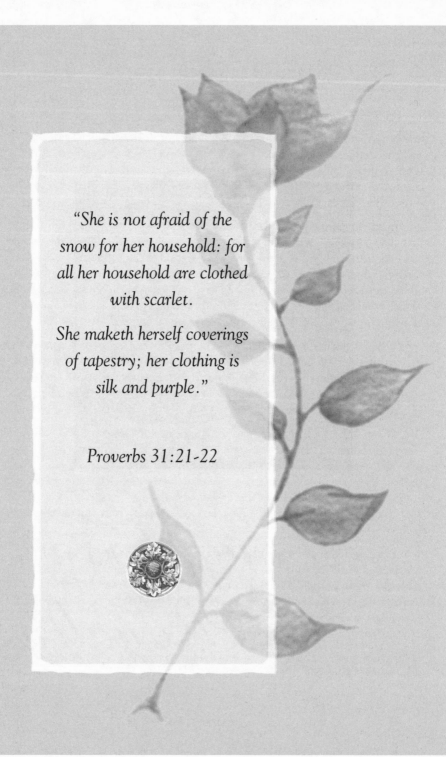

"She is not afraid of the snow for her household: for all her household are clothed with scarlet.

She maketh herself coverings of tapestry; her clothing is silk and purple."

Proverbs 31:21-22

Scotland's Angelic Queen

QUEEN MARGARET

When Malcolm Canmore had reigned over Scotland for nearly ten years, a great event happened in the neighboring kingdom of England. It was the conquest of England by William Duke of Normandy, in the year 1066. William Duke of Normandy took possession of all England, and Young Edgar the Atheling, the rightful heir to the throne, had to flee with his sisters, Margaret and Christina.

In the harshness of the day, their father and mother had been killed. The orphans purposed to set sail in a ship to Hungary, where they knew they would be kindly received. But a great storm arose. Their ship was battered and driven about by wind and waves they knew not whither, and at last, when they had lost all hope of ever seeing land again, they were driven upon the shores of Scotland. They landed at a place on the Firth of Forth which to this day is called Margaret's Hope, from the name of Edgar's sister the Princess Margaret.

When Margaret and her brother and sister found themselves in Scotland they were uncertain what to do. They did not know if they would be received in a friendly manner or not. The country people gathered round and stared at them. They were astonished, and a little afraid too at their grand clothes, and at the great size of their ship.

When King Malcolm was told of the beautiful ladies and fine tall men who had come in the strange ship, he sent some of his nobles to find out who they were, where they came from, and what they wanted. When the nobles came to the ship, they were almost as much astonished as the common people had been at the splendid men and beautiful ladies. The King's nobles spoke gently to them, and asked them how it was that they had landed upon these shores.

Princess Margaret told their sad story. "We are English," she said, "the relatives of King Edward. He is dead, and his throne and crown have been taken by the cruel Duke of Normandy. We have fled from the country. The winds and the waves have driven us upon your shores, and we seek the help and protection of your most gracious King."

The outcast princess spoke so simply, and looked so sorrowful, that the nobles took pity on them. They talked kindly to them for some time, and then went back to King Malcolm and told him all that they had learned.

When Malcolm heard that the royal castaways were English, and relatives of the King who had been so kind to him, he called for his horse and set out to visit them. Malcolm brought Edgar and his sisters back with him, gave them rooms in his palace, and treated them as great and honored guests.

Margaret's wonderful beauty and her angelic modesty, much more than her royal birth and the accomplishments due to the careful education she had received, drew on her the admiration of the untutored Scottish nobles and their warlike king. Malcolm was attracted by the manifold graces of the royal maiden, and soon he came to love the Princess Margaret very much. She too loved the King, and a few months after her arrival in the court of Dunfermline, she became the queen of all Scotland, to the unbounded delight of every class in the community.

The wedding was very splendid. Such pomp and grandeur had never before been seen in Scotland as was seen at the marriage of Malcolm Canmore and Queen Margaret.

For the sake of his wife Margaret, King Malcolm treated all English people kindly. Because of this, many of the English, who were driven out of their own country by William of Normandy, came to settle in Scotland.

It was an unrefined age, in a country with a long series of invasions by the Northmen, frequent wars with England, and perpetual feuds between the native clans. In spite of its Christianity, it remained half-uncivilized.

Instead of sitting down to cower amid the turmoil round her, Margaret set herself to conquer the evils in her own feminine way, by the performance of her queenly duties. Malcolm revered her saintly purity even more than he loved her sweet, sunny, cheerful manner, or admired her surpassing beauty. He looked on her as something too precious and tender for his wild, rugged court.

The Scottish chieftains, who were least inclined to reform their lives or refine their manners, could not resist the influence which drew them to Dunfermline. They enjoyed the privilege of being addressed by their beautiful, royal mistress with a grace that borrowed more of its charm from piety than from courtesy. They were given trifling presents, which of infinite value in their eyes from the angelic goodness of the giver.

Queen Margaret also encouraged merchants to come to Scotland to trade. They brought jewels and gold and other beautiful things, and took away woollen cloth and whatever else the Scots had to sell. It was in the days of Queen Margaret that the Scottish people first began to wear the brightly colored checked cloths which we call tartans.

She effected in the thoughts, the sentiments, the manners, and the morals of these hitherto untamed and unruly nobles, many of the same change which had taken place in the mind and heart and conduct of the king. Thus the blessed influence of her virtue and gentleness spread from above downward, through every class, till the lowliest peasants and the remotest Highland glens were made to feel Margaret's refining and elevating effects. The court of Malcolm—that had been for centuries the boisterous meeting-place of turbulent and intemperate warriors—became blended and sanctified by the cross.

Not one of Queen Margaret's nobles ventured to use a profane word or make an unseemly jest before her. They had a rude, ungodly practice of leaving the table without waiting for grace. The gentle queen reformed them by sending, as a special gift from herself, a cup of wine to all who remained. In after times, the last cup was called, after her, St. Margaret's cup, or the grace-cup.

To improve the manners of the ladies, she gathered round her a number of young girls, whom she brought up under her own eye, and she used to sit in the midst of them, embroidering rich vestments for the service of the Church, and permitting cheerful talk with the nobles whom she admitted, all men of whose character she had a good opinion.

From these young ladies she exacted that their homes should, in turn, become so many centers of zeal for the good of others; and thus every home in Scotland was benefitted by the examples and teachings of the queen. But above all her other qualities shone her tender love for the poor and the sick for whom she founded hospitals and asylums.

From the first year of her reign, she bent herself to the task of making her missionary efforts flourish wherever the misfortunes of the times had caused it to languish. She would plant wherever the missionaries had not penetrated or had only had an imperfect success.

Every morning before she had her own breakfast she fed nine little beggar children. Often she took them in her arms and fed them with her own hands. At certain times in the year the King and Queen would give dinner to three hundred poor, and wait upon them as they sat at the table in the great hall of the palace. Queen Margaret too used to wash the feet of pilgrims and beggars, which in those days was thought to be a very holy action.

The Queen could not bear to see any one hungry, or cold, or in misery. She gave all her own money to the poor, and often, when she had nothing left to give, she would borrow from her lords and ladies in waiting. They were always willing to lend to her, for they knew that they would be paid back more than they gave. Sometimes too, the Queen would take the King's money to give to the poor. He knew very well that she took it, but he pretended not to miss it. But sometimes he would laugh and say that he would have her tried and imprisoned for stealing. Really he loved her so much that she might do anything she wished.

Queen Margaret was learned too. In those days, when few people could read, she could read both English and Latin. The King, although he could speak Latin, English and Scottish (which were different languages in those days), had never been taught to read. But he loved to take Margaret's books in his hand and sometimes he would kiss those which she liked the best. Sometimes too, he would take away one of her favorites and give it to a goldsmith, who would cover it in gold and set it with precious stones. Then Malcolm would bring the book back again and give it to Queen Margaret as a sign of his love for her. Malcolm was a good King, but he was rough and passionate, and sometimes cruel. But, however angry he was, the gentle Queen Margaret could always soothe and calm him again.

Of the nine children with whom her union was blessed, one, Ethelred, died in infancy, the eldest, Edward, was slain with his father before Alnwick Castle in 1093. Her three sons, Edmund, Edgar, and David, reigned successively on the throne of Scotland, continuing the Golden Age inaugurated by their parents. Edith, later known as "Good Queen Maud," became the wife of Henry I of England, and was her mother's living image. Mary, the youngest, was married to Eustace, Count of Boulogne, becoming in her turn the mother of her people.

While thus proving herself to be a true mother, both to her children as well as her adopted people, she was mindful of her English origin and of the sufferings and needs of her countrymen. The wars between the two kingdoms which she was powerless to prevent, left many English captives in Scottish prisons. But her generosity and her influence found means to alleviate their condition and to hasten their ransom. She founded a hospital for sick and infirm prisoners, where they were tenderly cared for till they obtained their freedom.

Thus the veneration and love felt for Margaret in Scotland spread beyond its borders to every part of England. From the nearest counties emigrants flocked across the boundary to settle in the Lowlands, and enjoy there the security and other manifold blessings bestowed on their subjects by Malcolm Canmore and his angelic queen.

Surely it was a beautiful life, this of the tempest-tossed royal child, born in exile far away from the land of her fathers, and then cast by the storm on the

Scottish coast. She was a treasure beyond all price to be cherished by king and people, who lived in the hearts of all succeeding generations.

Let a woman's hand trace the first outlines of the glorious picture of piety and patriotism offered in this queenly life of twenty-three years on the throne. With this most admirable life before us, let us see how every woman can, in like manner, make of her home a paradise, and be the loved and revered queen of the little kingdom which no one can take from her.

The Princess Who Dared

EDITH OF SCOTLAND

William Rufus, son of the Conqueror and second Norman king of England, was holding his summer council of his lords and lieges, in the curious old Roman-Saxon-Norman town of Gloucester. The court was lodged in the Abbey guest-houses, in the grim and fortress-like Gloucester Castle, and in the houses of the quaint old town itself.

On a broad and deep window-seat in the old Abbey guest-house, sat two young girls of thirteen and ten; before them, stood a manly young fellow of sixteen. The three were in earnest conversation, all unmindful of the noise about them.

The boy was shaking his head rather doubtfully as he stood, looking down upon the two girls on the broad window-seat.

"Nay, nay, beausire*; shake not your head like that," exclaimed the younger of the girls. "We did escape that way, trust me we did; Edith here can tell you I do speak the truth—for sure, 'twas her device."

Thirteen-year-old Edith laughed merrily enough at her sister's perplexity, and as the lad turned questioningly to her, said gayly, "Sure, then, beausire, 'tis plain to see that you are Southron-born and know not the complexion of a Scottish mist. Yet 'tis even as Mary said. For, as we have told you, the Maiden's Castle standeth high-placed on the crag in Edinburgh, and hath many secret passageways to the lower gate. So when the Red Donald's men were swarming up the steep, my uncle, the Atheling, did guide us, by ways we knew well, and by twists and turnings that none knew better, straight through Red Donald's array, and all unseen and unnoted of them, because of the blessed thickness of the gathering mist."

"And this was your device?" asked the boy, admiringly.

"Ay, but any one might have devised it too," replied young Edith, modestly. "Sure, 't was no great device to use a Scotch mist for our safety, and 't were wiser to chance it than stay and be murdered by Red Donald's men. And so it was, good Robert, even as Mary did say, that we came forth unharmed, from amidst them and fled here to King William's court, where we at last are safe."

"Safe, say you; safe?" exclaimed the lad, impulsively. "Ay, as safe as is a mouse's nest in a cat's ear—as safe as is a rabbit in a ferret's hutch. But that I know you to be a brave and dauntless maid, I should say to you—"

"fair sir": an ancient style of address, used especially toward those high in rank in Norman times.

But, before Edith could know what he would say, their conference was rudely broken in upon. A royal page, dashed up to the three, with scant courtesy seized the arm of the elder girl, and said hurriedly, "Haste ye, haste ye, my lady! Our lord king is even now calling for you to come before him in the banquet-hall."

Edith knew too well the rough manners of those dangerous days. She freed herself from the grasp of the page, and said, "Nay, that may I not, master page. 'Tis neither safe nor seemly for a maid to show herself in baron's hall or in king's banquet-room."

"Safe and seemly it may not be, but come you must," said the page, rudely. "The king demands it, and your nay is naught."

And so, the young Princess Edith was speedily brought into the presence of the king of England, William II, called Rufus, or "the Red" because of the color of his hair and from his fiery temper. Her friend, Robert Fitz Godwine, accompanied her as far as he dared.

Edith and Mary were both princesses of Scotland, with a history, even before they had reached their teens, as romantic as it was exciting. Their mother, an exiled Saxon princess, had, after the conquest of Saxon England by the stern Duke William the Norman, found refuge in Scotland. She married King Malcolm Cranmore, the son of that King Duncan whom Macbeth had slain.

When King Malcolm had fallen beneath the walls of Alnwick Castle, a victim to English treachery, and when his fierce brother, Donald Bane, had usurped the throne of Scotland, the good Queen Margaret died in the gray castle on the rock of Edinburgh. Her five orphaned children were only saved from the vengeance of their bad uncle Donald by the shrewd and daring device of the young Princess Edith, who bade their good uncle Edgar the Atheling, guide them, under cover of the mist, straight through the Red Donald's knights and spearmen to England and safety.

For years the Saxons and the Normans were enemies, and you would naturally suppose that the worst possible place for the Saxon fugitives to seek safety would be in Norman England. Edgar the Atheling, a Saxons prince, had been declared king of England by the Saxons, enemies of the Norman conquerors, and the children of King Malcolm and Queen Margaret—half Scottish, half Saxon—were, by blood and birth, of the two races most hateful to the conquerors. But the Red King in his rough sort of way—hot to-day and cold tomorrow—had shown something almost like friendship for Edgar the Atheling, the royal Saxon prince. Edgar might have been king of England had he not wisely submitted the greater power of Duke William the Conqueror and to William Rufus, his son. More than this, it had been rumored that some two years before, when there was truce between the kings of England and of Scotland, this harsh and headstrong English king, expressed a particular interest in the eleven-year-old Scottish girl—this very Princess Edith who now sought his protection.

So, when this wandering uncle boldly threw himself upon Norman courtesy, and came with his homeless nephews and nieces straight to the Norman court for safety, King William Rufus not only received these children with favor and royal welcome, but gave them comfortable lodgment in quaint old Gloucester town, where he held his court.

But when the royal fugitives deemed themselves safest were they in the greatest danger. Among the attendant knights and nobles of King William Rufus's court was Sir Ordgar, a Saxon knight and baronet of Oxfordshire. Because those who change their opinions—political or otherwise—often prove the most unrelenting enemies of their former associates, it came to pass that Sir Ordgar, the Saxon, conceived a strong dislike for these orphaned descendants of the Saxon kings, and convinced himself that the best way to secure himself in the good graces of the Norman King William Rufus was to slander and accuse the children of the Saxon Queen Margaret.

And so that very day, in the great hall, when wine was flowing and passions were strong, this false knight, raising his glass, bade them all drink saying, "Confusion to the enemies of our liege the king, from the base Philip of France to the baser Edgar the Atheling and his Scottish brats!"

This was an insult that even the heavy and peace-loving nature of Edgar the Atheling could not brook. He sprang to his feet and denounced the charge, "None here is truer or more loyal to you, lord king, than am I, Edgar the Atheling, and my charges, your young guests."

But King William Rufus was of that changing temper that goes with jealousy and suspicion. His flushed face grew still more red, and, turning away from the Saxon prince, he demanded, "Why make you this charge, Sir Ordgar?"

"Because of its truth, beausire," said the faithless knight. "For what other cause hath this false Atheling sought sanctuary here, save to use his own descent from the ancient kings of this realm to make head and force among your lieges? And his eldest kinsgirl here, the Princess Edith. Is it not true that she who is the daughter of kings shall be the wife and mother of kings? And is it not further true that when her aunt, the Abbess of Romsey, bade her wear the holy veil, she hath again and yet again torn it off, and affirmed that she, who was to be a queen, could never be made a nun? Children and fools, 'tis said, do speak the truth, beausire; and in all this do I see the malice and device of this false Atheling, the friend of your rebellious brother, Duke Robert, as you do know him to be. And I do brand him here, in this presence, as traitor and recreant to you, his lord."

The anger of the jealous king grew more unreasoning as Sir Ordgar went on.

"Enough!" he cried. "Seize the traitor, —or, stay; children and fools, as you have said. Have in the girl and let us hear the truth—Not seemly, Sir Atheling?" he broke out in reply to some protest of Edith's uncle. "Aught is seemly that the king doth wish." And with that he summoned his pages, "Run, one of you, and seek the Princess Edith, and bring her here forthwith!"

While Edgar the Atheling, realizing that this was the gravest of all his dangers, strove, though without effect, to reason with the angry king, Damian, the page, hurried after the Princess Edith.

"How now, mistress!" Broke out the King William Rufus, as the young girl was ushered into the banquet-hall, where the disordered tables, strewn with fragments of the feast, showed the ungentle manners of those brutal days. "How now do you prate of kings and queens and of your own designs—you, who are but a beggar guest? Is it seemly or wise to talk,—nay, keep you quiet, Sir Atheling; we will have naught from you,—to talk of thrones and crowns as if you did even now hope to win the realm from me—from me, your only protector?"

The Princess Edith was a very high-spirited maiden, as all the stories of her girlhood show. And this unexpected accusation, instead of frightening her, only served to give her more boldness. She looked the angry monarch full in the face.

"'Tis a false and lying charge, lord king," she said, "from whomsoever it may come. Naught have I said but praise of you and your courtesy to us motherless folk. 'Tis a false and lying charge; and I am ready to stand test of its proving, come what may."

"Even to the judgment of God, girl?" demanded the king.

And the brave girl made instant reply: "Even to the judgment of God, lord king." Then, skilled in all the curious customs of those warlike times, she drew off her glove. "Whosoever my accuser be, lord king," she said, "I do denounce him as foresworn and false, and thus do I throw myself upon God's good mercy, if it shall please him to raise me up a champion." And she flung her glove upon the floor of the hall, in face of the king and all his barons.

It was a bold thing for a girl to do, and a murmur of applause ran through even that unfriendly throng. For, to stand the test of a "wager of battle," or the "judgment of God," as the savage contest was called, was the last resort of any one accused of treason or of crime. It meant no less than a "duel to the death" between the accuser and the accused or their accepted champions, and, upon the result of the duel hung the lives of those in dispute. And the Princess Edith's glove lying on the floor of the Abbey hall was her assertion that she had spoken the truth and was willing to risk her life in proof of her innocence.

Edgar the Atheling, peace-lover, though he was, would gladly have accepted the post of champion for his niece, but, as one also involved in the charge of treason, such action was denied him.

For the moment, the King's former admiration for this brave young princess caused him to waver; but those were days when suspicion and jealousy rose above all nobler traits. His face grew stern again.

"Ordgar of Oxford," he said, "take up the glove!" and Edith knew who was her accuser. Then the King asked: "Who standeth as champion for Edgar the Atheling and this maid, his niece?"

Almost before the words were spoken young Robert Fitz Godwine had sprung to Edith's side.

"That would I, Lord King, if a young squire might appear against a belted knight!"

"Ordgar of Oxford fights not with boys!" said the accuser contemptuously.

The king's savage humor broke out again.

"Face him with your own page, Sir Ordgar," he said, with a grim laugh. "Boy against boy would be a fitting wager for a young maid's life."

But the Saxon knight was in no mood for sport.

"Nay, beausire; this is no child's play," he said. "I care naught for this girl. I stand as champion for the king against yon traitor Atheling; and if the maiden's cause is his, why then against her too. This is a man's quarrel."

Young Robert would have spoken yet again as his face flushed hot with anger at the knight's contemptuous words. But a firm hand was laid upon his shoulder, and a strong voice said, "Then is it mine, Sir Ordgar. If between man and man, then will I, with the gracious permission of our lord the king, stand as champion for this maiden here and for my good lord, the noble Atheling, whose liegeman and whose man am I, next to you, lord king."

Taking the mate to the glove which the Princess Edith had flung down in defiance, he thrust it into the guard of his iron skull-cap, in token that he, Godwine of Winchester, the father of the boy Robert, was the young girl's champion.

Three days after, in the tilt-yard of Gloucester Castle, the wager of battle was fought. It was no gay tournament show with streaming banners, gorgeous lists, gayly dressed ladies, flower-bedecked balconies, and all the splendid display of a tourney of the knights. It was a solemn and sombre gathering in which all the arrangements suggested only death and gloom, while the accused waited in suspense, knowing that halter and fagot were prepared for them should their champion fall.

In quaint and crabbed Latin the old chronicler, John of Fordun, tells the story of the fight, for which there is neither need nor space here. The glove of each contestant was flung into the lists by the judge, and the dispute committed for settlement to the power of God and their own good swords. It is a stirring picture of those days of daring and of might, when force took the place of justice, and the deadliest blows were the only convincing arguments. But, though supported by the favor of the king and the display of splendid armor, Ordgar's treachery had its just reward.

Virtue triumphed, and vice was punished. Even while treacherously endeavoring (after being once disarmed) to stab the brave Godwine with a knife which he had concealed in his boot, the false Sir Ordgar was overcome, confessed the falsehood of his charge against Edgar the Atheling and Edith his niece, and, as the quaint old record has it, "The strength of his grief and the multitude of his wounds drove out his impious soul."

So young Edith was saved; and, as is usually the case with men of his character, the King Rufus's humor changed completely. The victorious Godwine received the arms and lands of the dead Ordgar; Edgar the Atheling was raised high in trust and honor; the throne of Scotland, wrested from the Red Donald, was placed once more in the family of King Malcolm, and King William Rufus himself became the guardian and protector of the Princess Edith.

And when, one fatal August day, the King was found pierced by an arrow under the trees of the New Forest, his younger brother, Duke Henry ascended the throne of England as King Henry I. And the very year of his accession, on the 11th of November, 1100, he married, in Westminster Abbey, the Princess Edith of Scotland, then a fair young lady of twenty-one.

At the request of her husband she took, upon her coronation day, the Norman name of Matilda, or Maud, and by this name she is known in history and among the queens of England.

So scarce four and thirty years after the Norman conquest, a Saxon princess sat upon the throne of Norman England, the loving wife of the son of the very man by whom Saxon England was conquered.

"Never, since the battle of Hastings," says Sir Francis Palgrave, the historian, "had there been such a joyous day as when Queen Maud was crowned." Victors and vanquished, Normans and Saxons, were united at last, and the name of "Good Queen Maud" was long an honored memory among the people of England.

And she was a good queen. In a time of bitter tyranny, when the common people were but the serfs and slaves of the haughty and cruel barons, this young queen labored to bring in kindlier manners and more gentle ways. Beautiful in face, she was still more lovely in heart and life. Her influence upon her husband, Henry the scholar, was seen in the wise laws he made, and the "Charter of King Henry" is said to have been gained by her intercession. This important paper was the first step toward popular liberty. It led the way to the Magna Carta, and finally to our own Declaration of Independence.

In common with those of England, Americans can therefore look back with interest and affection upon the romantic story of "Good Queen Maud," the brave-hearted girl who showed herself wise and fearless both in the perilous mist at Edinburgh, and, later still, in the yet greater dangers of "the black lists of Gloucester."

The Crown Of Life

LADY JANE GREY

"SEVENTEEN—AND KNEW EIGHT LANGUAGES—IN MUSIC PEERLESS—HER NEEDLE PERFECT, AND HER LEARNING BEYOND THE CHURCHMEN; YET SO MEEK, SO MODEST, SO WIFE-LIKE HUMBLE TO THE TRIVIAL BOY MISMATCHED WITH HER FOR POLICY! I HAVE HEARD SHE WOULD NOT TAKE A LAST FAREWELL OF HIM; SHE FEARED IT MIGHT UNMAN HIM FOR HIS END. SHE COULD NOT BE UNMANNED—NO, NOR OUTWOMAN'D. SEVENTEEN—A ROSE OF GRACE! GIRL NEVER BREATHED TO RIVAL SUCH A ROSE; ROSE NEVER BLEW THAT EQUALED SUCH A BUD?"—*TENNYSON*

When the fair young Lady Jane mounted the scaffold at Tower Hill she was still in her teens—with the simplicity of girlhood still fresh upon her. She was the eldest daughter of Henry Grey, Marquis of Dorset (later duke of Suffolk). She was allied with royal blood from both her father and mother. Her mother, Frances, was the niece of Henry VIII.

Jane was born in the year 1537, at her father's stately mansion of Bradgate, near Leicester, but the exact day is not known. She was the eldest of three daughters—Jane, Katherine and May. At a very early age her budding gifts gave abundant promise of a fair womanhood; so serene her temper and so remarkable her love of knowledge. Her principal tutor John Aylmer, was as zealous as the pupil was diligent, Lady Jane soon gained a thorough acquaintance with Latin and Greek, and also some degree of proficiency in Hebrew, Arabic, Chaldaic, French and Italian.

These grave and serious studies were relieved by a cultivation of the arts. Her voice was melodious, and she sang with much skill and expression. She also played on various musical instruments. Her needlework and embroidery excited the admiration of her contemporaries. She prepared tasty dishes, preserves, and sweets. Her calligraphy was a marvel of ease and elegance.

But her tutors did not forget the spiritual side of her education. She was well grounded in the doctrines of the Church as well as in the truths and teaching of her Lord and Savior, Jesus Christ.

After the death of Henry VIII, Lady Jane went to live with the widowed Queen Katherine Parr at Chelsea. Katherine later married Thomas Seymour, Lord High Admiral of England, and Jane accompanied them to Hanworth

Palace. The Queen did not long survive after her second marriage. She died at Dudley Castle, September 5, 1548, at the age of thirty-six. Lady Jane acted as chief mourner at the funeral.

It was soon after this event that Lady Jane addressed the following letter to the Lord High Admiral:

October 1, 1548

My duty to your lordship, in most humble wise remembered, with no less thanks for the gentle letters which I received from you. Thinking myself so much bound to your lordship for your great goodness towards me from time to time, that I cannot by any means be able to recompense the least part thereof, I purposed to compose a few rude lines unto your lordship, rather as a token to show how much worthier I think your lordship's goodness than to give worthy thanks for the same; and these my letters shall be to testify unto you that, like as you have become towards me a loving and kind father, so I shall be always most ready to obey your godly monitions and good instruction, as becometh one upon whom you have heaped so many benefits, And this, fearing lest I should trouble your lordship too much, I must humbly take my leave of your lordship.

Your humble servant during my life,

JANE GREY.

Life was very different when Jane went back home. Her parents acted upon the maxim that to spare the rod is to spoil the child; and not withstanding her amiability and honorable diligence, subjected her to a very severe discipline. She was rigorously punished for the slightest defect in her behavior or the most trivial failure in her studies. Her parents taught her to fear, rather than to love them; and insisted upon reverence, rather than affection, as the duty of children. It is no wonder therefore, that she turned with ever-increasing delight towards her studies.

In the pages of the wise she met with divine words of encouragement and consolation. They soothed her sorrows, taught her the heroism of endurance, and lifted her into that serene realm where the glorious minds of old dwelt. "Thus," says she, "my book hath been so much my pleasure, and bringeth daily to me more and more pleasure, that in respect of it all other pleasures in very deed be but trifles and troubles unto me."

Roger Ascham, one of England's most learned professors, who tutored

Lady Jane in calligraphy, visited Bradgate in the summer of 1550 on his way to London. He found, on his arrival, the stately mansion deserted. The Lord and Lady, with all their household, were hunting merrily in the park to the music of horn and hound.

Making his way through the deserted chambers, he came at length upon a secluded apartment, where the fair Lady Jane was calmly studying the pages of Plato's immortal Phaedon in the original Greek. Surprised and delighted by a spectacle so unusual, the worthy scholar, after the usual salutations, inquired why she had not accompanied the gay lords and ladies in the park, to enjoy the pastime of the chase.

"I believe," she replied, smiling, "that all their sport in the park is but a shadow to that pleasure that I find in Plato. Alas! good folk, they never felt what true pleasure meant."

"And how came you, madam," quoth he, "to this deep knowledge of pleasure?"

"I will tell you," said she, "and tell you a truth which, perchance, ye will marvel at. One of the greatest benefits that ever God gave me is that He sent me so sharp and severe parents and so gentle a schoolmaster. For when I am in presence either of father or mother, whether I speak, keep silence, sit, stand, eat, drink, be merry or sad, be sewing, playing, dancing or doing anything else, I must do it, even so perfectly as God made the world, or else I am so sharply taunted, so cruelly threatened, and mistreated in ways which I will not name for the honor I bear them, that I think myself in hell till time come that I must go to Mr. Aylmer; who teacheth me so gently, so pleasantly, with such fair allurements to learning, that I think all the time nothing whiles I am with him. And when I am called away from him, I fall on weeping, because, whatever I do else but learning is full of grief, trouble, fear and whole misliking unto me."

Ascham did not see her again after this memorable interview. "I remember this talk well," he wrote, "both because it is so worthy of memory and because also it was the last talk that I ever had and the last time that ever I saw that noble and worthy lady."

Her illustrious rank, her piety and her learnedness made the Lady Jane an object of special interest to the leaders of the Reformed Church in England. Under the direction and counsel of great leaders of the Reformed Church, Jane pursued her theological studies with great success, so as to be able to give abundant reason for the faith that was in her.

On one occasion the Princess Mary presented her with a sumptuous robe, which she was desired to wear in recognition of the donor's generosity. "Nay," she replied, "that would be a shame, to follow my Lady Mary, who leaveth God's word, and leave my Lady Elizabeth who followeth God's word." A speech which the Lady Mary doubtless remembered.

Early in 1553, men clearly saw that the life and reign of Edward VI were drawing to an abrupt end, due to his poor health. His legitimate successor was his elder sister Mary; but her morose temper and attachment to the Catholic Church had filled the minds of the Reformers with anxiety. Her unpopularity, and the dangers to the Reformed Church, led Dudley (Duke of Northumberland), to devise an audacious plan. He resolved to raise his son to the throne. But for this purpose it was necessary to ally him to the blood-royal, and he therefore planned a marriage between his young son, Lord Guilford Dudley, and seventeen-year-old Lady Jane Grey.

They were a fit match and in June 1554 the bridal ceremony took place at the Duke of Northumberland's palace. The Duke then obtained from King Edward, by an appeal to his zeal for the Church, letters-patent excluding Mary and Elizabeth from the succession and declaring Lady Jane Grey heir to the throne.

A few days afterwards, the young king died; and on the evening of the 9th of July, the Duke of Northumberland, and other nobles, urged Lady Jane to accept the crown, which was fated to become, for her, a crown of thorns.

She afterwards wrote, "how I was beside myself, stupefied and troubled, I will leave it to those lords who were present to testify, who saw me overcome by sudden and unexpected grief, fall on the ground, weeping very bitterly; and then declaring to them my insufficiency, I greatly bewailed myself for the death of so noble a Prince, and at the same time turned myself to God, humbly praying and beseeching Him that if what was given to me was rightly and lawfully mine, His divine Majesty would grant me such grace and spirit that I might govern it to His glory and service and to the advantage of this realm."

Her prudent reluctance, however, was overruled. History records the brief nine days of her reign: Lady Jane was at first confined in the house of Partridge, a warden of the Tower. Then, after she and her husband had been tried for high treason and found guilty, they were removed to the Tower. During her captivity she occasionally amused herself with the graceful pursuits of her earlier and happier years. She engraved on the walls of her prison, with a pin, some Latin distich, which turned into English read :

"Believe not, man, in care's despite,
That thou from others' ills art free
The cross that now I suffer might
To-morrow haply fall on thee.

"Endless all malice, if our God is nigh:
Fruitless all pains, if He His help deny,
Patient I pass these gloomy hours away,
And wait the morning of eternal day."

Her execution was fixed for the 12th of February 1554. On the night preceding she wrote a few sentences of advice to her sister on the blank leaf of a New Testament. To her father she addressed the following beautiful letter, in which filial reverence softens and subdues the exhortations of a dying saint:

The Lord comfort Your Grace, and that in His Word, wherein all creatures only are to be comforted; and though it hath pleased God to take away two of your children, yet think not, I most humbly beseech Your Grace, that you have lost them; but trust that we, by leaving this mortal life, have won an immortal life. And I, for my part, as I have honored Your Grace in this life, will pray for you in another life.—Your Grace's humble daughter,

JANE DUDLEY.

The stern Lieutenant of the Tower, Sir John Brydges, had been subdued by the gentle graces of his prisoner. In a manual of manuscript prayers she wrote a few sentences of farewell:

Forasmuch as you have desired so simple a woman to write in so worthy a book, good Master Lieutenant, therefore I shall, as a friend, desire you, and as a Christian require you, to call upon God to incline your heart to His laws, to quicken you in His way, and not to take the word of truth utterly out of your mouth. Live still to die, that by death you may purchase eternal life, and remember how Methuselah, who, as we read in the Scriptures, was the longest liver that was of a man, died at the last; for, as the Preacher saith, there is a time to be born and a time to die; and the day of death is better than the day of our birth.—Yours, as the Lord knoweth, as a friend,

JANE

Mary and her advisers had originally intended that both Lady Jane and her husband should be executed together on Tower Hill. But reflection convinced them that the spectacle of so handsome and youthful a pair, suffering for what was rather the crime of others than their own, might powerfully awaken the sympathies of the multitude. It was ordered, therefore, that Lady Jane should stay within the precincts of the Tower until after Dudley's execution.

The fatal morning came. The young husband—still a bridegroom and a lover—had obtained permission to bid her a last farewell. But Jane refused to see him. She was afraid that so bitter a parting might overwhelm them, and deprive them of the courage needful to face death with calmness. She sent him, however, many loving messages, reminding him how brief would be their separation, and how quickly they would meet in a brighter and better world.

In going to his death on Tower Hill, he passed beneath the window of her cell, so that they had an opportunity of exchanging a farewell look. He remained calm and dauntless on the scaffold. After spending a brief space in silent devotion, he requested the prayers of the spectators, and laying his head upon the block, gave the fatal signal. At one blow his head was severed from his body.

Before being conducted to the scaffolding, Lady Jane quoted the following prayer:

> *"O merciful God, be Thou unto me*
> *A strong Tower of defense,*
> *I humbly entreat Thee.*
> *Give me grace to await Thy leisure,*
> *And patience to bear*
> *What Thou doest unto me;*
> *Nothing doubting or mistrusting*
> *Thy goodness towards me;*
> *For Thou knowest what is good for me*
> *Better than I do.*
> *Therefore do with me in all things*
> *What Thou wilt;*
> *Only arm me, I beseech Thee,*

With Thine armor,
That I may stand fast;
Above all things taking to me
The shield of faith;
Praying always that I may
Refer myself wholly to Thy will,
Abiding Thy pleasure, and comforting myself
In those troubles which it shall please Thee
To send me, seeing such troubles are
Profitable for me; and I am
Assuredly persuaded that all Thou doest
Cannot but be well; and unto Thee

Be all honor and glory. Amen.

The end was at hand. The officers summoned for Lady Jane to be brought before the executioner. The bystanders noted in her "a countenance so gravely settled and with all modest and magnificent resolution that not the least symptom either of fear or grief could be perceived either in her speech or motions; she was like one going to be united to her heart's best and longest beloved."

So, like a martyr, crowned with glory, she went unto her death. Her serene composure was scarcely shaken when, through an unfortunate misunderstanding of the officer in command, she met on her way her husband's headless trunk being borne to its last resting place.

"Oh Guilford! Guilford!" she exclaimed; "death is not so bitter that you have tasted, and that I shall soon taste, as to make my flesh tremble—it is nothing compared to the feast that you and I shall this day partake of in heaven." This thought renewed her strength and sustained and consoled; we might almost believe, by ministering angels, she proceeded to the scaffold with as much grace and dignity as if it were a wedding banquet that awaited her.

She was conducted by Sir John Brydges the Lieutenant of the Tower, and attended by her two ladies-in-waiting. While these wept and sobbed bitterly, her eyes were dry, and her countenance shone with the light of a sure and certain hope. She read earnestly her manual of prayers.

On reaching the place of execution she saluted the lords and gentlemen present with unshaken composure and infinite grace. No minister of her own Church had been allowed to attend her, and she did not care to accept the services of Feckenham, Queen Mary's confessor. She was not ungrateful, however, to his respectful sympathy and when bidding him farewell, she said:

"Go now; God grant you all your desires, and accept my own warm thanks for your attentions to me; although, indeed, those attentions have tried me more than death could now terrify me."

To the spectators she addressed a few gentle words, in admirable keeping with the gentle tenor of her life.

"Good people," she exclaimed, "I am come here to die, and by law I am condemned to the same. My offence to the Queen's Highness was only in consent to the device of others, which now is deemed treason. It was never my seeking, but by counsel of those who should seem to have further understanding of things than I, who knew little of the law, and much less of the titles to the Crown. I pray you all, good Christian people, to bear me witness that I die a true Christian woman, and that I look to be saved by none other means but only by the mercy of God, in the merits of the blood of His only son, Jesus Christ; and I confess, when I did know the word of God, I neglected the same, loved myself and the world, and therefore this plague or punishment is happily and worthily happened unto me for my sins; and yet I thank God of His goodness, that He hath thus given me a time and respite to repent. And now, good people, while I am alive, I pray you to assist me with your prayers."

She knelt to her devotions, and turning to Feckenham, inquired whether she may repeat the fifty-first Psalm. He replied in the affirmative and she said it with great earnestness from the beginning to end.

Rising from her knees, she began to prepare herself for the headman. When she was unfastening her robe, the executioner would have assisted her, but she motioned him aside , and accepted the last offices of her ladies-in-waiting, who then gave her a white handkerchief with which to bandage her eyes.

Throwing himself at her feet, the headman humbly begged her forgiveness, which she willingly granted. He then requested her to stand upon the straw, and in complying with his direction she for the first time saw the fatal block. Her composure remained unshaken. She simply entreated the executioner to dispatch her quickly. Again kneeling she asked him:

"Will you take it off before I lay me down?"

"No, Madam," he replied.

She bound the handkerchief round her eyes, and feeling for the block, exclaimed, "What shall I do, where is it?"

Being guided to it by one of the bystanders, she laid her head down, exclaiming, in an audible voice: "Lord, into Thy hands I commend my spirit."

In an instant the axe fell, and the tragedy was consummated. An involuntary groan from the assembled multitude seemed to acknowledge that vengeance had been satisfied, but justice outraged.

Lady Jane—or Queen Jane, as she should more properly be called—was little more than seventeen years old when she thus fell a victim to Mary's jealous fears and hate. Her heroic death demonstrated how well she had profited by the lessons in her early years. She did not waver in her faith, but rather drew strength from Christ, the Great Comforter. With this vision before her eyes, Lady Jane bore herself with serene dignity and with the true courage of a martyr.

"*...Fear none of those things which thou shalt suffer: behold, the devil shall cast some of you into prison, that ye may be tried; and ye shall have tribulation ten days: be thou faithful unto death, and I will give thee a crown of life.*" Revelation 2:10

Princess of the Forest

POCAHONTAS

Upon the barren sand
A single captive stood;
Around him came, with bow and brand,
The red men of the wood.
Like him of old, his doom he hears,
Rock-bound on ocean's brim—
The chieftain's daughter knelt in tears,
And breathed a prayer for him.

Above his head in air
The savage war-club swung:
The frantic girl, in wild despair,
Her arms about him flung.
Then shook the warriors of the shade,
Like leaves on aspen limb,
Subdued by that heroic maid
Who breathed a prayer for him!

"Unbind him!" gasped the chief:
"It is your king's decree!"
He kissed away the tears of grief,
And set the captive free!
'Tis ever thus, when in life's storm
Hope's star to man grows dim,
An angel kneels, in woman's form,
And breathes a prayer for him.

GEORGE POPE MORRIS

The first settlement of the English in America was made in the year 1607, at Jamestown, a few miles above the mouth of the James River, in Virginia. The place where the colony was established was well chosen. Safe and convenient harbors for their shipping were numerous, large rivers seemed to open vast tracts of the continent to their navigation, immense forests furnished timber for building, the soil was fertile and the climate hearty. Their neighbors were the Indians, several tribes of whom were united under the powerful chief Powhatan. He was a good ruler, full of devices and tact, and one who might be made a potent ally or a formidable enemy.

The leader of Jamestown was Captain John Smith, a man of daring adventure. He had traveled in every continent, and had beheld the cities and learned the manners of many men. He had a vigorous constitution, and a mind that was never appalled at danger nor depressed by defeat. He led numerous expeditions into the New World in search of food.

On one of these excursions, accompanied by only two attendants, Smith was surrounded by a numerous body of Indians, his companions were killed, and himself taken captive. After being led in triumph through several parts of the country, he was brought before Chief Powhatan. Upon consultation, the doom of death was pronounced against the prisoner, and Powhatan claimed the honor of executing it.

As tradition has it, a large stone was brought, and the head of the captive, securely bound, was laid upon it. The arm of the chieftain was uplifted to strike the fatal blow with his club, when his favorite daughter, a young maid named Pocahontas, rushed out, threw herself between her father and the victim, put her arms around the prisoner and placed her face against his, and by her entreaties and tears saved his life.

The beautiful Indian princess was then about thirteen years of age, tall, sprightly, agile, full of feminine tenderness and affection. After a few days' detention, Captain Smith was released and returned to Jamestown. But the young princess' bold act of mercy was not forgotten.

Once the savage chieftain devised a surprise attack, intending to capture or slaughter all the English residents within his dominions. Pocahontas, at the risk of her life, resolved to give timely notice to the Captain, that he might effect an escape. Alone, in the darkness of the night, through the rough and dangerous woods, this dauntless maiden walked nine miles to a neighboring Indian camp, where Captain Smith was trading for corn. With eyes filled with tears, she besought him to hasten his departure. Giving him the best advice she was able, she returned home. Acting upon her information, Smith was able to outwit the

Indians; and after obtaining a supply of provisions for the colony, finally reached Jamestown, having been absent about six weeks.

Pocahontas frequently visited the English settlements, where she was always received with respectful admiration. According to Captain Smith's own testimony, throughout a period of two or three years, Pocahontas was the primary instrument, used by God, to preserve the colony from death, famine, and utter confusion.

In order to effect peace with the Indians, one of the English leaders, in the year 1613, determined to seize Pocahontas, and hold her as a hostage and security for the good behavior of Powhatan. By stratagem, Captain Argall obtained possession of her person, while she was on a visit among the Potomacs, a tribe on friendly terms with the English. The Indian Sachem and his wife, with whom Pocahontas stayed, treacherously delivered her up on condition of her receiving kind treatment. When the young princess found herself betrayed, she wept bitterly. Argall told her that she must go with him to the colony, and compound a peace between her father and the English. Finding herself well treated, she recovered her composure, and even seemed cheerful at the prospect of accomplishing good.

After various negotiations for peace, two messengers were sent to Powhatan early in the Spring of 1614; but they were unable to come to any terms. One of these messengers was John Rolfe. An ardent attachment sprang up between Pocahontas and himself. During the period of her captivity, two of her brothers visited her, and were delighted to find her in good health and spirits. To one of them she confided the secret of her love. Rolfe gaining information of her sentiments toward him, was thus emboldened to ask for her hand. The idea of this connection pleased Powhatan so much, that, within ten days after Rolfe's visit, he sent his brother and two of his sons to witness and confirm the marriage on his behalf.

The Indian princess had, during her captivity, been instructed by her lover in the English language and the Christian religion. She made a profession of faith and was baptized in the little village chapel, receiving the Christian name, Rebecca. On April 5, 1614, not long after her baptism, the wedding took place. The church was handsomely decorated for the occasion with garlands of evergreen interspersed with white flowers. The bride was arrayed in a simple tunic of white muslin; over her shoulders was loosely thrown an elegant robe, presented by Sir Thomas Dale, and fancifully embroidered by herself and her maids. From her head drooped a veil of gauze and the plumage of birds. Her arms were encircled with simple bracelets and her feet covered with slippers of her own handiwork. Rolfe was attired as an English cavalier, and around his waist he wore the short sword of a gentleman of distinction in society. He was the personification of manly grace and courage as she was of womanly virtue and delicacy.

Nearly all the settlers of the colony, including the Governor and other officers were present. The bride's two brothers and uncle were also there, along with their native attendants. The result of this union was the renewal of the most friendly relations between the two nations, which continued as long as Powhatan lived.

In 1616, just two years after their wedding, John Rolfe and his princess accompanied Sir Thomas Dale to England. King James was offended because one of his subjects had, without his consent, married the daughter of an Emperor—as Powhatan was then called. But the affair passed off with some little murmuring, and Pocahontas herself was received at Court by both the King and Queen with the most flattering marks of attention. In London she was visited by Captain Smith. When she first beheld him, she was overcome with emotion, and turned aside to weep. Too much discomposed for conversation, she was left for two or three hours to her own meditations. She soon recovered her self-possession, and the politeness and attention of her visitor, along with the geniality of her own disposition soon restored her usual vivacity.

There is something touching in this interview between the gallant Captain and his Indian deliverer. She was among strangers, far from her kindred and her home, and amid associations widely different from any known in her own land. It is no wonder that this meeting stirred her to tears. In the course of the conversation, Pocahontas called Smith her father. He expressed himself unworthy of this distinction, but she insisted, saying, "You called Powhatan father, when you were in his land a stranger, and for the same reason so must I do you. Fear you I should here call you father? I tell you, then, I will, and you must call me child; and then I will be forever and ever your countrywoman."

John Rolfe and Pocahontas remained in England about a year. When preparing to embark with her husband for Virginia, she developed tuberculosis and died at Gravesend, at the age of twenty-two. She died, as she had long lived, a sincere and pious Christian. Her death was a happy mixture of Indian fortitude and Christian submission, affecting all those who saw her by the lively and edifying picture of piety and virtue which marked her latter moments. Her unwearied kindness to the English was entirely sacrificial. She encountered danger and weariness, and every kind of opposition and difficulty. No favor was expected in return for her benevolence, and no sense of obligation was permitted to mar the pleasure which it gave. She asked nothing of Smith in recompense for whatever she had done, but the blessing of being looked upon as his child. Of her character as a princess, evidence enough has already been furnished. Her dignity, her energy, her independence, and the dauntless courage which never deserted her for a moment, were worthy of Powhatan's daughter.

Pocahontas at her death left but one son, called Thomas, whose education was superintended by Sir Lewis Steukley, and afterward by his uncle, Henry Rolfe, of London. He became, in after years, a man of wealth and prominence in Virginia, having inherited a considerable tract of land that had belonged to his grandfather, Powhatan. From him in the female line—for he had no sons—descended many most noted families in Virginia—the Eldridges, Bollings, Murrays, Guys, and, above all the rest, the Randolphs. Apart from the usual interest attached to the history of Pocahontas, her name would be worthy of record from the fact that she was the first Indian convert in the British Colonies, the first native who learned to speak English, and the first who was united in marriage to an Englishman.

Heir of Splendor

QUEEN VICTORIA

One foggy, pitch black night, the London Express train was suddenly shaken by the unexpected jolting of an attempted stop. The engineer had been startled to behold, in the beam of the speeding engine's headlights, a frantic figure dressed in a black cloak, standing in the middle of the tracks and waving his arms. Finally bringing the train to a stop, the engineer and one of his crew men climbed down to investigate what all the fuss was about. The mysterious figure had disappeared; no one was in sight. Calling out for the ghostly figure to appear, they continued to walk up the train track. Suddenly, they stopped and stared into the fog in horror! The bridge ahead of them had been washed out in the middle and had crumbled into the torrential stream below! Whoever this mysterious figure was, the train men immediately recognized that, without his warning, the train would have plunged into the river, and with it, all the passengers including their beloved Queen Victoria! The men were gripped with awe.

Sometime later, while the bridge and the tracks were being repaired, the train crew made a more intensive search for the strange flag man, but nothing turned up and no one came forward to confess that he had saved the queen. The mystery was finally solved while the train was being inspected for another run. At the base of the engine's headlamp, the engineer discovered a huge, dead moth. He looked at it a moment, then on impulse pasted it to the glass of the lamp. Climbing back into his cab, he switched on the lamp and saw the "flag man" in the beam. He knew the answer now: the moth had flown into the beam just moments before the train was due to reach the washed-out bridge. In the fog, it appeared to be a phantom figure, waving its arms. When Queen Victoria was told of the results of the investigation, she said, "I'm sure it was no accident. It was God's way of protecting us." She recognized her life had been spared by God.

Queen Victoria, the longest reigning monarch of Great Britain, was born May 24, 1819. She was baptized by the Archbishop of Canterbury a month later and was given the name of Alexandrina Victoria. Little Victoria was still a baby when her father, Edward, Duke of Kent (fourth son of George III) died. Her mother, Mary Louise Victoria (daughter of the Duke of Saxe-Coburg-Saalfield) was not an Englishwoman. She had been a German princess before she married the Duke of Kent and came to live in the beautiful Kensington Palace in England. Now she must stay in England and fit her daughter for the life of a queen.

The Duchess learned that her husband had become deeply involved in debt before he died, leaving her penniless. He had tried to sell the beautiful palace home, hoping to be able to pay off the debt, but the law of England would not allow him to do this. Now she was left a poor woman, although she lived in a palace.

The courageous Duchess did not allow poverty to prevent her from doing her best to educate her little daughter just as she believed a future queen should be educated. She wanted Princess Victoria to become a good, sensible, wise ruler. So from Victoria's youth, the Duchess trained her in the Christian virtues that graced her life ever after.

The Duchess kept the child with her much of the time, day and night, for she believed that no nurse or governess, however skilled she might be, could take the place of a mother. Victoria was taught about her country—about its laws, its people, and the people of other countries with whom England dealt. She was taught great works of literature. She mastered the German language, learned Latin, and became an accomplished pianist. She even learned the art of housekeeping, and valued this bit of her education so highly that years later, when she became the mother of girls, she insisted that each one of them learn the same art.

When Princess Victoria was seven-years-old she was taken to the Windsor Palace to visit her "Uncle King"—George IV. This was a great event in her young life, and we may be sure that she knew how to conduct herself quite properly among her elders, for the king was delighted with her pleasing manners.

Victoria was eleven-years-old when King George died. Her uncle, William IV, succeeded the throne and Princess Victoria was told that she would be England's next heir to the throne. She knew something of the corrupt state of the Monarchy under George IV and now William IV. She resolved that her reign would be different. "I will be good," she announced.

On June 20, 1837, shortly after Princess Victoria's eighteenth birthday, King William IV died suddenly. The responsibilities of the empire had now fallen to her.

Upon receiving an unexpected summons early in the morning, Victoria scrambled from her bed, drew on her dressing gown and slippers, and, with her beautiful hair tumbling over her shoulders, she entered the room where her urgent callers were waiting. "Your Majesty!" was the salutation which greeted her from the archbishop, who represented the Church, and from the

Lord Chamberlain, who represented the state. Then she understood what had happened and, bursting into tears, she turned to the archbishop and said, "I beg Your Grace to pray for me." And there they knelt in the quiet room while the archbishop prayed fervently and tenderly for the eighteen-year-old girl on whom the care of the British realm had fallen so suddenly.

According to the required custom, Victoria was soon afterwards proclaimed Queen from a certain window of St. James's Palace, while the waiting throng below viewed Her Majesty for the first time. There she stood, dressed in simplest mourning, the tears running down her cheeks, while she was being presented to the people as their sovereign. At once she won the hearts of the nation by her simplicity and modest behavior.

Like so many other kings and queens throughout history, Queen Victoria suffered many difficult years of political turmoil. Her greatest security, apart from Christ, was her husband, Prince Albert, whom she married in 1840 at the age of twenty-one. Albert, Prince of Saxe-Coburg-Gotha, was also her first cousin. In 1857, Victoria conferred the title of Prince Consort upon her husband. Their model marriage was an inspiration to the English people. They produced nine children—four sons and five daughters. After twenty-one years of marriage, Prince Albert died tragically; and the heart-broken Victoria, in virtual mourning for many years thereafter, sought to avoid most public appearances.

When Victoria came out of mourning, she began to take a renewed interest in her nation's future. Under Queen Victoria, England grew to become the largest and most powerful nation in the world. There was a time that the "sun never set on the British empire."

Under her influence and able leadership, England grew in such proportions that the whole world took notice. Millions of square miles and more than two hundred million people came under British rule while she was queen. The Victorian Age witnessed the rise of the middle class and was marked by a deeply conservative morality and intense nationalism. Victoria's popularity among all classes in British society reached its height in the last two decades of her reign.

God used Queen Victoria in marvelous ways to bless the English people. The Lord blessed Queen Victoria and granted her desire for peace and goodwill towards her subjects. Not only did Victoria's England colonize the world, but they sent their greatest missionaries throughout the Empire to convert the inhabitants and to bring the Gospel of our Lord Jesus Christ to the heretofore lost heathen.

"England's success," she felt, was as a result of believing the Bible to be the book of the English people and, without God's mighty hand of blessing, England would not have risen to such heights.

While being hosted by Queen Victoria in London, a chief from one of Britain's African colonies asked her the secret of England's greatness. The queen did not take him to the Tower of London and show him the glittering crown jewels. She did not speak to him of the brilliant politicians who debated in Parliament. Instead, she presented the chief with a Bible and said, "This is the secret of England's greatness."

Victoria died on January 22, 1901, at the age of eighty-two. Her sixty-three-year reign was the longest in the history of England. Her descendants, including forty grandchildren, married into almost every royal family of Europe. With her personal example of Christian faith, honesty, patriotism, and devotion to family life, Victoria became a living symbol of the solidness of the British Empire.

CHAPTER SIX

Daughters of Stature

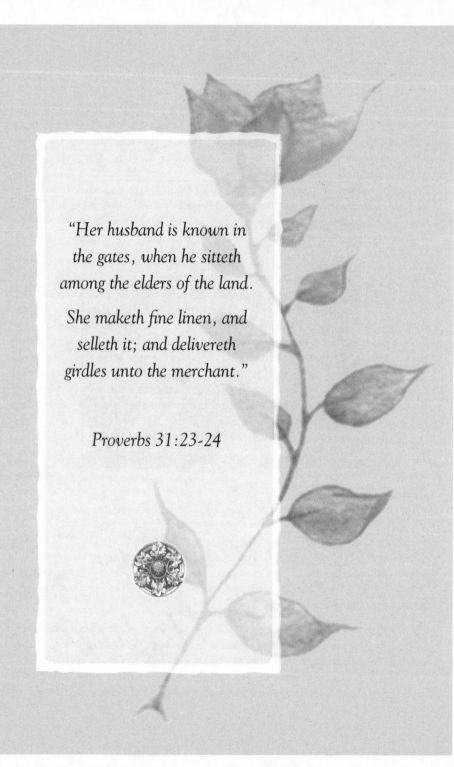

"Her husband is known in
the gates, when he sitteth
among the elders of the land.

She maketh fine linen, and
selleth it; and delivereth
girdles unto the merchant."

Proverbs 31:23-24

The Worthy Wife Of Luther

CATHERINE VON BORA

On the night before Easter, in 1523, a country wagon was slowly making its way from Nimtschen toward Torgau. It was managed by two stalwart Germans, who seemed to be something more than country farmers. The wagon itself was of capacious dimensions, and piled up with barrels, empty, in appearance. But that heavy movement of the team and the creak of the wheels indicated something more substantial than empty barrels. It was a freight of nuns who had just escaped from the Augustinian convent. They were nine in number. Among them was Catherine von Bora.

We must remember that the reformation of Luther was now in full blast. The light of truth had penetrated the dismal recesses of the cloister. These nuns had devoted themselves to the reading of God's Word. How wide the difference between the Christian life and the life they were compelled to lead! No wonder that they soon came to say to their friends, "Our continuance in the cloister is incompatible with the salvation of our souls." These nine women had entreated help from their parents and friends, but both had turned a deaf ear. They found help in two highly respectable citizens of Torgau, Senator Leonard Koppe and Wolff Tombitz. When the cavalcade drew up to the door of the old convent at Wittenberg, where Luther resided, he exclaimed aloud, "This is not my doing; but would to God I could, in this way, give liberty to enslaved consciences and empty the cloisters of their tenants! A breach is made however."

The eminent and noble family of Von Bora, from which Catherine was descended, had its residence at Stein-Laussig, near Bitterfeld, in Meissen, Germany. The date of her birth has been preserved to us by a silver-gilt medal, which her husband gave her to wear round her neck, as was the custom in those days. On one side was seen a representation of the brazen serpent with the wounded Israelites, and an inscription in Latin, purporting that the brazen serpent was a type of the crucified Savior; and on the other, Christ on the cross, with many figures of persons standing near, underneath which was written, "Christ died for our sins." On the rim were the words, "She was born on the 29th of January, in the year 1499."

Luther, at this time, had more thoughts of martyrdom than of marriage. Indeed, as late as 1521, he had written to Spalatin: "Our Wittenberg people are for giving wives to the monks, but they shall not force one on me." The story of his betrothment and marriage to Catherine is thus told: He came to Melancthon's house and requested to see Catherine alone. Margaret hastened to her and gave her the message. She entreated her friend to return with her. "That would not do," replied Margaret; "he said expressly alone; he undoubtedly has something very particular to say. Now, Catherine, take courage and open your heart."

Poor Catherine went with trembling steps to the presence of Luther. "I have sent for you, my child," said he, "to converse on the subject of matrimony. I hope you are convinced it is a holy state."

"Yes, sir," said Catherine.

"Are you prepared to embrace it?"

"No, sir," she replied.

"Perhaps you have scruples on the score of monastic vows; if so, I will mark some passages I have written on that subject, that may set your mind at rest." Catherine was silent. "I perceive that I do not make much progress in my purpose. I am little used to these matters, and I had better be direct. Do you mean to abide by your monastic vows, or will you marry, like a rational woman?"

This direct appeal seemed to arouse her courage. "Even Doctor Martin Luther has no right," said she, "to ask that question without explaining his motive."

"Well said, Kate," replied he, laughing. "I must tell you then. There is a person who would gladly take you, 'for better and for worse.'" Catherine's color rose, and her eyes sparkled with additional brightness. "Now say, has he any chance?"

"You have not told me who he is," said she, resolutely.

"And you have not told me whether you have any scruples of conscience on the subject; if you have, God forbid that I should urge you."

"When I left the convent," said she, in a low voice, "it was because it would have been hypocrisy in me to have remained there. I took the vows ignorantly, and almost by compulsion; I embraced the reformed religion with an inquiring and willing faith. God forgive me, that I so long offered him the worship of my lips while my heart was far from him."

"And now?" said Luther, after waiting for her to, finish her sentence.

"Now," she replied, "I need not ask his forgiveness for worshiping him in spirit and in truth. I am no longer a nun."

"Well," said Luther, "I suppose this is as direct an answer as I must expect. So, to my purpose." But even Luther stopped short, surprised at Catherine's emotion. "Perhaps, my dear," he said, kindly, "I do wrong in speaking to you myself; I had better commission Margaret. I suppose women converse on these matters better together; and yet, as I have begun, I will finish. The other day, Bodenstein, the nephew of Carolstadt, came to me to solicit my influence with you. He wishes you to marry him. I told him I could have no particular influence with you, unless you have scruples of conscience about marrying. He is a clever young man, and I see no objection. He is very unlike his fanatic uncle."

He might have talked an hour without receiving a reply. Catherine's manner had changed; there was no longer the emotion or the blush. "What shall I tell him?"

"Anything you please," said she, "so that I never see him again."

"Why, this is strange," said Luther; "you did not seem to have scruples of conscience just now. My dear Catherine, you must not forget that you have no natural relations here, and this young man can be a protector to you."

"I wish you would not speak of him," replied she.

"Is there any one else that you like better?" said Luther. She made no reply. "Nay, speak; I have ever disposition to serve you. Has any other person made the same proposition to you?"

"Yes," said Catherine, with a little womanly pride; "Counselor Baumgartner has made the same proposal."

"Do you prefer him?"

"Yes," she replied, rising; "but I am as happy as I ever expect to be. My friends assure me that I am no burden, but a help to them; so I wish you good morning."

Poor Catherine hastened to her room. Her dream was over. Luther, the austere, the insensible reformer, had awakened her from it. Margaret entered while her eyes were yet red with weeping. She tenderly approached, and embraced her; but neither exchanged a word. "There is no hope for Bodenstein," thought Luther; "it is evident Baumgartner is the object. Catherine is a child. If the Elector dies she is without a support, except by the labor of her hands, and they do not look as if they were made for labor. I will write to Jerome Baumgartner. He is well known as a young counselor at Nuremberg."

The young counselor received this letter with surprise and incredulity. The positive refusal of Catherine, some months before, had left no doubt on his mind, and he thought the wisest plan was to inclose the letter to her, and to inquire whether it was written with her sanction. In the mean time Luther's friends began to urge him to marry, particularly Melancthon. "You preach," said he, "what you do not practice." He protested, however, that he would not be caught in the snare that his time was now fully occupied.

When Catherine received the letter from her former lover, she was filled with astonishment, and requested Margaret to speak to Luther on the subject. He said he had done what he thought was right and would be agreeable to all parties; but he found there was one science he did not understand—the heart of a woman. "That is true," said Margaret, "or you would long since have perceived that Catherine's was yours; and now the mystery is out." It required all the evidence to convince Luther of the truth of this assertion. He was forty, and Catherine but little more than half that number of years. That she could prefer him to her young suitors seemed to him incredible. Margaret, however, had said it, and a new life opened to Luther, in the affection of a young and beautiful woman.

When he spoke to Catherine again on the subject of matrimony, he was more successful than before. He learned the history of her long attachment, which had become so much the reverie of her silent hours. The betrothment took place, and very soon the marriage followed.

This marriage, so singular in its origin, was a happy one. Both knew how much they possessed in each other. In order to be near her, Luther labored often at her side, or had her with him in his study. He regularly informed her of the progress of the Reformation, or at least so much of it as might afford her pleasure, and, when absent, wrote to her respecting it. He frequently read to her aloud, and occasionally also the writings of his opponents. In return, she reminded him of any urgent business, particularly as regarded the letters that were to be answered. Her sympathy in all that concerned him he repaid by a similar participation in her affairs, listening kindly to all she had to say, and, as appears from his letters, attending to many of her commissions on his journeys. In his social pleasures, walks, and recreations in the country, she was his constant companion, as much as was possible. It was one of his delights to aid his Kate in her intellectual advancement, and especially in her knowledge of the Word of God. She soon commenced regular reading of the Bible, and in one of his letters he says that "she shows great earnestness in the matter."

Their inward happiness cast its pure radiance over their outward circumstances, which were by no means brilliant. Luther had an income of two hundred florins. Till 1523 he had merely twenty-two dollars for his yearly salary. He inherited from his father only two hundred and fifty florins. His apartment was adorned with a stove of a pyramidal form. The windows were formed of little round panes of glass with small sashes; the boarded ceiling was carved. On a niche between two of the windows was a large bench, with two comfortable wooden seats, which were opposite to each other. In addition to this was a large, plain family table, with cross feet. This was the whole of the Reformer's furniture in his state-room, as preserved to this day. He was, however, assisted from time to time by his prince and his friends; so that he had a bare sufficiency. In the year 1536 the Elector John Frederick assigned him annually a hundred bushels of corn, malt sufficient for two brews of beer, and sixty fathoms of wood from the revenues of Wittenberg. John the Steadfast gave him, a year after his marriage, the Augustine convent for his habitation. In addition he frequently made him presents of money, jewels, furniture, clothes, provisions for the kitchen and the cellar, which the contented man often refused or returned.

Mr. Whipple, speaking of the domestic relations of authors, says that whenever a noble spirit has been fortunate in his domestic relations he has left testimonials in his writings that those human affections, which are the monopoly of none, are more productive of solid happiness than wealth, or power, or fame. This is illustrated in the relation of Luther to Catherine von Bora. Her piety, animation, vivacity, and activity in the management of her household, rendered her a spouse after his own heart; and a thousand letters and expressions of his prove how worthy she was of him. For instance, in August,1526, he writes as follows to his friend Stiefel: "Kate, my rib, sends you her greeting. Through mercy she is very well, and is complacent, obedient, and obliging in every respect, in a greater degree than I could have hoped for—God be thanked! So that, I would not exchange my poverty for the wealth of Croesus."

While laboring at his Exposition of the Epistle to the Galatians, he exclaimed, "She is my epistle, to which I have betrothed myself: she is my Catherine von Bora!" And subsequently, in 1538, to a friend, "If I were a young man, I would rather die than marry a second time, although a queen were offered me after my Kate."

That which increased the happiness of this marriage was the birth of six children, which Luther regarded as a blessing from the Lord. He was an extremely tender father, and the many expressions on record of his susceptible and affectionate heart render him particularly worthy of our esteem. But with the high ideas he possessed of the end for which mankind was created, he was necessarily strict in the education of his children, and in forcibly repelling the development of that which was evil in them. Though Catherine perfectly agreed with him with regard to the end to be obtained, yet, under the influence of maternal feelings, she occasionally sought to soften his mode of treatment. Still she did not remain blind to any faults that were committed, and the beneficial results of the education which the children received showed that the parents had not mistaken the proper means.

We have not yet spoken of the personal appearance of the spouse of Luther. She possessed an intensely German countenance, marked with practical sense and good temper. Erasmus speaks of her as being "wondrous fair." But she possessed an even greater beauty of heart and intellect. She was of middle size, oval countenance, bright and lively eyes. She had not enjoyed the advantages of a superior or learned education, but she was sensible, docile, and possessed great simplicity. She was well experienced in domestic matters, and very expert at her needle. There was formerly at Wittenberg a neatly-worked likeness of Luther in silk, by her hand; and in Luther's room are still shown, several other works and specimens of her skill. Her character and history to the latest hour and the last act of life vindicated the choice of Luther, and showed her to be a woman worthy of the great Reformer.

During all the years of his married life Luther suffered much from bodily affliction, and often from great depression of spirits. But his "faithful Catherine" showed herself equal to every emergency. This noble-minded woman also practiced faithfully the virtue of self-denial; for she had little of his society in reality even when he was well, since he was daily immersed in books, so that windows, seats, and furniture lay full of them; and he had so many letters to write, that he had need almost of two shorthand typists. The works he wrote fill more than twelve volumes of the largest size; add to which, his lectures for the students, his sermons, his numberless visits, and the various journeys he undertook, and hence we may easily infer how much his wife was deprived of his society. But instead of murmuring, she did all in her power to alleviate and cheer him.

Whenever he was mentally disturbed, his prudent and sensible wife invited Dr. Jones, an intimate friend, to dine with him, in order that the latter might amuse him with his lively conversation. Although he was generally cheerful and happy in his God, yet occasionally he experienced such painful temptation as to induce him to suppose that the Lord was no longer propitious to him. On these occasions his wife was enabled to reprove, encourage, and comfort him. Once, nothing would avail, and Luther left home for a few days, in order to recover his cheerfulness, but returned deeply grieved in spirit. On entering the house, he found Catherine seated in the middle of the room, dressed in a black gown, with a black cloth thrown over her, and looking very sad. A white handkerchief which she held in her hand was wet, as if moistened with her tears. When Luther urged her to tell him what was the matter, she held back at first, but then replied, "Only think, dear Doctor, the Lord in heaven is dead; and this is the cause of my grief." On which he laughed, and said, "It is true, dear Kate; I am acting as if there was no God in heaven." From that moment his melancholy left him. She not only assisted in relieving him of his sorrow, but she also participated in his joy, thus doubly enhancing it.

Luther was thoughtless of worldly concerns. When he was reminded that he ought to lay up a small capital for his family, he answered, "I will not do so: for otherwise they will not depend upon God and their own hands." From the same principle he became surety for others; pledged his four silver cups, one after the other; pressed together with all his might, for a begging student, a gilded cup he had just received from the Elector, and gave it to a needy young man, notwithstanding his hesitation to accept it, and the warning looks of his wife, saying, "I require no silver goblets; there, take it to the goldsmith's." When a person who was exiled on account of his faith entreated alms of him, and he had only a Joachim dollar, which he had long preserved in his purse, after a brief reflection he exclaimed, "Out with thee, Joachim—the Lord hath need of thee!"

In the same manner, he presented all his manuscripts gratuitously to the publishers, and rejected their offer of four hundred florins yearly, saying, "I will not sell the grace of God; I have quite enough already." Nor would he take any pay from the students for his lectures. When the Elector John was desirous of bestowing upon him a gainful vein in the silver mines of Schneeberg, for his translation of the Bible, he replied, "If I did not labor hard for His sake who died for me, the world could not give me gold enough to write a book, or translate something from the Bible. I will not be rewarded by the world for my labor: for it is too mean and poor for such a purpose." When a friend presented him with two hundred florins, he distributed them among the poor students; and when another rich man gave him a hundred florins, in 1529, he shared them with Melancthon.

When a tax was imposed in support of the war against the Turks, and Luther was exonerated from it, he expressly offered to bear his part from the proceeds of his little farm. On another occasion, when a person in distress solicited his aid, just at the time when his wife was confined, he took the money which the sponsors had left for the infant, and presented it to him. After some time, his wife observed the emptiness of the cash-box, and spoke rather sharply to him respecting it; to which he meekly replied, "My dear Kate, God is rich: he will bestow it in some other way."

Catherine was careful, without being covetous. In her capacity of housewife, she occasionally gave lectures to her husband; and Luther, who preached so much himself, was a cheerful and submissive hearer. "I must have patience with the Pope," cried he, once; "I must have patience with the fanatics; I must have patience with the scavengers; I must have patience with the servants; I must have patience with Kate von Bora; and altogether so much patience is required, that patience constitutes my whole life."

About the year 1544 Luther became so disgusted with living in Wittenberg, that he was desirous of leaving it, and disposing of every thing. With the concurrence of her friends, the Elector, and the University, she succeeded, with much difficulty, in bringing him to think otherwise. He had already reached Leipsic, and when at Torgau, suffered himself to be persuaded by the Elector to return home; which he did in a state of illness and discomposure, and was received with open arms by his family and his friends. But Catherine's joy was not of long continuance.

On the 17th of January, 1546, Luther, though still indisposed, was under the necessity of undertaking his last journey to Eisleben to settle some disputes between the heirs of the Count of Mansfeld's estates. His three sons accompanied him. On the 28th of January he arrived, much indisposed, in Eisleben. John hastened home with the alarming intelligence. His mother, who had often assisted many with her advice and medical aid, sent her husband a variety of restoratives from her domestic medicine-chest, which had frequently been of good service to him on previous occasions. On the 6th of February he wrote her in good spirits, stating that every thing was going on well; and that they would have been spending their time pleasantly, were it not for the disagreeable litigation. Again, on the 10th of February he wrote:

Grace and peace in Christ, dearest consort! We are very grateful for the anxiety you felt respecting us, which prevented you from sleeping. For since the time you so well provided for us, we had almost been consumed by fire at our inn, close to my room-door; and yesterday, doubtless because of your care for us, a stone fell on my head and caught it like a rat-trap. For the roof giving way over my private chamber, we engaged people, who touched the stone, which was of large size, with two of their fingers, on which it fell down, and had like to have rendered your kind care of us unavailing, had not the holy angels prevented. I fear that if you do not leave off caring, the earth at last will swallow us up, and all the elements conspire against us. The Lord be with you.

After this cheerful letter, she must necessarily have been the more surprised and shocked at the news of his decease. He was born in Eisleben, and there he also died, on the 18th of February, 1546, aged sixty-three years. Thus Catherine was not permitted to attend him in his last extremity, nor to see his face any more.

No record has been preserved of the state and condition of the widow at that time. She is recorded as being present at his funeral. Luther in his last will, dated the 6th of January, 1542, had bequeathed to her the little farm at Zuellsdorf, a house in the town on which there was a debt of two hundred florins, and goblets and jewels to the value of a thousand florins. "I do this," he writes, "because, as a pious and faithful wife, she has always loved, esteemed, and treated me well; and, by the blessing of God, has borne and brought up five living children; and most of all, because I will not that she should look to the children, but the children to her; and that they should honor and be in subjection to her, as God hath enjoined. For I have seen and experienced how the devil incites and urges on the children to act contrary to his commandment even though they are pious, by wicked and envious tongues, particularly when the mothers are widows, and the sons and daughters get wives and husbands."

The Elector confirmed this last will of Luther. And, as the provision was entirely inadequate to the support of the family and the education of the children, he promised such assistance as was needed. But, after the unfortunate battle near Muhlberg—in April, 1547—the Elector, John Frederick, was taken prisoner; and after a short siege, Wittenberg was entered by the Emperor, with his Spaniards, on the 25th of May. Catherine fled to Magdeburg, and from thence to Brunswick, accompanied by Melanethon, with the intention of seeking protection in Copenhagen from Christian III. But on an Imperial announcement that no harm should happen to them, she returned, with the rest of the fugitives, to Wittenberg. From that time her life was only a series of afflictions. Her sovereign could do nothing more for her; heavy taxes were imposed upon her little property; she was obliged to borrow a thousand florins. She then rented out single apartments in her house, and also boarded those who lodged with her at their request.

In the beginning of the year 1548, in conjunction with Melanethon, she besought the Imperial commander-in-chief to grant a reduction of the war-tax, which was very heavy. When the solicitations of her friends, who applied to the King of Denmark on her behalf, proved unavailing, she herself petitioned him on two successive occasions for aid in her severe distress, since every one acted as if she were a stranger to them, and no one would take her part. Bugenhagen also wrote to his Majesty in support of her statement; and this time he appears to have felt for her in her destitute situation. A reply, with some pecuniary assistance, soon followed, which Bugenhagen gratefully acknowledged on the 22nd of March of the same year.

That which grieved Catherine more than the infamous falsehoods propagated by her mortal enemies, the Papists, was the conduct of her friends toward her. This appears from the funeral address of the Wittenberg University at her burial: "During the war she wandered about with her orphan children, exposed to the greatest difficulties and dangers; and, besides the manifold distresses of a state of widowhood, she experienced great ingratitude from various quarters, while by those from whom she might have expected assistance, on account of the immense and manifest benefit which her husband had been to the Church, she was often shamefully deceived." Hence she the more fully experienced the truth of her late husband's assertion, when she complained that she could not acquire any relish for the Psalms, with their numerous complaints against enemies, false friends, etc. "Wait," replied he, "till thou art a widow; thou wilt then be able to value them." She later felt doubly grateful to him for having given her the thirty-first Psalm to commit to memory, the contents of which she certainly was unable to appreciate at the time.

After the treaty of Passau, in August, 1552, when tranquillity was restored for a time, an infectious plague prevailed to such a degree in Wittenberg, that the whole of the members of the University removed to Torgau. Catherine resolved to follow them, accompanied by her two younger sons, Martin and Paul, and her daughter Margaret, since the epidemic had broken out in her house. On the journey the horse took fright, and ran away with the carriage. Catherine, anxious for her children, jumped out of the vehicle, and fell violently on the ground, and afterward into a ditch, which was full of water. The shock and the chill she received operated so painfully upon her frame, that she arrived at Torgau in a very weak state, and fell dangerously ill while there. Her disorder increased, and tuberculosis set in. During the three months she lay ill "she comforted and sustained herself by the Word of God, and anxiously longed for a peaceful dismission from this vale of tears. She often commended the Church and her children to God, and prayed that the pure doctrine, which the Lord had caused to be promulgated by her husband, might be handed down unadulterated to posterity. During the last years of her life she had the great pleasure of hearing that the pious Elector, John Frederick, had been set at liberty, and the freedom of the Protestant confession and of Divine service established.

From the few words which are left on record of what she said during her last illness, we learn how firmly her heart cleaved to her beloved Savior, in the firm belief on whom she expired on the 20th of December, 1552, in the fifty-fourth year of her age. She was buried in the parish church of Torgau, and her funeral was attended by the students of the University whom the vice-rector Paul Eber had invited by a public placard, to show her this last mark of respect, in of her own worth, as well as from honored consideration for the memory of Luther. A beautiful tombstone, which is still to be seen, was erected over the spot where she lies. Along the side is a simple German inscription, of which the following is a translation: "In the year 1552, the 20th of December, here in Torgau, fell asleep, blessed in God, Catherine von Bora, the blessed widow of Dr. Martin Luther."

Catherine Luther fulfilled a truly historical task. The world saw in Luther's honorable housewife and her excellent management, and religious training up of her children, the evident proof that not the convent but matrimony is the Divine order for mankind. The thousands who either traveled through or studied at Wittenberg carried home with them to all parts of Germany a lovely image and pattern of domestic felicity. As Luther became the venerable patriarch of all the Protestant clergy of Germany, so Catherine stood in the same position with reference to the numberless clergymen's wives, and the immense and incalculable benefits, both mental and spiritual, which have flowed upon the whole of Protestant Germany from the consecrated homes of its clergy. Neither shining by beauty, riches, nor learning, nor even rising above the narrow limits of her domestic circle, she fulfilled the divine mission of the woman, with that meek and quiet spirit which is before God of great price. Catherine, a German housewife, both in life and death, with the Bible in her hand, was thus not a faultless, but a human fulfillment of the model which the Scripture gives us of a prudent and pious, economical, and modest woman, who places her hope in God.

The Mother Of Reformers

SUSANNAH WESLEY

It matters little as to the descent of any individual. We estimate one's life by what it is, not by the ancestry; yet this is of interest in tracing the character and personal traits. Susanna Wesley, the daughter of Dr. Samuel Annesley, a distinguished Non-Conformist minister, was born in London 1669 or 1670. Her father was cousin to the Earl of Anglesea, and of an ancient and honorable family that existed before the Norman conquest. Better, however, than this ancient lineage is the story of the simple devotion of Dr. Annesley's life, linking his devotional childhood with a fruitful and vigorous old age. He read twenty chapters of the Bible a day, begun by the boy of six, and not forgotten by the man of sixty. He was a man of noble demeanor, vigorous health, abstemious and self-denying habits, and devoted piety. He ministered with great success to two of the largest congregations in London, till the Act of Uniformity, in 1662, deprived him of his vicarage. He continued, however, to reside in London, and was most eminent and useful among the Non-Conformists, having, in some measure, the care of all the Churches. For thirty years he enjoyed uninterrupted peace in his soul, and a blessed assurance of God's favor; and he could say on his death-bed that he had been faithful in the work of the ministry for fifty-five years. Susannah was the youngest and the latest survivor of twenty-five children.

Susannah was the father's most beloved child, and we may imagine the blooming girl, a privileged guest in her father's study—a diligent reader of her father's books. That she did not adopt all her father's opinions we learn from the fact that, at the age of thirteen, she reviewed the controversy between the Dissenters and the Established Church, and decided in favor of the latter, thus becoming "a zealous Churchwoman, yet rich in a dowry of Non-Conforming virtues." Prayerful she was; for she conscientiously gave as much time to devotion as to recreation. She was faithful in her studies, and Greek, Latin, Logic, and Mathematics, with their severe discipline, gave strength and tone to a mind destined to stamp enduring impressions on the character of one who was to stand "prominent among the worthies of all time."

Nobly descended, carefully and piously educated, highly gifted, graceful in form, and beautiful in face Susanna Annesley was:

> "A perfect woman, nobly planned,
> To warn, to comfort, and command,

And yet a spirit still and bright,
With something of an angel light."

She attracted the regards and won the, affections of Samuel Wesley, a minister of the Established Church, though, like herself, brought up among the Dissenters. Mr. Wesley was a curate in London, with an income of thirty pounds, increased to sixty by his writings. He was introduced to Miss Annesley by her brother-in-law, John Dunton, with whom he had become associated by his publications. No higher degree did his literary labors ever bring him than this acquaintance, which soon ripened into a mutual attachment. In 1690, about six years before her father's death, Susannah Annesley left the untroubled home of her early years, and became the wife of Samuel Wesley.

In 1702 the Wesley family was subjected to a severe trial. It was the last of July; the weather had been very hot and dry. Mrs. Wesley was in the study with her children, her husband having gone to visit a sick person, when fire broke out in the floor under their feet. Mrs. Wesley took two of the children in her arms, and calling to the rest to follow, ran through the smoke and fire. One child left in the burning house was rescued by the neighbors, who also saved the books and papers of the rector, and most of his goods. The fire, which was kindled by some sparks falling on the dry thatch, consumed one wing of the house, and into the remaining portion the family were crowded.

In 1709 a still more disastrous fire took place. Mrs. Wesley, who was ill at the time, was awakened by her husband, who was gathering the children together to save them from the devouring element. Unable, from her weakness, to climb to the window through which they escaped, she endeavored three times to make her way to the street door, but was as often beaten back by the fury of the flames. In her distress she besought her blessed Savior, if it was his will, to preserve her from that death, and then waded through the fire, which only scorched her hands and her face.

How affecting was the father's thanksgiving when they brought to him John, the little fellow of five, the last rescued from the falling house! "Come, neighbors, let us kneel down; let us give thanks to God. He has given me all my eight children; let the house go; I am rich enough." Without a roof to shelter them, the children found temporary homes among neighbors and relations. Mr. Wesley rebuilt the parsonage-house in a year, and the family removed into it, "with very little more," said he, "than Adam and Eve had when they first set up housekeeping." Furniture, clothes, books, and papers, all were gone, and their limited income was insufficient to make good these losses, so that for many years the rectory was but half furnished, and Mrs. Wesley and her children but scantily clothed.

In answer to the Archbishop of York's question whether she had ever been in want of bread, Mrs. Wesley replied, "My lord, I will freely own to your Grace, that strictly speaking, I never did want bread; but then I have had so much care to get it before it was eat, and to pay for it after, as has often made it very unpleasant to me. And I think to have bread on such terms is the next degree of wretchedness to having none at all."

Mr. Samuel Wesley was a faithful pastor and an earnest student, especially of the Scriptures in the original tongues. For three years he attended the convocation in London at an expense he could ill afford of fifty pounds a year. This absence threw the whole weight of family care and government upon his wife. However, it was no unwonted burden to her. Feeling it to be her duty to pay more attention to the children, especially on Sunday when there was no afternoon service in the church, she read prayers and a sermon, and conversed with them on religious subjects. Accidental hearers requested permission to become stated ones, till the house was filled, and many had to go away for want of room.

A stranger, on entering the rectory at Epworth, might, at the first sight of its half-furnished rooms, have thought it a cheerless home; but he would soon perceive that this was no ordinary household. Peace and quietness reigned there—no child was allowed to cry after it was a year old—the law of order regulated their rising and their rest, their morning and their evening prayers—their simple meals taken with thankful hearts—their hours of study and of exercise. The firm yet gentle influence of the mother harmonized every jarring string, till the family that owned her potent sway had the name of being the most loving family in Lincoln.

Her first object was to subdue their wills and bring them to an obedient temper, and that done the rest was comparatively easy. Her remarks on this subject are very forcible, and are quoted by her son, John Wesley, in his sermon on the education of children. "I insist," she says, "upon conquering the will of children early, because this is the only strong and rational foundation of a religious education, without which both precept and example will be ineffectual. But when this is thoroughly done, then a child is capable of being governed by the reason and piety of its parents till its own understanding comes to maturity, and the principles of religion have taken root in the mind. As self-will is the root of all sin and misery, so whatever cherishes this in children insures their after wretchedness and irreligion; whatever checks and mortifies it promotes their future happiness and piety. This is still more evident if we further consider that religion is nothing else than the doing the will of God and not our own; that the one grand impediment to our temporal and eternal happiness being this self-will, no indulgences of it can be trivial, no denial unprofitable. Heaven or hell depends on this alone. So that the parent who studies to subdue it in his child works together with God in the renewing and saving a soul. The parent who indulges it does the devil's work, makes religion impracticable, salvation unattainable, and does all that in him lies to damn his child forever."

John Wesley speaks of the calm serenity with which his mother transacted business, wrote letters, and conversed, surrounded by her thirteen children. The order and system so ingrained in her character enabled her to assign to every duty its own time.

Six hours a day this faithful mother devoted to the education of her children, and no child was allowed to leave its seat in the school-room without permission. The alphabet was taught to the child the day it was five years old; and from letters to words and from words to sentences, he proceeded till he could read well in a quarter of a year. Most of the daughters, as they grew up, had the rare accomplishment of reading with propriety and elegance, and Emilia, the eldest daughter, was said by her brother, John Wesley, to be the best reader of Milton he ever heard. She was remarkable, too, as well as her youngest sister Kizzie, for the beauty of her handwriting. Sons and daughters, accomplished and learned, testified to the excellence of their mother's educational discipline. She was doing a great work in the rectory at Epworth—a work for which successive generations might call her blessed. With the mother of the Gracchi the mother of the Wesleys could say, "These are my jewels," and day after day witnessed her work of faith and labor of love in polishing those precious stones, whose kindling radiance was to flash bright and strong in the eyes of a wondering world, and was afterward, and in a more glorious casket, to be enshrined above, to shine there as the brightness of the firmament, and, as the stars, forever and ever. And scarcely ever, in this world's history, has such a group of children demanded a mother's care. Her toil was rewarded amply by the fine development of character in her children, but her heart was dampened by their unhappy marriages. Charles's marriage seemed almost the only prosperous and happy one.

Susannah's source of strength came in the hour of devotional retirement, which she conscientiously observed every morning and evening. The varied duties of wife, mother, and mistress of the family might have served as a good excuse for spending less time in her closet, but it was the very pressure of these, accumulated responsibilities that led her to seek that anointing which could alone qualify her for her work. Five o'clock in the afternoon was the hour sacredly observed in the Wesley family for the hour of devotion: father, mother, and children reading the Psalms and lessons of the day.

When her duties allowed, Mrs. Wesley retired at noon for meditation and prayer; and some of these quiet meditations, which she committed to writing, have been preserved: "I sometimes think," she writes, "that if it were not on account of Mr. Wesley and the children, it would be perfectly indifferent to my soul whether she ascended to the supreme Origin of being from a jail or a palace, for God is every-where. No walls, or locks, or bars, nor deepest shade, nor closest solitude, excludes His presence; and in what place soever He vouchsafes to manifest Himself, that place is heaven. And the man whose heart is penetrated by divine love, and enjoys the manifestation of God's blissful presence, is happy, let his outward condition be what it will. He is rich as having nothing, and yet possessing all things. Upon the best observation I could ever make, I am induced to believe that it is much easier to be contented, without riches than with them. It is so natural for a rich man to make gold his god; it is so very difficult not to trust in, not to depend on it for support and happiness, that I do not know one rich man in the world with whom I would exchange conditions." Were such hours, so inviolably sacred to prayer, more frequently redeemed from sleep and from petty cares, mothers would assuredly, see their children endowed with the gift of power, won by their patient and persevering supplications—sons going forth, if not with the greatness of the Wesleys, yet girded valiantly for the battle of life—princes prevailing with God.

Mrs. Wesley did not lose sight of her sons when they left her for school and college. The maternal hand that had molded their youthful minds ceased not its loving work. The correspondence exhibits the wisdom of her counsels, and the deference with which they were received, and is characterized by high principle, good sense, and severe conscientiousness. "I hope," she writes to her son Samuel, in 1709, "you retain the impressions of your education, nor have forgot that the vows of God are upon you. You know that the first-fruits are Heaven's by an unalienable right, and that as your parents devoted you to the service of the altar, so you yourself made it your choice when your father was offered another way of life for you. But have you duly considered what such a choice and such a dedication imports? Consider well what a separation from the world, what purity, what devotion, what exemplary virtue, are required in those who are to guide others to glory! I say exemplary, for low, common degrees of purity are not sufficient for those of the sacred function. You must not think to live like the rest of the world; your light must so shine before men, that they may see your good works, and thereby be led to glorify your Father which is in heaven. I would advise you as much as possible, in your present circumstances, to throw your business into a certain method, by which means you will learn to improve every precious moment, and find an unspeakable felicity in the performance of your respective duties. Begin and end the day with Him who is the alpha and omega, and if you really experience what it is to love God, you will redeem all the time you can, for His more immediate service. Appoint so much time for sleeping, eating, and company. In all things endeavor to act upon principle, and do not live like the rest of mankind, who pass through the world like straws upon a river, which are carried which way the stream or wind drives them."

"Endeavor," she writes to him the next year, "to get as deep an impression on your mind as is possible of the awful and constant presence of the great and holy God. Consider frequently that wherever you are, or whatever you are about, He always adverts to your thoughts and actions, in order to a future retribution. He is about our beds and about our paths, and spies out all our ways; and whenever you are tempted to the commission of any sin, or the omission of any duty, make a pause and say to yourself: 'What am I about to do? God sees me.' Consider often of that exceeding and eternal weight of glory that is prepared for those who persevere in the paths of virtue. And when you have so long thought on this that you find your mind affected with it, then turn your view upon this present world, and see what vain, inconsiderable trifles you practically prefer before a solid, rational, permanent state of everlasting tranquillity. Could we but once attain to a strong, lively sense of spiritual things, could we often abstract our minds from corporeal objects and fix them on heaven, we should not waver, and be so inconstant as we are in matters of the greatest moment; but the soul would be naturally aspiring toward a union with God as the flame ascends; for He is alone the proper center of the mind, and it is only the weight of our corrupt nature that retards its motion toward Him. Meditate often and seriously on the shortness, uncertainty, and vanity of this present state of things. Alas! had we all that the most ambitious, craving souls can desire, were we actually possessed of all the honor, wealth, strength, and beauty that our carnal minds can fancy or delight in, what would it signify, if God should say unto us: 'Thou fool, this night shall thy soul be required of thee?'"

"I heartily join with your small society," she writes to her son, John, of the society known afterward as Methodists, "in all their pious and charitable actions, which are intended for God's glory. May you in such good works go on and prosper! Though absent in body, I am present with you in spirit, and daily recommend and commit you all to divine Providence. Your arguments against horse-races do certainly conclude against masquerade-balls, plays, operas, and all such light and vain diversions, which, whether the gay people of the world will own it or no, do strongly confirm and strengthen the lust of the flesh, the lust of the eye, and the pride of life, all of which we must renounce, or renounce our God and hope of eternal salvation. I will not say it is impossible for a person to have any sense of religion, who frequents those vile assemblies; but I never, throughout the course of my long life, knew so much as one serious Christian that did; nor can I see how a lover of God can have any relish for such vain amusements." These are words to which it would be well for many to take heed in these days, when the distinctions between the Church and the world are, in so many instances, thrown down."

In 1735 Mr. Wesley died in great peace, and his wife, who for some days had fainted whenever she entered the room of her dying husband, was enabled to bear this severe stroke with Christian resignation and fortitude. She was now to leave the home where, for forty years, she had known much of joy and sorrow—where she had seen ten of her nineteen children grow up to man's and woman's estate. Thronging must have been the memories of the past, as Mrs. Wesley, still beautiful in advancing years, passed away from the home she had so adorned and blessed. After residing a short time with her daughter, Emilia, at Gainesboro, she spent the serene evening of her life in the humble dwelling connected with the Foundery, in London, with her sons, John and Charles, greatly edified and blessed by their ministry. A woman of uniform piety, and of deep experience in the things of God, she obtained in her latter days clearer views than she had before enjoyed of justification by faith, and an abiding evidence of her acceptance with God.

In July, 1742, about seven years after her husband's death, Mrs. Wesley went to be with him in glory. Her son, John, and five of her daughters, were present at the closing scene. "My dear Savior," she exclaimed about twelve hours before her death, "are you come to help me at my extremity at last?" The remainder of her time was spent in praise.

"About three in the afternoon," writes John Wesley, "I went to my mother, and found her change was near. I found her pulse almost gone, and her fingers dead, so that it was easy to see her spirit was on the wing for eternity. After using the commendatory prayer, I sat down on her bedside, and, with three or four of our sisters, [sang a hymn] to her departing soul. She was, in her last conflict, unable to speak, but I believe quite sensible. Her look was calm and serene, and her eyes fixed upward, while we commended her soul to God. Then, without any struggle, or sigh, or groan, the soul was set at liberty. We stood round the bed and

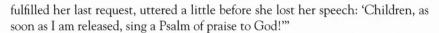

fulfilled her last request, uttered a little before she lost her speech: 'Children, as soon as I am released, sing a Psalm of praise to God!'"

Her grave is near that of John Bunyan, in Bunhill-Field, nearly opposite the City Road Chapel, where her son, John Wesley, lies buried. "Almost an innumerable company of people being gathered together," says Mr. Wesley, "about five in the afternoon, I committed to the earth the body of my mother, to sleep with her fathers. It was one of the most solemn assemblies I ever saw, or expect to see on this side eternity."

Well may we call her the mother of reformers. Nobly did she accomplish her mission. The names of John and Charles Wesley are not more indissolubly connected with one of the greatest moral and spiritual reforms in the history of the Church, than is that of the noble Christian mother who, under God, trained and fitted them for their work.

Her son Charles wrote the following lines for her epitaph:

"In sure and certain hope to rise,
And claim her mansion in the skies,
A Christian here her flesh laid down,
The cross exchanging for the crown.

The daughter of affliction, she,
Inured to pain and misery,
Mourned a long night of griefs and fears,
A legal night of seventy years.

The Father then revealed his Son,
Him in the broken bread made known;
She knew and felt her sins forgiven,
And found the earnest of her heaven.

Meet for the fellowship above,
She heard the call, Arise, my love!
I come, her dying looks replied,
And lamb-like as her Lord, she died."

Mother Of The Father Of Our Country

MARY WASHINGTON

If, indeed, "the hand that rocks the cradle rules the world," what a stupendous debt of gratitude this nation owes to the mother of George Washington!

Let us not doubt that Mary Washington herself found full compensation for all she did that helped to make her son great and good. It is the proudest day in any woman's life, when she sees her son exalted to an honorable position among his fellows, and hears his praises sung by mankind. Mary Washington was no exception to the rule. How honored she must have felt with the chain of events which led her son from military hero, to commander-in-chief of the American armies, to the first President of the nation!

Upon his occupation of the presidency, the mother's prayers were more fervent than when he went away to fight his country's battles with musket, cannon and sword. The victories of peace are harder to win than the victories of war. Therefore she prayed that the God of battles who had spoken from the cannon's mouth, and had led the sword of Washington to triumph over his enemies, would now guide the hand and temper the scepter with which he should rule his brethren in peace.

It was in the blaze and glory of this, her son's proud ascendency, that Mary Washington—mother of the Father of his Country—passed the cloudless hours of the gathering twilight-age which ushered her, without an intervening night, from the glories of time into the glories of eternity.

It is a matter of regret that more of the details of his mother's life are not known. It is natural to suppose there must have been something extraordinary in the mother of so great a son. But we must be content with those scant incidents which history furnishes us. These would never have been known had not the greatness of her son called them out. For she was a plain old Virginia housewife, as devoted to her humble duties and as devoid of selfish ambition, as persistent in truth, as noble, as brave, as firm and uncompromising in the right as Washington proved himself to be. These principles were the keys to his greatness—and they, with his qualities of mind and physical vigor, were a heritage from his mother.

Augustine Washington, a country gentleman of vast fortune and land estate, lived near the Widow Ball, who had a beautiful daughter by the name of Mary. She is said to have been always a great favorite with Mr. Washington.

He had known her father, who died when she was a child. The little girl was known in the neighborhood as "Sweet Molly," for her amiable disposition and sunny beauty. An old letter from Williamsburg, dated October 17th, 1720, gives us the only description of sixteen-year-old Molly's personal appearance. This letter, written from one girl friend to another, we copy just as it has been read:

> "Madam Ball, of Lancaster, and her Sweet Molly have gone hom. Mama thinks Molly the Comeliest Maiden she Knows. She is about sixteen years old, and taller than Me, is verry sensable, Modest and Loving. Her Hair is like unto Flax. Her eyes are the Color of Yours, and her cheeks are like May Blossums."

Hence, we conclude that "Sweet Molly," with all of her beauty, had little opportunity to acquire an education in the modern sense of that term. She is said to have been a poor speller and to have read very few books. Few of her letters remain, and it is possible very few were ever written. The only letter of her girlhood which seems to have been preserved was written at seventeen years of age to her half brother, Joseph Ball, in England, in which she says:

We have not had a schoolmaster in our neighborhood until now in four years.

Though she may not have been well educated, she was fully trained in various homemaking skills. She mastered cooking and spinning, weaving, making clothing, and everything that was useful to learn in preparation for when, if the Lord willed, she would be a wife and mother. Her religious training was also regarded as most important. Mary Ball became a church member early in life. Her mother was deeply devoted to God, and her ancestors were Covenanters.

The Sabbath was the day most filled with important duties. There was a solemnity and seriousness about their worship unknown in modern times. They studied the Bible almost to the exclusion of other literature, and the children learned to repeat large portions of it from memory. Such was the early training of Mary Ball.

When Mary had grown to womanhood the name of "Sweet Molly" was dropped, and she was christened, in the flowery language of those times, as "the Rose of Epping Forest." "Epping Forest" was the name of their country home and plantation. She was not only the flower of her home, but the reigning social queen of the community. The family of Ball was an old and an honorable one. Their ancestors came to America from England in 1650, seven years before the Washingtons. The two families had been neighbors for three-quarters of a century. When Mary was twenty-two years of age her mother died. Soon after, she married the widower Augustine Washington, and assumed, with the duties of wife, those of stepmother to his four children.

An old family Bible gives the record as follows: "Augustine Washington and Mary Ball was married the 6th of March, 1730—31."

Mary Ball was eminently fitted for the position she had assumed as wife and stepmother. She was a consistent Christian, and from beginning to end, through eighty-three eventful years, she was a devoted wife and mother—loved by all she came in contact with. She, like the mothers of nearly all great men, was a praying woman. Her Bible was her constant companion; its precepts ever on her lips. This is why she was so silent, self-respecting, reserved and serious a woman. The sentence defining Mary's ideals on life, written by De Tocqueville, declares that life is: "A state of neither pain nor pleasure, but a serious business, to be entered upon with courage in the spirit of self-sacrifice."

It is doubtful that she ever read many books besides her Bible, but it is certain that De Tocqueville's definition was the molding of both her and her son's great characters.

The home to which Augustine conducted his young wife was one of the most comfortable in that section of the country. The house was situated about half a mile from the Potomac River, and commanded a view of the Maryland shore for many miles. On the 22nd of February, 1732, in their pretty country home, Mary and Augustine's first child, George, was born.

During the next ten years, five other children were born to Mr. and Mrs. Washington. All except one lived to maturity. When George was six years old the family moved to a large tract of land on the Rappahannock River, opposite Fredericksburg. It was not a thickly settled portion of Virginia at the time, and the Indians, though ostensibly friendly, were still a menace to the settlers. The conversation of the parents, which their little son listened to with interest, was often on this subject, and it was in this new home that he first exhibited his strong liking for military life.

Mr. Washington owned many slaves, and it required an industrious housewife to manage and provide for her family as well as these slaves. The spinning-wheel and the weaver's loom, the sewing-room and the seamstresses required constant watching. There could be no better position for the development and cultivation of order, discipline, habits of economy, and method than this one filled by Mrs. Washington. Her husband could safely trust in her and have no worry of spoil.

It was a very religious household; both father and mother were members of the Episcopal Church, and were strict observers of the rules of their denomination. Family prayers were said morning and evening. The Bible was read, and the servants of the household were always present. The old Bible which Mrs. Washington read is still preserved, with its curious old-fashioned pictures, its yellow leaves, and pencil-marked pages. On the outside it is covered with a piece of homespun cloth, no doubt crafted by her own hands.

Mr. Washington died at the age of forty-nine years, leaving his young wife with the responsibility of raising the family and managing his affairs. George was then about eleven years old. He said afterward that he remembered little of his father, except that he was tall in stature, of manly proportions, fair complexion, and very fond, loving, and indulgent to his children, but left their training entirely to the mother.

Mrs. Washington found little difficulty in bringing up her children. They were disciplined to obedience, and a simple word was her command. She was not given to any display of petulance or rage, but was steady, well balanced, and unvarying in her mood. Not only did her own children look up to her and venerate her, but her stepchildren seemed equally devoted and obedient to her, as were also the neighbor boys who came to play with her sons.

That she was dignified, even to stateliness, is shown us by the statement made by Lawrence Washington, a relative and playmate of George in boyhood, who was often a guest at her house. He says: "I was often there with George—as his playmate, schoolmate, and young man's companion. Of the mother I was ten times more afraid than I ever was of my own parents. She awed me in the midst of her kindness, for she was indeed truly kind. I have often been present with her sons—proper tall fellows, too—and we were all as mute as mice. And even now, when time has whitened my locks and I am the grandparent of a second generation, I could not behold that remarkable woman without feelings which are impossible to describe. Whoever has seen that awe-inspiring air and manner so characteristic in the Father of his country will remember the matron, as she appeared when the presiding genius of her well-ordered household, commanding and being obeyed."

Allied to this spirit of command were gentle qualities which made obedience to her wishes an easy task. Her servants and slaves rendered the same implicit obedience. It is related of her that on one occasion, having ordered a person in her employ to do a piece of work in a certain way, she was surprised to find that he had disobeyed her. He explained that he had a better plan, when she reminded him that she had commanded, and there was nothing left for him but to obey. There was no occasion for a second reprimand in that direction.

George Washington Parke Custis, the adopted son of Washington, said of her: "The mother of Washington, in forming him for those distinguished parts he was destined to perform, first taught him the duties of obedience, the better to prepare him for those of command . . . The matron held in reserve an authority which never departed from her, not even when her son had become the most illustrious of men . . . The chief never dissent from these truths, but to the last moment of the life of his venerable parent, he yielded to her will the most dutiful, implicit obedience, and felt for her person and character the most holy reverence and attachment."

Though she objected to his joining the British navy at age fourteen, Mrs. Washington was not deaf to the call of patriotic duty. When the French and Indian war broke out George Washington received not only his mother's consent, but her blessing when he made known his desire to go. From that time henceforth he was with her only on occasional visits, for he soon after married and settled at Mount Vernon, while his mother remained on her own farm. But, it is almost certain that there were many meetings and visits back and forth. Washington, we know, was often a guest in his mother's house at Fredericksburg.

When the Revolutionary War broke out, Washington, fearing his mother would not be safe on the farm, induced her to remove to a house in the city of Fredericksburg, where she ever afterward continued to reside. It was here he paid her, as has been said, a visit and received her blessing before starting North to assume command at Boston. When Benedict Arnold with the British vessels ascended the Potomac River and began his devastations not far from Fredericksburg, the anxiety of Washington for his mother was very great. When she heard of it she said: " My good son should not be anxious about me, for he is the one in danger, facing constant peril. Tell him I am safe enough. It is my part to feel most anxious and apprehensive over him."

In the long years that passed before she saw him again he wrote her repeatedly, and lost no opportunity to relieve her mind of anxiety concerning him, but we have no letters of hers to him. The lavish praises bestowed upon him by all who saw her hardly ever received any other recognition than a quiet reminder that Providence was ordering all things. She spent much of her time alone, in prayer.

The surrender of Cornwallis at Yorktown was the auspicious event that hastened their reunion. A messenger was sent to tell her of the fact, and as soon as possible public duties were laid aside and Washington visited her, attended by his staff. She was alone, her aged hands employed in the works of domestic industry, when the good news was announced, and it was further told that the victor-chief was in waiting at the threshold. She bade him welcome by a warm embrace and by the well-remembered and endearing name of George—the familiar name of his childhood.

His presence in Fredericksburg aroused the enthusiasm of all classes. For the first time in nearly seven years mother and son met, and it may be imagined that her heart rejoiced over the meeting. She was then over seventy years of age, erect and well preserved.

The foreign officers were anxious to see the mother of their chief. How they were surprised when, leaning on the arm of her son, she entered the room, dressed in the very plain, yet becoming garb worn by the Virginia lady of the old time! Her address, always dignified and imposing, was courteous, though reserved. She received the complimentary attentions which were paid to her, without evincing the slightest elevation. The matron's simple grace won all hearts and the foreign officers were impressed with her. It was a moral spectacle such as the European world furnished no examples. Names of ancient lore were heard to escape from their lips, and they declared, "If such are the matrons in America, well may she boast of illustrious sons."

The most beautiful as well as the most pathetic of all the scenes in the lives of the illustrious chief and his venerable mother is the following, given also as related by Mr. Custis:

> Immediately after the organization of the present Government, the Chief Magistrate repaired to Fredericksburg to pay his humble duty to his mother, preparatory to his departure for New York. An affecting scene ensued. The son feelingly remarked the ravages which a torturing disease had made upon the aged frame of the mother, and addressed her with these words: 'The people, madam, have been pleased, with the most flattering unanimity, to elect me to the Chief Magistracy of these United States, but before I can assume the functions of my office I have come to bid you an affectionate farewell. So soon as the

weight of public business which must necessarily attend the outset of a new Government can be disposed of, I shall hasten to Virginia, and—'

Here the matron interrupted with, "And you will see me no more; my great age, and the disease which is fast approaching my vitals, warn me that I shall not be long in this world; I trust in God that I may be somewhat prepared for a better. But go, George, fulfill the high destinies which Heaven appears to have intended for you; go, my son, and may that Heaven's and a mother's blessing be with you always."

The President was deeply affected. His head rested upon the shoulder of his parent, whose aged arm feebly, yet fondly, encircled his neck. That brow on which fame had wreathed the purest laurel virtue ever gave to created man relaxed from its lofty bearing. That look which could have awed a Roman Senate in its Fabrician day was bent in filial tenderness upon the time-worn features of the aged matron. He wept. A thousand recollections crowded upon his mind, as memory, retracing scenes long passed, carried him back to the maternal mansion and the days of youth, where he beheld that mother, whose care, education and discipline caused him to reach the topmost height of laudable ambition. Yet, how were his glories forgotten while he gazed upon her whom, wasted by time and malady, he should part with to meet no more! Her predictions were but too true. The disease which so long had preyed upon her frame, completed its triumph, and she expired at the age of eighty-five, rejoicing in the consciousness of a life well spent, and confiding in the belief of a blessed immortality.

Another biographer tells us that as Washington left his aged parent on the above memorable occasion he pressed into her hand a purse filled with gold. She handed it back, saying, in kindly remonstrance, "I don't need it, my son. I have enough."

"Let me be the judge of that, mother," he said. "Whether you need it or not, keep it for my sake," and the chief strode off to conceal his emotion, while she, with tearful eye, stood in the door and watched him walk away. It was the last time her eyes beheld him on earth.

Mrs. Washington died at the age of eighty-five, on the 25th of August, 1789 at the home of her daughter, Mrs. Lewis. She had been a widow for forty-six years.

There was a place between her home in Fredericksburg and the house of her daughter where she is said to have resorted almost daily for meditation during the latter years of her life, and there she often knelt in prayer to Him alone on whom she was willing to depend. Her grandchildren said they never disturbed her when they saw her there. For many years she had expressed a desire to be buried in this sacred spot, and here, in accordance with her wish, she was laid to rest.

America's Most Gracious First Lady

DOLLY MADISON

Theodore Tilton said: "I once watched an artist while he tried to transfer to his canvas the lustre of a precious stone. His picture, after his utmost skill, was dull."

Such the writer feels his effort must be in trying to paint the picture of Dolly Madison—a radiant and sparkling woman, full of beauty, wit, reason and heroism—she was a whole crown of jewels. She was the only woman who, for sixteen years, through four Presidential terms, held sway as the social queen at our National Capital, and for many years thereafter she was, perhaps, the most esteemed and celebrated woman in Washington.

It was in the State of North Carolina, on the 20th of May, 1772, that a little May blossom came into the home of John and Mary Payne. They were good, religious people. There home was a simple old Southern mansion. They owned a number of slaves and distributed Southern hospitality according to the generous customs of the times.

They named the little baby "Dorothy." We do not know if John and Mary Payne were at that time Quakers. Accounts differ. If so, the first sight which greeted little Dorothy's eyes was the Quaker cap and sweet, somber face of her mother, and her father's yet more solemn countenance and straight-brimmed Quaker hat. Had these been all she saw, felt and heard in her infancy, how different might her life have been! But her eyes and ears were open to every beauty and every voice of nature.

Even in childhood her buoyant spirits bubbled and gushed out from under her Quaker cap, and her friends ceased to call her Dorothy. "Dolly" suited her better. Years passed, and everyone referred to her as "Sweet Dolly." Then when she entered the White House, "Queen Dolly" was the only title that well-suited the gracious lady.

The parents of Mrs. Madison were native Virginians, and, though born in North Carolina, she claimed for herself also the honor of being a granddaughter of the Old Dominion, a title dear to all its possessors. Her parents removed to Philadelphia in Dolly's childhood, and, if they had not done so before, they now joined the Society of Friends. John Payne, her father, freed all his slaves, abiding the law enacted in 1774 by the Society of Friends.

By this religious denomination no graceful accomplishments were deemed necessary to a girl's education. Jewelry, dancing and music and all light-heartedness and gaiety were forbidden by the tenets of their faith. As a dutiful daughter, Dolly regretfully submitted to the will of her parents. Attired in the close-fitting dress of her order, she would demurely attend to the duties imposed upon her, and the wonderful undertone of sweetness in her character kept the brow serene and the heart ever bright and hopeful. But nothing could conceal her beautiful, genial, sunny character. Nor could the quaint bonnet of the Friends hide her sparkling eyes and the perfectly rounded features from the admiring gaze of her young acquaintances. Nor—shall we say it?—could any restraint check the joyful flow of spirit in Dolly, nor her love of what the Friends called "carnal pleasures."

When Dolly was eighteen years of age, she became acquainted with John Todd, a young lawyer of good estate, who began to show interest in Dolly.

John Todd was not permitted by the custom of the Friends to go at once to Dolly, but he began to court the father. He heaped many favors on him, and finally gained Mr. Payne's permission to approach the winsome Dolly. In the language of one of her biographers, let us tell the story of this and another later love which came to brighten the life of "Sweet Dolly."

In true Quaker fashion, John Todd pressed his suit and asked her hand. "I never mean to marry," was the demure reply.

Her father was more persuasive, and soon John Todd bore away a bride. For three years she lived the secluded life of a proper Quaker matron, and became the mother of two babies. Then the yellow fever epidemic broke out in Philadelphia. John Todd sent away Dolly and her babies, but lingered himself to do what a man and a Christian might. When he knew the fever to be burning in his veins he followed his wife, with the cry, "I must see her once more." In a few hours he was dead, and soon Dolly and a baby lay battling with the fever. When the disease was stayed, Dolly, now widowed with one baby, went home to her mother.

The married years had turned the shy girl-bride into a beautiful woman. Men would station themselves where they might see her pass. Her companion maid often said: "Really, Dolly, thou must hide thy face, there are so many staring at thee."

It was on one of these walks that her bright beauty first flashed upon Madison. Its effect is shown by a note, written the next day by Dolly: "Dear Friend: Come to me. Aaron Burr says the great-little Madison has asked to be brought to see me this evening."

Dolly was in mulberry satin, silk tulle, with curls creeping from beneath the dainty Quaker cap, brimming with fun and sparkling with wit. Soon a strange rumor spread through the city. The President and Mrs. Washington shared in the amusing surprise, and to be assured, sent for Dolly. "Is it true?" asked Mrs. Washington.

In the same manner with which she had once answered John Todd, she said, "No, I think not." Confusion and blushes told the tale she would hide, and Mrs. Washington bade her not to be ashamed; it was "an honor to win a man so great and so good; he will make thee a good husband, and all the better for being so much older. We both approve of it. The esteem and friendship existing between Mr. Madison and my husband is very great, and we would wish thee to be happy."

Soon, with her child, sister, and maid, she was driven from the city in an open carriage, and the "Father of the Constitution," mounted, rode at her side. At the home of her sister, who married a nephew of Washington, she became Mrs. Madison. Guests came from far and near, and the merry-making went on for days.

Party spirit never ran so high, but in the drawing-room of Mrs. Madison, under her gracious tact, men who would meet at no other place forgot their bitterness. She made foes friends. Her civilities were never influenced by party politics, and at her social board, where she dispensed her lavish hospitality with quiet dignity and elegance of manner, the subject was never mentioned.

When she was congratulated on her husband's occupation of the White House, with her ready wit she answered: "I don't know that there is much cause for congratulation. The President of the United States generally comes in at the iron gate and goes out at the weeping willows." At that time there was a side entrance, a stone archway, with a weeping willow on each side of it.

Whatever the end was to be, the beginning was very brilliant. Mrs. Madison, in buff velvet and bird-of-paradise plume, looked and moved with queenly elegance.

"Sweet Dolly" had high-bred airs and refinement, was beautiful in form and features, always richly and elegantly dressed, as became her position. At her marriage, by her husband's request, she laid aside the Quaker dress, retaining only the dainty cap, which was very becoming, but even that was put aside in the Executive Mansion. The Quakers charged her with "an undue fondness for the things of this world;" but by her sweetness and affability she retained their favor. She was remarkable for rarely forgetting a name, would even remember little incidents connected with her guests.

The first term, which had passed for Mrs. Madison in unclouded happiness, was drawing to a close. It was said that Jefferson chose his own successor, but he had passed the Government to him with Pandora's box wide open, and had also reduced the means of stamping out the evils which had escaped and were working bitter results. George III, who went insane, was harmless in his padded cell, but his son laid a heavy hand upon the new and struggling nation.

The war of 1812 came on. The British offered bounties for American scalps. Battles on the Canadian border were fought with varying fortunes to land forces and brilliant victories to our ships. General Jackson defeated and destroyed the Creek Nation. Attempts were made to invade Canada, but in vain, and the British tried as vainly to enter the United States. The British had blockaded and ravished the Atlantic coast from North to South. Lighthouses only benefitted the enemy, and the lighting of lamps was forbidden.

Meantime things at the capital went on undisturbed, until the crowning humiliation of the war came when the British sailed up the Potomac and burned Washington, August 24th, 1814. For several days before grave fears had been entertained. Our soldiers and fleet were in the North and East, where the war was raging, and our National Capital was unprotected. Suddenly the news was spread, "Cockburn, the marauder," is coming up the Chesapeake Bay to attack the capital. "What!" exclaimed General Armstrong, Secretary of War, "the enemy attack Washington? Nonsense!" This quieted the fears of the people, and little preparation was made to defend the city.

Suddenly, on the morning of August 19th, a horseman dashed through the villages forty miles below the capital shouting, "To arms! To arms! Cockburn is coming!" It was true. Cockburn and Ross had landed with 5,000 men and were marching for the capital. Stirring appeals were made, and citizens at home were quickly congregated for defense, and these, under General Winder, were expected to drive back the marauders. General Armstrong had no doubts of its being done. But they drew nearer.

On the afternoon of the 22nd President Madison bade his wife good-by and hurried to the front to join General Winder. Scarcely had he taken his departure when news came that the American ships below the city had been destroyed to prevent their falling into the hands of the enemy, and the latter were in close proximity to the capital. Mrs. Madison now for the first time manifested fear. Her husband was in danger. The work of saving records was now inaugurated.

All day and all night the work went on. Every one was busy and every available transport was summoned for use. Carts, wagons, and wheelbarrows were loaded with the precious documents.

A hurried note from the President came: "Be ready at any moment to enter your carriage and leave the city. The British may destroy it." With busy, nervous haste, the entire household scurried about gathering Madison's papers and records and packing them in as many trunks as Dolly's carriage would hold.

Excitement grew more intense. In the outskirts of the city a skirmish was in progress. With eager eyes from an upper window Mrs. Madison scanned the field with a glass. She could see the moving troops, but could not distinguish individuals. Night came. The firing ceased. Friends urged her to fly. She would not until she heard from her husband.

In great alarm and amid the gloomiest forebodings Mrs. Madison awaited the return of the President. Two messengers, covered with dust and exhausted with heat, arrived at the White House, and, breathlessly informing her of the fate that had overtaken the Americans, implored her to leave the place at once. Bidding them make good their own escape she still refused to go, determined to brave her situation to the last in the hope of her husband's return.

In the mean time she resolved to save the famous life-size portrait of General Washington that hung in one of the rooms. Finding the task of unscrewing it from the wall too tedious a process for such perilous moments, she ordered one of her servants to break the heavy gilt frame with an axe, and then with her own hands removed the canvas. Scarcely had this been accomplished when the sounds of rapidly approaching troops were heard, and the same instant two gentlemen, bent upon urging her immediate flight, entered the room.

"Fly! Fly at once, madam!" they exclaimed. "The British are upon us!" The time for her departure had come; to remain longer would be useless. "Save that picture!" she cried, addressing her two friends. "If you cannot save it, see that it is destroyed; but remember, under no circumstances allow it to fall into the hands of the enemy."

It was at this moment, just as she was in the act of hurrying away, that Dolly Madison was seized with an inspiration that ever will cause her name to live in the heart of every true American. She stopped to think that she had packed up all of the valuable personal and official papers of the President. The records were safe. Was there anything more? What if the White House should be burned? Did it contain anything of value to the Government that she had neglected? The Declaration of Independence! In a flash she called to mind this most precious of all documents. Carefully treasured in a case apart from the other papers, it had been overlooked in the worriment and confusion. It must be saved at all hazards! Without a moment's hesitation she turned and rushed back into the house.

Her friends, vainly endeavored to intercept her. Regardless of their entreats, regardless of her danger, the brave woman sped to the room containing the treasure for which she was willing to sacrifice her life. Without attempting to open the glazed door of the case, she shattered the glass with her clenched hand, snatched the priceless parchment, and waving it exultantly above her head hurried to the door, where she entered her carriage and was rapidly driven away in the direction of Georgetown.

Learning, however, that the British had not yet entered the town, she compelled her terrified coachman to return toward the White House, in the hope of finding the President. Great was her joy when she beheld him proceeding along the road on horseback, accompanied by several gentlemen, on his way from the White House, where he had gone to assure himself of her safety. He, like hundreds of others, was a forlorn fugitive, anxiously seeking a place of refuge. Accompanying him and his party to the river, where they embarked for the Virginia shore, Mrs. Madison set off toward a point several miles up the river, where it was planned she and the President should meet the next day. So crowded was the roadway with retreating troops, horses, and wagons that she was frequently obliged to leave her carriage and tramp through the heat and intolerable dust. She was surrounded by a crowd of rough soldiers, who rudely pushed her aside and insulted her with coarse and angry remarks. Suffering greatly and thoroughly exhausted with the hardships of the day, she bravely continued her unhappy flight. Then, late in the evening, when overcome with fatigue, she took shelter in a farm-house where she remained all night.

The last glimmer of twilight was fading away when into the nearly-deserted city rode the dreaded Cockburn at the head of his band of marauders. Elated at their decisive victory over a force nearly twice as large as their own, and thirsting for spoils, the red-coated soldiers marched triumphantly toward the Capitol. Suddenly from the window of a house came the report of a musket, and the horse General Ross rode dropped dead. "Fire the house!" shouted Cockburn, and the next moment it was in flames.

Heedless of the remonstrances of General Ross, who was averse to such methods, the invaders followed the lead of their Admiral and rushed toward the Capitol, which stood upon the brow of a hill overlooking the city in every direction. Even at that early period of its construction it was a building of unusual magnificence. Discharging their firearms at the windows the reckless soldiers burst in the doors and with a wild shout of triumph carried their leader to the Speaker's chair, from which with mock gravity he put the question, "Shall this harbor of the Yankee democracy be burned?"

A yell of affirmation rang through the hall, and without further preliminaries papers and other combustibles were piled under the desks and set on fire. In a few minutes this noble edifice, that had been in course of construction more than twenty years, and containing the library of Congress and vast quantities of official documents of great historical value, was enveloped in a seething mass of flames that shot up into the sky in unmistakable proclamation of the awful fate that had come upon the capital of the nation.

Now thoroughly aroused to their work of plunder, a howling crowd of the desperate marauders hurried to the White House in the hope, perchance, of capturing the President and his wife. Finding the house locked and deserted, they battered down the doors, and, consoling themselves for the loss of their distinguished captives by a ruthless destruction of the furniture, they raided the pantry and treated themselves with a hastily prepared feast in the state diningroom. Then, destroying the remaining provisions and ransacking the place from garret to basement, breaking and mutilating whatever they could readily lay their hands on, they concluded their visit by setting fire to the home of the President. Fanned by the gust of a coming storm, the fires that had been kindled in all directions burned and spread with increasing fury, lighting up the streets with a glare more brilliant than that of day. The next day, a terrific hurricane completed the ruin.

Overawed at the terrible devastation wrought by their hands and the forces of nature, the British stole silently forth from the city on the night of the 25th of August and beat a hasty retreat to their ships. Slowly and mournfully the hopeless inhabitants returned to their desolate homes. According to appointment, the President had rejoined Mrs. Madison at a small tavern about sixteen miles from the city on the day following the invasion. At first Mrs. Madison had been refused entrance, and it was only the breaking of the storm that finally induced those who had taken refuge in the house to grant her entrance, though not without gross insults and much remonstrance. Leaving this place in disguise, and accompanied only by a friend and one soldier, she reached Washington on the night of the 26th. She stopped a moment to gaze at the smouldering ruins of her once beautiful home and then drove to the house of her sister, where she awaited the President. He was returning by another route, having left her again the day before upon learning that the British had discovered his hiding-place and were in pursuit of him.

American pride and determination built again the city that Cockburn had burned, but never could they have replaced that priceless parchment which the noble Dolly Madison gladly risked her life to save.

At last the war was over, and though her husband's reputation had seriously suffered, the last years of Queen Dolly's reign were more dazzling than ever. She seemed to invest the city itself with a courtly tone, and something of a royal flavor clung to the manners and presence of all social events which she managed.

On retiring from the Presidency, Madison, like Washington, repaired to his country estate at Montpelier, where he and his charming wife dispensed old Virginia hospitality. So much loved was Mrs. Madison that not only her country's best, but distinguished guests from abroad came, and simple country people begged the privilege of seeing her, which she never denied them. One farmer's wife came from a distance and asked to kiss her, that her daughters might tell of it in years to come, to which Dolly graciously acquiesced.

Death came for the old President in the form of a lingering illness. For eight months his faithful wife watched and nursed him with tender care. On June 28th, 1836, in the eighty-sixth year of his age, President James Madison died and Dolly arranged his letters and manuscripts for publication. At length she returned to Washington to be among her old friends, and it was always an honor to be a guest where she was present. She was so popular that when she offered the manuscripts and letters of her husband for sale, both parties in Congress, out of compliment to her, voted to purchase them, and paid her thirty thousand dollars for them. They also gave her a seat on the floor of the Senate, a mark of favor and esteem no other woman had ever enjoyed from our nation.

The press of the country went so far as to accuse Congress, as a body, of flirting with Mrs. Madison. But since every man, woman or child who met her, either in youth or age, fell in love with her, no editor who knew "Queen Dolly" had any censure against Congress for favoring her. She was the honored guest of succeeding Presidents as long as she lived. When the great cannon, Peacemaker, exploded on the Princeton, killing and wounding many, she was on board as the guest of President Tyler. Preserving her presence of mind while others were fainting about her, she assisted heroically in the care of the wounded, soothed their friends, and went home, where she found a host of friends had preceded her, anxious to learn of her own safety. She appeared before them smiling, but pale as death, and begged them not to ask her to speak of the awful scene, and she was never afterward known to mention it.

The last years of her long and happy life were saddened by the dissolute habits of her only son, Payne Todd, for whom President Madison had often paid debts, and she was finally forced to sell Montpelier to save him from further disgrace. With a sore and grieved heart over this one cloud on the sky of her life, she died, at the age of eighty-two, in Washington, July 12th, 1849, the name of this dissolute son, whom she called her "poor boy," on her dying lips. Her funeral was attended by a large concourse of people, and her remains were taken to Montpelier and laid beside those of her husband.

Two years later typhoid fever carried this disgraceful son away. The faithful servants of his mother, for her sake, tended him in his illness, and they alone, followed him to his grave.

CHAPTER SEVEN

Daughters of Liberty

"Strength and honour are her
clothing; and she shall rejoice
in time to come."

Proverbs 31:25

The First Flag Of Liberty

BETSY ROSS

Betsy, born January 1st, 1752, was the sixth daughter of Samuel and Rebecca Griscom, Quakers from Philadelphia, Pennsylvania. Her father was a noted builder, who assisted in the erection of Independence Hall. Betsy was a bright girl, and grew to be a beautiful woman, noted for her amiable and lady-like manner. Skillful with the needle, she was fond of embroidery and other kinds of fancy work. Among her many admirers was John Ross, a young man who, though poor, was possessed of such qualities as made him worthy of Betsy Griscom. His uncle was the Hon. George Ross, one of the signers of the Declaration of Independence. Young Ross was an upholsterer. One day he noticed the young women in his employment were puzzled over some work. He told them he knew a young woman who could arrange it. They sent for her. Her mother consented to let her learn the business. Thus, Betsy became an upholsterer.

In December, 1773, John and Betsy were married. For marrying "out of meeting" the Quakers disowned her. Her husband being an Episcopalian, she attended Christ Church with him, occupying a pew near General Washington's. The young couple soon embarked in the upholstery business, and moved into the house at 239 Arch Street. In January, 1776, while at his home, John Ross died from an injury received while guarding military supplies. The young widow heroically determined to continue the business alone.

When Washington wanted a sample flag made, Betsy Ross was recommended by the Hon. George Ross. Directed by Colonel Ross, a short walk brought General Washington and Governor Morris to the upholstery shop. Imagine Betsy's surprise at the entrance of these two highly distinguished guests! Her uncle pleasantly explained the purpose of their visit and they asked her if she could make a flag.

"I don't know," she humbly replied, "but I will try."

Washington then drew from his pocket a small paper with a hurried pencil sketch, showing the outlines of a flag of thirteen stripes with a field dotted with thirteen stars; thirteen, for the number of States at this time in the Union. Betsy noticed that the stars drawn by Washington had six points. She suggested that they have only five. He supposed a six-pointed star could be more easily made, but Betsy quickly folding a piece of paper, with one clip of her scissors displayed a perfectly formed pointed star. This point was then yielded in her favor and the design redrawn. She was left to make the sample flag according to her own ideas of proportion.

It was soon completed, accepted by the committee, and adopted by Congress June 14th,1777. Then, Congress drew an order on the treasury to pay Betsy Ross seventy-three dollars for flags for the fleet in the Delaware. She soon received the contract to make all the government flags, and held it many years. Her daughter, Mrs. Clarissa Wilson continued the business until 1857. Betsy Ross was married three times, her second husband was Captain Ashburn, and after his death she married John Claypole.

The colors of the flag were specially chosen to symbolize what their nation stood for. Red stands for love; some people say it means divine love. It is the same language of bravery and the emblem of war. Red was the field color of England's and the colonial army's flag. Red denotes daring and defiance; and tells of the blood our forefathers shed for their rights. This meaning appears in the crimson stripes of the flag. White means truth and hope. It is the language of purity and the emblem of peace. Blue means loyalty, sincerity, justice. Blue was the color of the Covenanter's banner of Scotland, adopted by them in opposition to the scarlet of the royalty. Its choice is based on Numbers 15:38, "Speak unto the children of Israel, and bid them that they make them fringes in the borders of their garments, throughout their generations, and that they put upon the fringes of the borders a ribband of blue." Other nations, to be sure, had previously used these colors, but never in such a beautiful design as Old Glory.

One writer describes the flag in a simple, but true statement, "Every color means liberty; every thread means liberty; every form of star and beam or stripe of light means liberty. It is not a painted rag." Let us uphold our liberty and raise the standard of excellence.

BETSY'S BATTLE-FLAG

From dusk till dawn the livelong night
She kept the tallow dips alight,
And fast her nimble fingers flew
To sew the stars upon the blue.
With weary eyes and aching head
She stitched the stripes of white and red,
And when the day came up the stair
Complete across a carven chair

Hung Betsy's battle-flag.

Like shadows in the evening gray
The Continentals filed away,
With broken boots and ragged coats,
But hoarse defiance in their throats;
They bore the marks of want and cold,
And some were lame and some were old,
And some with wounds intended bled,
But floating bravely overhead
Was Betsy's battle-flag.

When fell the battle's leaden rain,
The soldier hushed his moans of pain
And raised his dying head to see
King George's troopers turn and flee.
Their charging column reeled and broke,
And vanished in the rolling smoke,
Before the glory of the stars,
The snowy stripes, and scarlet bars
Of Betsy's battle-flag.

The simple stone of Betsy Ross
Is covered now with mould and moss,
But still her deathless banner flies,
And keeps the color of the skies.
A nation thrills, a nation bleeds,
A nation follows where it leads,
And every man is proud to yield
His life upon a crimson field
For Betsy's battle-flag!

MINNA IRVING

The Spy Who Saved The American Army

LYDIA DARRAH

When the British army held possession of Philadelphia, the assistant general, selected a back chamber in the house of Mrs. Lydia Darrah, for private conference. Suspecting that some important movement was on foot, she took off her shoes, and putting her ear to the key-hole of the door, overheard an order read for all the British troops to march out, late in the evening of the fourth, and attack General Washington's army, then encamped at White Marsh.

On hearing this, she returned to her chamber and laid herself down. Soon after, the officers knocked at her door. She rose only at the third summons, having pretended to be asleep.

Her mind was so much agitated that, from this moment she could neither eat nor sleep. It was in her power to save the lives of thousands of her countrymen, but she did not know how she was to carry the necessary information to General Washington. For the sake of the safety of her loved ones, she dared confide her discovery to no one.

The time left was short, and she quickly determined to make her way as soon as possible to the American outposts. She informed her family, that, as they were in want of flour, she would go to Frankfort for some. Her husband proposed that she take with her the servant maid, but to his surprise, she decisively declined.

Gaining access to General Howe, she obtained a pass for a visit to a mill for flour. Leaving her bag at the mill she went safely through the British lines. Once safe on the American side she encountered Colonel Craig, who, with some of his men, was on the lookout for information. He knew her, and inquired whither she was going. She answered, in quest of her son, an officer in the American army; and petitioned the Colonel to dismount and walk with her. He did so, ordering his troops to keep in sight.

To him she disclosed her momentous secret, after having obtained from him the most solemn promise never to betray her individually, since her life might be at stake. He conducted her to a house near at hand, directed a female in it to give her something to eat, and hastened to head-quarters, where he made General Washington acquainted with what he had heard. Washington made, of course, all preparation for baffling the meditated surprise, and the contemplated expedition was a failure thanks to the courage of Lydia Darrah

Guided By A Southern Girl

EMMA SANSOM

It was in 1863. There was war in the land. The soldiers of the gray were on their famous raid from Tennessee to Georgia, in pursuit of the soldiers of the blue. To their dismay the fleeing Union forces burned a bridge after they had passed over it in safety, and left their pursuers on the opposite side of a deep creek.

The country was wild and rugged. The pursuing general searched the banks for a place to cross, but the stream was too turbulent and deep to allow them to pass on horseback. A short distance away was a little farm-house. As he approached this humble dwelling, he saluted a young girl who was standing on the porch.

"Is there any place above or below the destroyed bridge where we can ford or pass over the creek?" he asked.

Emma Sansom, the southern girl with flashing eyes and cheeks aglow, excitedly gave her directions, emphasizing her words with gestures. Her old mother, in the half-open doorway, stood peering out in wonderment at their strange visitors.

The general sat with his leg thrown over the saddle-pommel, while his faithful followers, weary and weather-worn, were gathered in groups along the roadside. Every moment was precious to the confederate general, and after further inquiry, wishing not to lose a second, he asked the maiden if she would not ride with him and guide them to the crossing.

Eager to be of service to her country, Emma turned to her mother and said: "I am not afraid to trust myself with so brave a man as General Forrest. Please let me go."

Mrs. Sansom, who at first was hesitant to release her daughter, finally gave her consent. "Go, dear one," she said. "My prayers and the God of peace be with you."

General Forrest brought his charger to Mary's side. She grasped the gallant chieftain's hand and he lifted her up to the saddle behind him. She waved a farewell to her anxious mother and instantly they were on their way through the dense woods. The ride was exceedingly difficult, but the maiden kept her seat quite as well as her experienced companion. The cruel undergrowth caught her clothing and lashed her cheeks, but the fair guide did not heed these trifles as she fearlessly led the cavalry forward. Soon they came in sight of the ford, but General Forrest's quick eye espied the Federal sharpshooters on the high precipice opposite. A bullet whistled by their heads.

Still, on they pressed, as long as they could force a road through the tangled brambles and towering shrubs. At last, they were obliged to dismount and make their way on foot. The general hitched his horse to a tree and followed his fair guide.

"Let me go first, for they would not fire upon me, and they might fire if you went," she urged.

"No," exclaimed the general emphatically. "I cannot use a brave girl for my protection."

With the general in the lead, they advanced through the almost impenetrable underbrush to the ford. Around them, the bullets of the concealed enemy were falling in rapid succession. Having reached the crossing in safety, they returned to the spot where they had left the soldiers, who immediately went to work with their tools and soon had cut a path to the ford wide enough to admit of their passage. When general Forrest had sent his company safely to the other side of the creek, he returned to the girl.

"Is there anything that I can do for you in return for your invaluable services?" he inquired.

"The Yankees, on ahead, have taken my brother prisoner, and if you will only release him, I shall be more than repaid," replied the fair young guide.

The gallant general reached for his watch and gazed at it for a moment. "It is now just five minutes to eleven," he said. "To-morrow at five minutes to eleven o'clock your brother shall be returned to you."

The girl made her way swiftly to her home. The Confederate cavalry proceeded on their raid. The following morning on May 8, 1683, at ten o'clock, General Forrest overtook the Union forces under General Streight, in the vicinity of Rome, Georgia. The Confederate cavalcade was so far out-numbered by its Federal prisoners that it was obliged to call all the citizens that could be mustered to form a sufficient guard for them.

General Forrest passed along the lines of prisoners. "Is there a young man

named Sansom in the ranks?" he asked.

"I am here," answered a voice.

"My lad," exclaimed the general, "you are wanted at home. You have just fifty-five minutes to get there. Take the fastest horse in the command and do not rest a moment until you have reached your sister."

When the lost brother entered his home, the heart of his sister, Emma Sansom, was filled with delight.

"I knew," she said, "that General Forrest would do it. I knew he would do it."

In token of the heroism of this Southern girl, and her service to her army, the legislature of Tennessee granted her a valuable plot of land.

Roll a river wide and strong,

Like the tides a-swinging,

Lift the joyful floods of song,

Set the mountains ringing.

Run the lovely banner high,—

Crimson morning glory!

Field as blue as yonder sky,

Every star a story.

By the colors of the day,

By the breasts that wear them,

To the living God we pray

For the brave that bear them!

Run the rippling banner high;

Peace or war the weather,

Cheers or tears, we'll live or die

Under it together.

The Daring Messenger

EMILY GEIGER

The bearing of important dispatches through an enemy's country is an enterprise that always requires both courage and address. Such a feat was performed during the American Revolution, by Miss Emily Geiger, under circumstances of peculiar difficulty.

General Greene had retreated before Lord Rawdon. When Green passed Broad River, he was desirous to send an order to General Sumter, to join him, that they might attack Lord Rawdon, who had divided his force. But the General could find no man in that part of the state who was bold enough to undertake so dangerous mission.

The country to be passed through for many miles was full of blood-thirsty Tories, who, on every occasion that offered, drenched their hands in the blood of the Whigs. At length Emily Geiger presented herself to General Greene, and proposed to act as his messenger. The general, both surprised and delighted consented to her proposal. He accordingly wrote a letter and delivered it, and at the same time communicated the contents of it verbally, to be told to Sumter in case of accidents.

She pursued her journey on horseback on a side-saddle. But on the second day she was intercepted by Lord Rawdon's scouts. Coming from the direction of Greene's army and not being able to tell an untruth without blushing, Emily was suspected and confined to a room.

The officer sent for an old Tory matron to search her for papers. As soon as the door was closed and the bustle a little subsided, she ate up the letter, piece by piece. After a while the matron arrived. She carefully searched Emily, but nothing was found of a suspicious nature about the prisoner, and she would disclose nothing. Suspicion being then relieved, the officer commanding the scouts allowed her to depart.

Emily took a route somewhat roundabout to avoid further detentions and soon after struck into the road leading to Sumter's camp, where she arrived in safety. Emily told her adventure, and delivered Greene's verbal message to Sumter, who in consequence, soon after joined the main army at Orangeburgh.

The Heroine Of Monmouth

MOLLY HAYS

Mary Ludwig, the daughter of John George Ludwig, was born on October 13th, 1744, near Trenton New Jersey. When Mary, or "Molly," was old enough to work, she was employed as a house servant at Carlisle, Pennsylvania, in the family of General William Irvine. In the Summer of 1769, at twenty-five years of age, she was married to John Hays. He was originally a barber, but later enlisted in Proctor's First Pennsylvania Artillery. Molly, not wanting to be separated from her beloved husband, decided to go with him.

It was not unusual, during the American Revolution, for women, generally wives of private soldiers, to follow the armies into the field as laundry women. Every regiment had women who did duty in laundering for the officers. The women had lodgings assigned them and wagons to carry them from place to place.

No account of the battle of Monmouth is complete without this story of Molly Hays. The battle of Monmouth was fought June 28th, 1778, under the command of General Washington. The enemy, commanded by General Clinton, had attacked the Americans brigades, which lined a hedgerow across an open field. Some American artillery took post on a knoll in the rear of this fence, but the British cavalry and a large body of infantry, skilled in the use of the bayonet, charged upon the Americans and broke their ranks. It was during this part of the action that Molly displayed great courage and presence of mind.

Molly's husband was in charge of firing one of the cannons. The day was sweltering and the artillerymen were suffering from the heat. Molly was not far away from watching the fight and could see that the men were thirsty. She obtained a bucket—or "pitcher"—and began to bring water for them from a neighboring spring. Whenever the men were thirsty they would call out, "Molly—pitcher." And this is how the well known name of Molly Pitcher was formed.

While thus engaged, she saw her husband fall. She ran to his aid, but he was dead when she reached him. Just then poor Molly heard an officer order the gun removed; there was no one else to take the place of the valiant cannoneer. Molly's patriotism got the better of her, and, facing the officer, she asked to be allowed to take her husband's place. Her request was granted, and she handled the job with such skill and courage that all who saw her were filled with admiration. She attended the cannon until the battle was won.

Molly's brave act was brought to General Washington's attention. Men were expected to do the fighting and women to do the nursing, but under these circumstances Molly was commended. It has been said that General Washington gave her the rank of sergeant, and she was granted half-pay during her life. She was known afterward as Captain Molly.

Some years after the thrilling incident at Monmouth, Molly married George McCauley, another soldier. She continued to serve her country, living for many years at the Carlisle Barracks after the Revolution, cooking and washing for the soldiers. Molly died January 22, 1823, at seventy-nine years of age.

Pitcher the gunner is brisk and young;
He's a lightsome heart and a merry tongue;
The ear of a fox, the eye of a hawk,
A foot that would sooner run than walk,
And a hand that can touch the linstock home
As the lightning darts from the thunder-dome.
He hates a Tory—he loves a fight—
The roll of the drum is his heart's delight,
And three things rule the gunner's life,
His country, his gun, and his Irish wife.

Oh! Molly, with your eyes so blue;
Oh! Molly, Molly, here's to you!
Sure, honor's roll will aye be richer
For the bright name of Molly Pitcher.

The sun shoots down on Monmouth fight
His brazen arrows broad and bright.
They strike on sabers' glittering sheen,
On rifle-stock and bay'net keen;
They pierce the smoke-cloud gray and dim
Where stand the gunners swart and grim,
Firing fast as balls can flee
At the foe they neither hear nor see.

Where all are brave the bravest one,
Pitcher the gunner, serves his gun.

Oh! Molly, Molly, haste and bring
The sparkling water from the spring,
To drive the heat and thirst away,
And keep your soldier glad and gay!

A bullet comes singing over the brow,
And Pitcher's gun is silent now.
The brazen throat that roared his will,
The shout of his warlike joy, is still;
The black lips gape, but they shoot no flame,
And the voice that falters the gunner's name
Brings only its echo where he lies
With his ghastly face turned up to the skies.

Oh! Molly, Molly, where he lies,
His last look meets your faithful eyes;
His last thought sinks from love to love
Of your darling face that bends above.

"No one to serve in Pitcher's stead?
Wheel back the gun," the Captain said.
When like a flash before him stood
A figure, dashed with smoke and blood,
With streaming hair, with eyes of flame,
And lips that cry out the gunner's name.
"Wheel back his gun, who never yet
His fighting duty would forget?
His voice shall speak, though he lie dead.
I'll serve my husband's gun!" she said.

Oh! Molly, now your hour is come.
Up, girl, and send the linstock home!
Leap out, swift ball, away, away!
Avenge the gunner's death today!

All day the great guns barked and roared;
All day the big balls screeched and soared;
All day, 'mid the sweating gunners grim,
Who toiled in their smoke-shroud dense and dim,
Sweet Molly labored with courage high,
With steady hand and watchful eye,
Till day was o'er, and the setting sun
Looked down on the field of Monmouth won,
And Molly standing beside her gun.

Now, Molly, rest your weary arm!
Safe, Molly, all is safe from harm.
Now, woman, bow your aching head,
And weep in sorrow o'er your dead!

Next day on that field so hardly won,
Stately and calm stands Washington,
And looks where the gallant Greene doth lead
A figure clad in motley weed—
A soldier's cap and a soldier's coat
Masking a woman's petticoat.
He greets our Molly in kindly wise;
He bids her raise her fearful eyes;
And now he hails her before them all
Comrade and soldier, whate'er befall,
"And since she has played a man's full part,

A man's reward for her loyal heart,
And Sergeant Molly Pitcher's name
Be writ henceforth on the shield of fame!"

Oh, Molly, with your eyes so blue,
Oh, Molly, Molly, here's to you!
Sweet honor's roll is aye the richer
For the bright name of Molly Pitcher.

LAURA E. RICHARDS

Angel Of The Battlefield

CLARA BARTON

"A Christmas baby at the Bartons"—this was the news which spread through a certain New England neighborhood in the winter of 1821, when little Clara was born. The Bartons were farmers, living several miles from Oxford, Massachusetts. She was the youngest of five children, who were nearly all grown up when their baby sister was born.

Because she had no playmates in her early childhood, little Clara often watched others at their work and learned from them how to do simple tasks. She found more joy in helping others by running errands and doing little chores than in playing alone. Always she would hurry back and ask more questions, hoping to find something else to do.

When the weather was warm and sunny Clara enjoyed being out of doors. The one person she liked best of all to follow about his work was her big brother David. He was seldom too busy to take her along with him, and sometimes he allowed her to help him drop potatoes down the long rows, or hold the lines as they drove the wagon across the fields. He would take her with him on horseback when he rode to the pasture after the cows. He would try to answer her funny little questions in a kind, big-brotherly manner.

Clara was such an eager little helper that David taught her how to do many things. He taught her how to drive a nail straight, how to tie a knot that would hold, and one evening he taught her how to milk a cow. Clara felt happy when he praised her for learning so quickly everything he tried to teach. One day he placed her in the saddle all alone and taught her how to ride a horse.

When Clara learned to ride well she enjoyed being outside more and more. Now she could bring the cows from pasture alone, and she could carry messages across the field in a hurry. No one would have guessed, to see the little five-year-old girl dash away on the wildest pony in her father's pasture, that she knew the meaning of fear.

But at heart little Clara was timid and afraid. The world seemed so great and mysterious, and the people seemed so hard to understand. They did not talk in terms of child knowledge, and often their sayings perplexed her. When strangers came on the place she shrank away out of sight, for she felt afraid of them. Then there were the awful thunderstorms in summer—how she trembled as she crouched in the darkest corner alone, trying to hide! Sometimes, strange as it may seem, Clara felt afraid of her own little self, for there were no other little children near with whom she could romp and play and whose feelings she could understand. After all, the carefree little girl who often raced madly across the New England hills on her fleet-footed pony was not always happy.

Clara's father had been a soldier in the great Revolutionary War. When his baby girl grew old enough to beg for "more stories, Papa," he would take her on his knee and tell her about the time when he went out to fight against the enemy and help gain independence for his country. He would tell about his daring leader, Mad Anthony Wayne, who led him into many a battle. He would tell of the clouds of black smoke which rose over the battlefields and how the hills and woodlands reechoed with the sound of their flintlock guns. Then the birds would leave their nests in fright, and the furry woodland folk would rush pell-mell, here and there, trying to find places of safety. Little Clara would listen with solemn eyes, and then she would ask, "What happened to the men who got shot, Papa?" And he would shake his head sadly and reply, "alas, my little daughter, I cannot tell; for we had to leave them while we chased the Redcoats away from our beloved land." Clara would shudder as she cuddled up closer in her father's strong arms, for she would think about the suffering men who had no one to wash their wounds, no one to bring them a drink of cool water, and no one to offer them a bit of comfort in their dying hour.

Two miles up the road from the Barton home stood a country schoolhouse. There Clara learned how to overcome some of her shyness, for she was enrolled as a pupil. Both summer and winter terms of school she attended, while the wonders of the book world began to unfold before her eager mind. Then she studied for a while at home, with her teacher brother for instructor. She learned her lessons well, and she also learned how to sympathize with other children, for now she understood that children think and feel different from their elders. This helped her to be kind and patient with other children when she became a schoolteacher herself.

When Clara was eleven years old, one day her big brother David fell from a tall building and injured himself. The men with whom he was working carried him home, and there he was placed in a clean, white bed to get well. But instead of getting well he grew worse, and for two years he suffered as an invalid. Clara remembered the kind things he used to do for her when she was a tiny girl following him about the place, and now she asked permission to become his nurse. Day after day she smoothed his pillow, brought him cool water from the well when he was thirsty, and entertained him by reading stories from her schoolbooks or by telling him the happenings about the farm. She willingly denied herself the pleasure of many horseback rides just to stay in his sickroom and try to make him comfortable.

One who knew Clara well, said of her: "I believe I have never looked upon a happier face than that of Clara Barton." Yet it is certain she never sought her own happiness. Perhaps that is the reason she found it. Her whole long busy life was employed in making less unhappy the lives of miserable ones and in sharing the burdens of those in need.

After David recovered from his invalidism Clara decided to become a schoolteacher. She studied harder than ever and learned everything that was taught in the country schoolhouse. Then, although still a very young girl, she lengthened her dresses, wound her hair in neat coils about her head, and pretended to be quite grown up, for she wished to teach the neighborhood school. "We will let her try," agreed the members of the school board, although they knew she was not yet sixteen years old. And in trying, Clara succeeded, for she won the love of the children and the respect of the big, rude boys who used to make trouble in the schoolroom. They found out that she was not cross or unreasonable, but that she had the courage to demand of them an honest effort to learn. Soon they quit trying to provoke her, as they had done former teachers; for they liked her frank, earnest manner and were glad to treat her as a friend.

Clara saved her small earnings until she had enough money laid aside to pay her way through a school in Clinton, New York. After graduating from that school she went still farther from home, to open a free school for girls and boys in Bordentown, New Jersey. She began teaching there in a tumble-down building with only six pupils. "Everyone is welcome, rich or poor," said she, and after a few weeks passed she had more pupils than the room would hold. At the end of the year a free school building was erected, and five hundred children enrolled to attend the first term. Clara was asked to be the principal of the school, and she continued to teach there for a number of years. Perhaps she thought she would teach school all the rest of her lifetime, for she loved children and understood how to encourage them in well-doing.

She went to Washington, D.C., to visit relatives and take a rest from teaching. While there, the great Civil War broke out. Soon the roar of cannons could be heard, and black clouds of smoke could be seen rising above the battlefields near Washington. Clara remembered the stories her father used to tell about his soldier life. She remembered, too, the sadness which used to steal into her heart when she thought of the wounded men who died without anyone to comfort them on the bloody battlegrounds. Now she knew this same horrible thing was happening again, and she felt a great longing to help the wounded men.

At her first opportunity Clara visited an army hospital, where doctors and nurses were caring for the sufferers who were brought in from the battlefield. Some of them had been left so long that they were nearly dead when at last they reached the hospital. Clara felt that they had suffered needlessly, and she decided that help should be sent to other wounded men on the battlefields directly, just as soon as the smoke would clear away enough for wounded men to be found. Because the doctors and nurses were unwilling to go nearer the danger line than the army hospitals, for a while Clara had to be content with taking provisions in a boat up the Potomac River to the sufferers and bringing back as many of the wounded as the boat could accommodate. Only a few could she relieve in this way, but as long as the fighting continued along the shores of the Potomac she bravely rowed her boat across the water and back again, risking the fire from the guns.

After a while the battle front drew away from the river. Then Clara begged permission to follow the cannons and be ready to minister help as soon as the fight would end. Her aged father had encouraged her to attempt this great work, and with tears in her eyes she pleaded for the privilege, saying, "My father was a soldier." Finally, quite contrary to army regulations, she was allowed to take a supply of bandages and other necessities and pitch her tent with the regular army drawn up for battle.

On these bloody fields Clara began her great lifework. Although a timid little woman, she forgot her own fears in her eagerness to relieve the sufferings of others. She bound up ugly wounds, bathed fevered brows, and cooled parched lips from her own canteen. Day after day she worked, and often far into the night. Sometimes she traveled on horseback, sometimes in an army wagon; but on and on she went, keeping at the battle front with her first aid to the wounded.

Once when no food supplies had been sent, Clara found that the medicine bottles had been packed in fine meal, so she borrowed several big kettles from a farmhouse near by and cooked the meal to serve to her half-starved patients until other supplies reached them. She did not hesitate to go with her own throat parched and her face blackened by sulphurous smoke to answer the groans of a dying soldier. She ministered to all alike, whatever uniform they wore, not just with the men who fought in the cause which she believed to be right. No wonder she was called the "Angel of the Battlefield."

Although Clara risked her life on sixteen battlefields during the Civil War, not once was she injured. Often her clothing was torn by shells, and once when she stooped to lift the head of a wounded soldier a bullet whizzed between her arm and her body, instantly killing the man. So near she followed the horrible trail of death, but always she escaped when risking her own life to save others who, left unattended, would have died.

After the War ended, Clara spent several years helping to trace missing soldiers. Many letters came to her from mothers whose sons had been killed and who wished to learn where their bodies lay buried. Clara helped to identify and mark the graves of about nine thousand soldiers. She answered bushels of letters—bushel sacks full of them—and returned many keepsakes to mothers and wives and sweethearts which had been given to her by dying men.

When at last this sad task was finished Clara felt quite worn out. She went to Europe to rest and to try to forget the misery she had seen. There again she was called by the cruel demands of war to bind up more wounds and comfort other sufferers, for the Franco-Prussian war began to rage. Clara found that there were Red Cross societies in Europe to whom permission was given to care for the wounded and dying on any battlefield. She was pleased with the good work of this society and wished that her own people in America would organize such a society too.

Clara returned to America full of enthusiasm to organize a Red Cross society in her native land. She talked to everyone whom she met about the wonderful work which the Red Cross accomplished in Europe. To her great surprise and disappointment, few people seemed interested.

"We shall never have another war," many told her when she talked about the benefits of such a society.

"But we may have disasters," she would reply, "and people who suffer from flood, or from famine, or earthquake, or from any other calamity are just as needy and deserving of our organized interest and ready relief as are soldiers on a battlefield." After years of waiting and working Clara finally convinced the people that an American Red Cross society would be a worthy organization. She was chosen to serve as its first president and remained in that office until she retired at the age of eighty-three years. She lived on at her Red Cross home in Glen Echo, Maryland, until her death, April 12, 1912. She died just two years before the first world war called forth the best efforts of all the Red Cross societies to minister to the needs of sufferers from both hemispheres.

CHAPTER EIGHT

Daughters of Lyrics

"She openeth her mouth with wisdom; and in her tongue is the law of kindness."

Proverbs 31:26

Nearer, My God, To Thee

SARAH F. ADAMS

Many people consider this hymn, so full of trust and aspiration, to be the best ever written by a woman. The gifted and romantic author was the daughter of a talented and fearless English journalist, Benjamin Flower. While still a young man, he wrote several articles expressing political views too radical for his times, and as a result, was sentenced to serve six months in a London prison. His friends and political sympathizers did not desert the young liberal at this misfortune, however, but came frequently to his prison to visit him. Among these friends was a young English girl with whom he fell in love, and later married, after his release from prison.

Their daughter Sarah Flower (1805-1848) gave early promise of a brilliant and varied career. The dream of her youth had been to go on the stage, for she believed the drama, as well as the pulpit, could teach religious truths. Her very uncertain health, however, soon forced her to abandon all thought of the stage as a career. Greatly disappointed, at first, she turned her talents to writing, little realizing that in this field was to lie her greatest achievement.

Her hymn, "Nearer, My God, to Thee," written in 1841, is based on the story of Jacob, as told in Genesis 28:11-17. Jacob, fleeing from Esau's wrath, went to sleep on a lonely hillside, with a stone for a pillow, and dreamed that he saw a ladder reaching up to heaven, with angels ascending and descending on it. In the morning he arose refreshed and named the place of his vision, "Bethel, the house of God."

Few hymns have such a rich heritage of associations surrounding its use. It was the favorite hymn of the martyred President William McKinley, and brought comfort and peace to him in his last hours. His physician, Dr. M. D. Mann, reported that the dying president softly sang "Nearer, My God, to Thee", saying afterwards,"This has been my constant prayer."

On the day of President McKinley's funeral, September 19, 1901, this hymn was sung in his memory in countless churches, large and small, all over the land. In England, too, by the order of King Edward VII, the hymn was sung at the McKinley memorial services held in Westminster Abbey.

In the last moments of the Titanic tragedy, on Sunday, April 14, 1912, the ship's band played this hymn, while the vessel was slowly sinking after having struck an iceberg on its maiden voyage across the Atlantic. The prayer and perfect trust in these verses have helped men meet the greatest crises of human life.

The hymn is a supreme and triumphant expression of the message that even in darkness and trouble may we be lifted nearer to God; the golden "steps unto heaven" may be revealed to us. Yet the hymn has been so often used in times of sadness that we overlook sometimes the real note of joy, of exaltation, which soars upward to a climax in the last stanza. In times of joy as well as in sorrow our song should still be "Nearer, My God, to Thee."

Nearer, my God, to Thee, nearer to Thee,
E'en though it be a cross that raiseth me;
Still all my song shall be, nearer, my God, to Thee,
Nearer, my God, to Thee, nearer to Thee.

Though like the wanderer, the sun gone down,
Darkness be over me, my rest a stone.
Yet in my dreams I'd be, nearer, my God, to Thee,
Nearer, my God, to Thee, nearer to Thee.

There let the way appear steps unto heav'n;
All that Thou sendest me in mercy given;
Angels to beckon me, nearer, my God, to Thee.
Nearer, my God, to Thee, nearer to Thee.

Then with my waking thoughts, bright with Thy praise,
Out of my stony griefs Bethel I'll raise;
So by my woes to be, nearer, my God, to Thee.
Nearer, my God, to Thee, nearer to Thee.

Or if on joyful wing, cleaving the sky,
Sun, moon, and stars forgot, upward I fly,
Still all my song shall be, nearer, my God, to Thee,
Nearer, my God, to Thee, nearer to Thee.

The Swedish Nightingale

JENNY LIND

A little Swedish girl sat near the window in her grandmother's room in Stockholm one day, singing to her pet cat. She had sat near the same window doing the very same thing many times before. And quite as often she had seen people who were hurrying along the street below stop suddenly and stare at her in wonder. She did not understand why they should stare so.

One of the listeners on this particular day chanced to be a servant girl of Mademoiselle Lundberg's. She stopped, stared, and listened, just as other people had done. Then she hurried home to her mistress and told what she had seen and heard. "No child ever lived who had a sweeter voice," she declared emphatically, after describing the scene she had viewed through the window. Mademoiselle Lundberg was deeply interested. She was a prominent woman who loved music. "I must hear the child for myself," she said.

Jenny Lind was born in Stockholm nine years before, on October 6, 1820. The first three years of her life she spent in a small village ten miles from the city. Then, because her hard-working mother was not always able to provide a home for her, sometimes Jenny stayed with her grandmother in Stockholm.

It was the grandmother who first discovered that Jenny possessed unusual musical talent. She made the discovery in this way: A square piano stood in her best room, and one day not long after three-year-old Jenny came to stay awhile with her she heard somebody playing a tune on the instrument. She had forbidden the child to trum on the piano, thinking her scarcely more than a baby. Jenny's elder half sister sometimes practiced her music lessons on the piano, and now the grandmother supposed that it must be she who was picking out a melody with one finger instead of attending to her lesson properly. So she called to her from the next room, but received no answer. Wondering at the strangeness, she went into the room to investigate and was surprised to find no one. Before leaving the room, however, she stooped down and looked under the piano. There, crouched on the floor in a trembling heap, lay her little granddaughter Jenny.

"Child, was that you?" the astonished woman asked as she drew the little one from her hiding place. Jenny, sobbing out her story on her grandmother's knee, told how she had heard the music of the military buglers who paraded through the streets each day, and how she had felt the tune linger in her mind. She had wanted oh, so much, to try to find it on the piano keys, but she had feared to disobey her grandmother. The longing had grown so urgent that she watched for an opportunity to be alone in the house. Then, creeping up to the piano, she had been delighted to pick out the melody with one finger on the keys. While thus engaged she did not hear her grandmother re-enter the house, and so had been caught.

"Don't cry, child," soothed the astonished woman. "It is I who did the wrong. Hereafter you may play whenever you feel a tune stirring in your soul."

Not long afterwards Jenny's mother came to the city to see her children, and the grandmother told her of this incident. "Mark my word," she concluded, "this child will bring you help someday."

As much as Jenny was delighted with her success in coaxing melodies from the keys of her grandmother's piano, she enjoyed singing still more. From morning until night as she skipped about her play, she sang. Indoors and out of doors her childish voice rang clear and sweet, just as if her soul were overflowing with happiness. Sometimes, when she was still a tiny girl, the neighbors came in to hear her play. But the music of her singing would float to them at any hour of the day. As she grew older they often shook their heads and said, "Too bad that nothing is being done to train that child's remarkable voice."

Jenny's grandmother was an earnest Christian. Often she talked to the little girl about the heavenly Father. She told her that her wonderful talent for music was a gift from God. All through her lifetime Jenny believed that her grandmother was right. She tried to use the wonderful gift God had given her just as she believed he wanted her to use it.

When Jenny grew old enough to enter school she returned to her mother, who was then teaching. For several years she enjoyed the rare privilege of having her mother with her at home and in the schoolroom, too. She studied her lessons thoroughly and was a bright pupil, but just as soon as her lessons were done and school was dismissed she bounded away to frolic and sing.

The time came when Jenny's mother could no longer earn enough money teaching school to pay expenses, so she sought other employment and sent the child back to live again with her grandmother in Stockholm. At first Jenny must have felt lonely in the city, and so she whiled away the hours singing to her pet cat. And that is how she happened to be singing when the servant girl saw and heard her through the window.

Not many days afterwards Jenny's mother received a note from Mademoiselle Lundberg. The note read: "Will you please bring your little girl to sing for me?" This was Jenny's first invitation to sing before someone capable of judging musical talent, and how eager she was to go! The fact that she would be singing to a wide-awake, critical lady instead of to a sleepy cat did not make one bit of difference. She dressed in her Sunday frock, combed her hair neatly, and set out with her mother in time to reach the lady's apartment at the appointed hour.

And how she did sing! The lady sat listening in amazement, tears trickling down her cheeks.

"Wonderful!" she exclaimed, when the song was ended. Then turning to Jenny's mother, she said, "Your child is a genius indeed. You must have her educated for the stage."

"Not for the stage," came the quiet reply, for, like her grandmother, Jenny's mother was a Christian, and she feared that the influence of stage life would be harmful to her little daughter.

"Then at any rate she should be taught singing by the most competent instructor," the Mademoiselle insisted.

For a long time Jenny's mother had wished to give her a musical education, but she could not earn enough money to afford this. She explained how impossible this had been, and the kind lady replied, "Perhaps we may find some other way." She then asked permission to write a note of introduction to her friend, Herr Croelius, the court secretary and singing master of the Royal Theater. "Take this to him," she said. "It may lead to something."

Jenny's eyes grew wide with anticipation as they bade their new friend good-bye and turned their footsteps toward the opera house. She was going to see a singing master! And perhaps he would ask her to sing for him as the Mademoiselle had done. She wondered whether he, too, would like her singing.

When they reached the studio and presented the note of introduction, they met the gentleman and chatted for a while with him. He seemed friendly and cordial. He asked questions about his little visitor, and by and by he brought a sheet of music and asked her please to sing for him. Jenny glanced at the music and saw that it was familiar. Then she threw back her little head and sang her very best, right out of her heart. When she finished the song she saw that big tears had been rolling down the cheeks of her astonished listener.

"I must take her at once to Count Puke, the head of the Royal Theater," said he to Jenny's mother, "and tell him what a treasure I have found."

But the busy count did not receive his visitors as graciously as had the singing master. When he saw the shy, plain-faced little girl standing before him he did not look pleased. He asked her age, and upon hearing that she was nine years old (she looked younger) he said impatiently, as if wishing to dismiss them from his presence, "This is not a nursery; this is the King's school."

"Very well," replied Herr Croelius, turning away in disappointment, "if you refuse to hear her now I shall teach her myself, and someday she will astonish you."

The count was surprised at these words flung at him so bitterly from the singing master. He glanced a second time at the shy, plain-faced little visitor about to leave the room. "Stay," he called, "and let me investigate the matter further."

It had been easy to sing for the Mademoiselle, who had invited Jenny to her apartment. It had been a joy to sing for Herr Croelius, the kind singing master. But when this critical, stern, great man asked her to sing for him, that was quite a different matter. However, Jenny resolved again to try to do her best. She sang with all her heart, and the count stared at her in wonder, just as the listeners had often stared at her from the streets below her grandmother's window. She did not mind that he stared, for she saw his hard face soften, and presently the tears began to trickle down his cheeks, too. He had been convinced just as the Mademoiselle and Herr Croelius, that little Jenny Lind was no ordinary child.

Now the count was very eager to enroll Jenny as a pupil of the King's school. He proposed that she be adopted into the school of pupils attached to the Royal Theater. Thus all her expenses would be paid and she would receive the very best training. At first her mother felt very unwilling to consent to this arrangement, but finally she agreed, and Jenny Lind's musical education began.

For eleven years Jenny drilled at the Royal Theater in voice and motion, studying earnestly and always trying to do her best. She believed that although God had given her a talent for music he expected her to improve it as much as possible, and that was her reason for studying so faithfully. During this time she lived in an apartment near the Royal Theater, where her mother kept several other pupils as boarders. In this manner she was permitted to be with her Christian mother every day, and she resolved never to allow the influence of the theater to spoil her life. She admired the beautiful Christian character

of her mother and of her grandmother, and she determined to become a good woman as well as a great singing artist.

By and by Jenny Lind began to make concert tours through Sweden. Wherever she went she thrilled the hearts of her listeners, but she felt that she was not yet prepared to do her best. She wanted to continue her studies in Paris under a master artist, so she saved the money which she earned from these concert tours to pay her expenses in Paris.

No student was ever more determined to succeed than was this Swedish maiden. When she arrived in Paris she found out that she had nearly lost her voice. Instead of giving way to discouragement she set to work in earnest to study the French language, and at the end of three months she was able to go on with her music lessons. Now she studied under a noted master in Paris for ten months. She received some benefit from his teaching, but she declared that she sang after no-one's method. She loved to watch the birds sing, and she approved of their method, which had been taught to them by the Master of all creation.

The first concert which Jenny Lind gave outside of her native Sweden was in Copenhagen, where she had gone to visit friends. She had not intended to sing in public while there, but was urged to do so by Hans Anderson, the renowned writer of Fairy Tales, and his friend, A. A. Boumonville. The concert which she gave was such a success that her fame soon spread all over Europe and invitations came flooding to her from everywhere.

Words of praise and the thrill of fame did not turn the head of this noble Christian girl. She went just as willingly into the humble room of a sick man to sing for him when he could not go to the concert to hear her as she went to her most successful concert. She tried just as hard to please one listener as thousands.

With the coming of fame, Jenny Lind entered upon a busier life than she had known before. Because of the invitations which came from all over Europe and from across the sea to give concerts to music-loving people, she traveled from one country to another, singing her way into the hearts of her listeners wherever she went. In her own country she was treated like an empress. Thousands of people lined the streets to see her pass through her home city, Stockholm, when on her way to England. Even the warships in the harbor were decorated for the occasion, and all fired salutes, just as they did when the king himself was being honored.

When the "Swedish Nightengale", as Jenny came to be called, sang at court before the royalties of Europe, she manifested the same naturalness and simplicity which marked her singing elsewhere. She attended the receptions given by members of the royal family in her honor, and entered into the social life of the fashionable people. But always she remained the same unspoiled, simple-hearted, noble-minded singer who first won the applause of the people.

At the beginning of her career as a singer, Jenny Lind sometimes disappointed her audience when she first appeared on the stage. Then she was a thin, shy, plain-featured girl resembling somewhat a nervous, awkward country schoolgirl. But when she rose to sing, her face and form seemed to undergo a change, just as if the grace and purity of her soul were shining through and transforming her being. No one who saw and heard her sing said that she was plain. They felt that she sang with all her heart in the joy of her soul, and they realized that they were listening to the voice of an artist who cherished in her heart a reverence for God.

The vast sums of money which Jenny Lind received from her concerts she did not use selfishly. It is said that no woman ever gave away such wealth from her own earnings as this singer did. In America alone, her earnings amounted to about one quarter of a million dollars. Much of this she gave away at once, and the remainder she reserved as a charity fund to be distributed after her death. She gave the receipts of many of her public entertainments to objects of charity, and in her native country she founded a school in which the poorest girls could receive an education. She urged the cultivation of art and virtue in this school, especially of virtue, for she believed that it was of more value in one's life than all things else.

For nearly half a century, Jenny Lind's wonderful voice thrilled the hearts of audiences wherever she sang. She lived to see her grandchildren cluster about her knee while she told them about the loving Father-God whom her own dear grandmother had introduced to her when she was a little child. Then, when the last days on earth approached and she lay on her deathbed, she thought longingly about the time, so soon to come, when she would be singing again, forever free from pain.

Raising herself on her pillow one day when the window blinds had been opened to let in the sunlight, she sang in a voice still sweet a song she loved—"An den Sonnemschein" ("And Then Sunshine"). Soon afterwards her happy spirit took its flight to the realm where eternal sunlight never fades and songs of gladness never die.

Blind And Content

FRANCIS JANE CROSBY

"Aunt Fanny," called a cheery voice, "here comes the postman with a letter for you!"

"Where is it from?" asked the dear old lady, never stopping her knitting to adjust her spectacles, for she knew she could not read it.

"It bears a foreign postmark—England, I believe."

"Then by all means read it at once," urged Aunt Fanny, leaning forward in her low rocking chair. For the moment she dropped her knitting, so eager was she to hear who had sent her this message from across the sea.

"Oh, it's a poem, a long poem," exclaimed her friend, as soon as she had torn open the envelope and unfolded its contents, "from that wonderful Christian woman in England, Frances Ridley Havergal.

> *"Sweet blind singer over the sea,*
>
> *Tuneful and jubilant; how can it be,*
>
> *That the songs of gladness, which float so far,*
>
> *As if they fell from the evening star,*
>
> *Are the notes of one who never may see?"*

And while it was being read the old lady sat very still in her low rocking chair, smiling happily. She felt pleased to hear how much her songs were being appreciated and sung in England.

Fanny Jane Crosby, the hymn writer, was blind. She had been blind ever since she was a tiny baby, only a few weeks old. In spite of this affliction she had grown up to become one of the most cheerful, lovable, and noble Christians, and she wrote some of the most beautiful hymns that the world has ever sung. How did she do it? Perhaps we can answer that question when we read the story of her life.

The low, rural cottage in which Fanny Jane Crosby was born March 24, 1820, stood near the bank of a gay little brook that rambled through Putnam County, New York. Fanny's parents were poor, although they and their ancestors were numbered among the brave New England families who helped to make America great. Fanny could not remember her father, for he died before she was a year old. Then her grandmother, a dear Christian woman, came to live in the little cottage and care for the blind baby while her mother was at work.

As baby Fan grew older she often sat on her grandmother's knee, listening to stories about the great, wide, wonderful, beautiful world in which she lived. For Grandmother knew Fan could never see the beauties of nature with her eyes, and she wanted the child to begin early to see them with her imagination. She wanted to train little Fan to think about the word pictures which she tried to paint so patiently, day after day.

And so it was through Grandmother's stories that Fanny caught her first idea of the glorious sunrise and sunset pictures which are flung upon the sky canvas for us to view. She learned about the twinkling stars which shine so bravely through the long, dark nights, and about the silvery moon which rides around the earth with never a stop. She learned about the clouds with their various shapes and colors—the fleecy white summer clouds, the murky rain clouds, and the dark storm clouds. She learned about the beautiful rainbow, too, which God placed in the sky as a bow of promise to mankind.

From Grandmother, Fanny also learned about the little feathered songsters that came every springtime to nest in the shade trees near by. Together they would listen to the birds sing, and then Grandmother would explain how each bird looked. Soon Fanny learned how to recognize each bird by its song. "Oh, there is a meadow lark!" she would shout, just as happy as if she could see him balancing himself on the slender twig. One day Fanny heard an unfamiliar bird call down in the meadow. "Grandmother," she cried excitedly, "come and listen! A new bird is here."

"He is saying, 'Whippoorwill!'" exclaimed Grandmother, "and that is how he got his name." Then she told little Fan that he had specked wings and a reddish brown breast and a white, bristled tail. Thus one at a time Fanny came to know the mockingbird, the redheaded woodpecker, the robin, the red-winged blackbird, the song sparrow, the meadow lark, the goldfinch, the yellow warbler, and the wren. How many little girls with two good eyes can describe each of these birds?

In pleasant weather Grandmother often took Fanny for long walks over the hills and through shady lanes. Sometimes they stopped to examine gay wild flowers, and in the springtime they spent happy hours picking violets down by the brook or gathering bouquets of apple, cherry, and peach blossoms in the orchard. Fanny examined every kind of blossom carefully while Grandmother told its name and described its color.

When Fanny grew old enough to romp and play she learned how to find her way alone through the grassy meadow. She learned how to ride horseback, how to climb rail fences, and even how to walk the top rail! One day her mother brought home from the pasture a shivering little lamb. Fanny had been wishing for a pet, so she begged to have the lamb for her very own. "I cannot give it to you to keep always," said her mother, "but you may care for it and play with it until it grows up." Then she told Fanny the rhyme story about "Mary's Little Lamb." This story pleased Fanny, and she too, soon trained her pet to follow her wherever she went. What lively frolics they had out in the meadow! When the pet lamb grew up to be a sheep, then it was too valuable to keep any longer, so it had to be sold. Then a very lonely little girl went to bed one night and cried herself to sleep!

Fanny did not waste much time shedding tears. She soon found other things to play with. When only eight years old she wrote these lines:

> *Oh, what a happy soul am I!*
> *Although I cannot see*
> *I am resolved that in this world*
> *Contented I will be.*

> *How many blessings I enjoy*
> *That other people don't;*
> *To weep and sigh because I'm blind*
> *I cannot, and I won't!*

We see that Fanny began to make rhymes when she was a very little girl. She loved the musical rhythm of poetry. One day her mother told her that some of the world's greatest poets were blind. She read to Fanny the lines which Milton wrote on his blindness, and Fanny learned to repeat them from memory.

Because Fanny's mother was often very busy, her grandmother continued to be her most constant teacher. From Grandmother she learned much about the love of the heavenly Father. With Grandmother's assistance she memorized long portions of Scripture. "Child, you will never be able to take the Book from the shelf and read it as I do," Grandmother would say, "but you can store much of it in your bright mind, and then it will be with you wherever you go."

With this encouragement Fanny studied until she could repeat from memory many of the Psalms, the Proverbs of Solomon, the Book of Ruth, and much of the New Testament. The stories of the Old Testament she knew word for word. All through her lifetime she prized these memory treasures which her dear old grandmother had helped her to store away. One day she wrote these lines about the Bible:

> *O Book, that with reverence I honor,*
> *What joy in thy pages I see!*
> *O Book of my childhood devotion,*
> *More precious than rubies to me.*

"How splendid it would be," thought Fanny one day, "if I could read for myself!" But there was no school for the blind near her home, and the expense of sending her away to school was more than her mother could afford. Fanny continued to learn from hearing others read and explain the meaning of things which she could not see. However, the desire to study in a school for the blind grew stronger in Fanny's heart every day, and she began to talk to the heavenly Father in prayer about this desire. She believed he could help her mother find a way to send her to school.

Fanny did not grow discouraged or quit praying when her prayer was not answered at once. She kept right on reminding her heavenly Father of this desire to learn more than could be taught to her at home. Then one glad morning her mother said, "Fanny, we shall begin preparations today to send you to the Institution for the Blind in New York City."

"Thank God, he has answered my prayer!" exclaimed Fanny, clapping her hands for joy.

School days brought new experiences to the sightless girl. She had never been alone among strangers before, and we may be sure that at first she felt homesick. The unfamiliar rooms and halls she feared to venture through in the self-confident manner of other days. Soon she became acquainted with her new surroundings, and then she felt very much at home. She enjoyed the companionship of other young people who, like herself, were searching after knowledge with unseeing eyes. She studied her lessons eagerly and drank in the beautiful poetry which her teachers often read. As soon as she was able to choose her own reading she began a careful study of poetry.

At first Fanny's teachers did not encourage her to write rhymes.

They thought she spent too much time with poetry, and occasionally they would assign her other work and take the poetry from her. This made her feel very unhappy.

Then one day a doctor from Boston, who came to the Institution to examine the pupils, said to Fanny's teachers: "You will do well to teach this pupil to appreciate the finest there is in poetry. Read the best books to her, and give her every possible encouragement. You will hear from this young lady someday."

Fanny was delighted. Now she knew her teachers would no longer discourage her in doing what she liked best of all to do. They would help her, rather than hinder, when she tried to write rhymes. She felt that this was the happiest moment of her school life, and she began more earnestly than ever to study and write.

Everything seemed to be going along pleasantly with Fanny now. Her classmates were saying flattering things about her poems, and words of commendation were coming from other people, too. Fanny was feeling very well pleased with herself when one day a teacher asked her to remain after class. She felt sure that he was going to say something good about her poems, as everyone else was doing. To her surprise, he began to talk to her about the harm which sometimes results from receiving too much flattery. He kindly showed her that her poems were weak in some places, and that they could not honestly be ranked with the best poetry. Fanny listened quietly, feeling very much ashamed. When he finished, she thanked him heartily, through her tears and resolved to profit by his reproof.

For twelve years Fanny studied in the Institution, spending much time with music, art, and literature. Then she accepted a position as teacher in the same school, and remained eleven years longer. At once she became a favorite among her pupils, for she always encouraged them to do their best. She was cheerful and patient, and understood their struggles because she had passed through similar struggles herself.

Fanny's love for sacred music had begun when she was a very small child. She used to fancy that the birds were singing songs of praise to their Creator and that the brook which flowed past her home also sang His praise. She felt that she would like to sing words of her very own heart language—words which she had put together into rhyme. The time came when she began to write such words, and then they were set to music. She heard them sung by others, too, wherever she attended religious services. How her heart thrilled with joy when she heard that the world was singing her songs of praise and worship to Jehovah! Her hymns were translated into other languages and sung all around the world.

Fanny's first hymn to win world-wide favor was, "Pass Me Not, O Gentle Savior." Missionaries carried it across the seas and translated the words into the languages of the people among whom they labored. Thus Chinese and Japanese Christians began to sing the hymn just as enthusiastically as their brothers and sisters in America did.

One day a missionary who was on furlough in the United States called to see Fanny. He told her about a little blind girl whom he had met in Korea. "She does not write hymns," said he, "but she uses her wonderful voice to sing them for others to hear. And they call her 'little blind Fanny Crosby,' because she sings your hymns with all her heart. People come for more than a hundred miles just to hear her sing: "Praise Him, praise Him, Jesus our blessed Redeemer."

We may be sure that Fanny Crosby felt very happy when she heard about the little blind singer over the sea who was using her hymns to sing the gospel story into the hearts of her fellow men.

Another of Fanny Crosby's best-loved hymns came to be written this way: Mr. Doane, a gentleman who composed sacred music, said to her one day, "I have a tune that I should like to have you write words for."

He played the melody softly, and Fanny said, "That seems to be saying, 'Safe in the arms of Jesus.'" She hurried to her room and there she wrote the beautiful words which we sing in his hymn.

Sometimes the blind hymn writer visited missions in crowded cities and spoke to the poor people who assembled there. One hot August evening she attended the services at the Bowery Mission in New York City. Although unable to see the audience, she felt that she was addressing some young man who had been reared in a Christian home but had wandered far from its teachings. At the close of her address she said, "If there is a lad here tonight who has wandered away from his mother's teachings I should like to meet him after the service." Sure enough, a boy about eighteen years old came forward, and said, "Did you mean me?" He told her that he had promised his dying mother to meet her in heaven, but that now he was a guilty sinner, unprepared to die. Fanny talked long and earnestly with him; then they knelt to pray. She did not leave him until he knew that his sins were forgiven. After going home that night, she wrote the words of this familiar hymn:

> *Rescue the perishing, care for the dying,*
> *Snatch them in pity from sin and the grave;*
> *Weep o'er the erring one, lift up the fallen,*
> *Tell them of Jesus, the mighty to save.*

This hymn is numbered among the five most famous of her writings which are sung in many lands. The others are: "Blessed Assurance, Jesus Is Mine!" "Pass Me Not, O Gentle Savior," "Safe in the Arms of Jesus," and "Saved by Grace."

One evening a traveler in the Sahara Desert heard a familiar melody floating to him from a distant campfire around which sat a group of rough-looking Bedouins. He had been dreading the prospect of spending a night in the desert among these fierce men, but when he heard their song he urged his camel along with all possible persuasion; for the men were singing one of Fanny Crosby's hymns! However rough-looking they were, he knew that they had come into contact with Christianity and that their hearts had been touched by the love of God.

Fanny Crosby lived to be ninety-four years old. In all, she wrote over eight thousand hymns. Some of them will never cease to be sung to the end of time. She died on Friday morning, February 12, 1915. The following is a poem which truly depicts Fanny's outlook on life from beginning to end:

NEVER GIVE UP

Never be sad or desponding,
If thou hath faith to believe,
Grace, for the duties before thee
Ask of thy God and receive.
Never give up, never give up,
Never give up to thy sorrows,
Jesus will bid them depart,
Trust in the Lord, trust in the Lord,
Sing when your trials are greatest,
Trust in the lord and take heart!

FANNY CROSBY

Author Of Elsie Dinsmore

MARTHA FINLEY

Martha Finley was born on April 26, 1828, in Chillicothe, Ohio. She was the daughter of Dr. James Brown Finley and his wife and first cousin, Maria Theresa Brown Finley. The Finleys, who were of Scotch-Irish bloodline, were descendants of two famous leaders. Samuel Finley, Martha's great-uncle, had been president of Princeton Theological Seminary and Martha's grandfather had been a general in the War of 1812 and the Revolutionary War, and was a personal friend of George Washington.

Martha had three older sisters and one younger brother. At the age of eight Martha moved with her family to South Bend, Indiana. Here mother died when she was quite young. Her father remarried a kind and caring widow named Mary, who had two daughters and a son. Mary was instrumental in young Martha's life and nurtured her desires to become a writer.

While in Bend, Martha received her education in the form of private schooling. She spent one year at a boarding school in Philadelphia. Then, in 1851, misfortune hit her once more, taking the life of her beloved father. What was life to be like now, with neither father nor mother? She was a professed Christian and knew that God would be by her side—be a father to the fatherless.

Though now an orphan, Martha's bright and cheerful disposition left little room for feeling sorry for herself. Not being one for wasting time, Martha served as a school teacher from 1851-1853. She moved to New York for a short time to live with an older sister, then traversed to Philadelphia to stay with her stepmother. Eventually, she made her way to Phoenixville, Pennsylvania, where she taught school for a year. Martha devoted much time to serving her many friends, as well as the local Presbyterian Church.

In 1853 Martha began her literary career by writing a newspaper story and a small book published by the Presbyterian Board of Publication. She spent most of her life in the service of the church, writing Sunday school material for girls. She was dedicated to writing uplifting literature, which came to be widely known across the country. Martha wrote nearly one hundred highly moralistic volumes for young girls. Her most famous series was Elsie Dinsmore.

When Miss Finley wrote her first "Elsie" book in 1867, she was an invalid and living in poverty. She used her nieces as models to create her fictionalized account of a devoted, motherless Southern heiress named her fictionalized account of a devoted, motherless Southern heiress named Elsie Dinsmore. Elsie's simple womanliness and devotion to Christ reflects the heart of Miss Finley.

The Elsie Dinsmore Series swept the country by storm. For over forty years Miss Finley sold more books than any other juvenile author of her day, with the exception of Louisa May Alcott. Because of the strong Christian content that surfaces throughout Elsie's life, Miss Finley was blackballed. She was ignored by contemporary critics and by such popular children's magazines of her day as St. Nicholas and Youth's Companion.

Despite being rejected by the critics, she was extremely popular and successful among her readership. In fact, Elsie Dinsmore was originally written as a single volume, but because of the readers' demand for "more," Martha continued writing.

In 1876, she visited some relatives in Elkton, Maryland and loved the area so much that she decided to stay. She lived in a spacious house with beautiful grounds, and here is where she finished the "Elsie" series.

At the peak of her popularity, her books were estimated to have been read by twenty-five million readers on both sides of the Atlantic, and to have earned her close to a quarter of a million dollars. Finally, in 1905, after forty-eight years of writing "Elsie" books, Miss Finley ended the series. Four years later, the little pleasant-faced, white-haired woman, departed from this world.

Though she did not have children of her own, she left a legacy of true devotion to the daughters of America, by the bright example of her writings of which were over one hundred.

When speaking about her first publications, Miss Finley remarked, "Elsie was sent out with many an anxious thought regarding the reception that might await her there. But, she was kindly welcomed, and such has been the favor shown her ever since. May my readers who have admired and loved her as a child find her still more charming in her fresh young girlhood; may she prove to all a pleasant companion and friend; and to those of them now treading the same portion of life's pathway, a useful example also, particularly in her filial love and obedience."

ELSIE DINSMORE

CHAPTER NINE

Her father's arm was around her, and she had been standing silently, through her mind, and the little heart going up in prayer to God for him and for herself.

"What is my little girl thinking of?" he asked presently.

"A good many things, papa," she said, raising her face, now quite peaceful and happy again. "I was thinking of what you had just been saying to me, and that I am so glad I know that you love me dearly; and I was asking God to help us both to do His will, and that I might always be able to do what you bid me, without disobeying Him," she added simply; and then asked, "May I say my lesson now, papa? I think I know it quite perfectly."

"Yes," he said, in an absent way; "bring me the book."

Elsie brought it, and putting it into his hands, drew up a stool and sat down at his feet, resting her arm on his knee, and looking up into his face; then in her sweet, low voice, she repeated slowly and feelingly, with true and beautiful emphasis, the chapters he had given her to learn; that most touching description of the Last Supper, and our Saviour's farewell address to His sorrowing disciples.

"Ah! papa, is it not beautiful?" she exclaimed, laying her head upon his knee, while the tears trembled in her eyes. "Is not that a sweet verse, 'Having loved His own which were in the world, He loved them unto the end?' It seems so strange that He could be so thoughtful for them, so kind and loving, when all the time He knew what a dreadful death He was just going to die; and knew besides that they were all going to run away and leave Him alone with His cruel enemies. Oh! it is so sweet to know that Jesus is so loving, and that He loves me, and will always love me, even to the end, forever."

"How do you know that, Elsie?" he asked.

"I know that He loves me, papa, because I love Him, and He has said, 'I love them that love me;' and I know that He will love me always, because He has said, 'I have loved thee with an everlasting love,' and in another place, 'I will never leave thee, nor forsake thee.'"

"But do you think you are good enough, daughter, for Jesus to love you?"

"Ah! papa, I know I am not at all good. I have a very wicked heart, and often my thoughts and feelings are all wrong, and Jesus knows all about it, but it does not keep Him from loving me, for you know it was sinners He died to save. Ah! papa, how good and kind He was! Who could help loving Him..."

Daughters
of
Purpose

"She looketh well to the ways
of her household, and eateth
not the bread of idleness."

Proverbs 31:27

For The Want Of A Bible

MARY JONES

Mary Jones was born in 1784, in a small village called Llanfihangel, lying in a picturesque valley on the southern side of Cader Idris, Wales.

When she was ten years old, she first went to a Sunday-school which had been started in a village two miles off, and there soon committed to memory whole chapters of the Bible.

The poor Welsh people in those days did not know any English, and there were very few Welsh Bibles, and these were very expensive indeed. The nearest whole Bible which Mary was allowed to read was in a farmhouse a mile or more from her home. Little Mary visited that farmhouse a great deal that she might read the precious book. But the one thing she desired more than anything else was that she might have a Bible of her own. For that purpose she saved every penny that came into her possession, and great was her joy when, at last, she thought she had enough money to buy one. But she was told that no copy of the Welsh Bible could be had nearer than Bala, where the Rev. Thomas Charles might have one, though even that was doubted. Mary, however, determined to try to get one. Mary rose with the dawn one morning, and walked thirty miles barefooted—carrying her rustic shoes which were to be put on when she reached her journey's end. She reached Bala late in the evening. She had been told to go first to the house of a poor but highly respected Methodist preacher of the name of David Edwards. He was much touched and interested when she told him the object of her journey.

"Well, my dear little girl, it is too late to see Mr. Charles tonight," he said. "He always retires to bed early, but he rises in the morning with the earliest dawn. You must sleep here tonight, and we will go to Mr. Charles as soon as I see light in his study window tomorrow morning, so that thou may reach home before night."

Accordingly, the next morning, the good man roused the little stranger at earliest dawn, and together they went to Mr. Charles's house. There was light in the study window; the clergyman was up and at work with his books. When they knocked at the door he came to it himself.

Edwards having explained the object of their early visit, Mr. Charles asked Mary many questions, and was surprised to find how much she knew about the Bible. He asked how she could have learned so much of it by heart when she did not possess one. When she told him of her constant visits to the farmhouse, and how she had tried to carry away in her memory what she read there, and how she had treasured up her pence and halfpence in the hope of being able one day to have one of her own, he was much affected.

"It truly grieves me," he said to Edwards, "to see the little girl come all the distance from Llanfihangel here to buy a Bible, and I without a Bible to give her. The last supply of Welsh Bibles I received last year from London has been all sold out months ago, excepting a few copies I have kept for friends whom I must not disappoint. The society in London, which has for years supplied Wales with Bibles, has now positively refused to print for us a single copy more. What I shall do for Welsh Bibles for my country again I know not."

Upon hearing this, poor Mary began to cry very bitterly. Was all her labor to be in vain? Would she have to return without the precious book for which she had saved so long and walked so far?

In spite of his obligations to other friends, Mr. Charles felt that he could not let poor Mary go home thus disappointed.

"My dear child," he said, "I see you must have a Bible. Difficult as it is for me to spare you one, it is impossible to refuse you."

Mary's joy was now so great that she could not say a word, but her eyes shone with delight and gratitude, and the good clergyman understood.

"If you, my dear girl," he said, "are glad to receive that Bible, truly glad am I also to be able to give it you. Read it and search it diligently, and treasure up its chapters in your memory, and be a good girl.

"David Edwards," he went on with emotion, "is not such a sight as this enough to melt the hardest heart; a girl, so young, so poor, so very intelligent in the Bible, compelled to walk all the distance from Llanfihangel to Bala to get a Bible? From this day I can never rest until I find out some other means of supplying the crying wants of my country for the word of God."

And the good clergyman worked harder than ever for that end. Often, very often, when making his appeals for help, he related the story of Mary's brave struggle to obtain a Bible, and this aroused much sympathy and enthusiasm for the cause he advocated. He wanted to found a society to supply Wales with Bibles and Testaments; but, one day, when he had been appealing for this, and ended as usual with telling the meeting about Mary Jones, a venerable man made the suggestion: "Mr. Charles, if a society for Wales, why not a society for England, and for the whole world?" And that led to the establishment of the great British and Foreign Bible Society—all because of Mary Jones and the want of a Bible.

The Stormy Night Rescue

GRACE DARLING

Tumultuous waves crashed against the North Sunderland lighthouse one dismal September night in 1838. The heavens blew forth such a ferocious wind that even Grace Darling's usually cheery face looked as grim as the sea. She was not afraid of peril to herself, for the faithful lighthouse stood strong and firm enough to brave the worst of storms. But as the white sea spray crashed against the walls, even to the high lantern, she thought of the poor fishermen at sea, and of the troubled women in the villages round about, whose hopes might even now be buried under the raging waves. Her own father and mother were also listening uneasily.

The land in which the Darling's lived was the largest of the Farne Islands, off the main shore of Northampton, England, and neighboring Holy Island. The Darlings were the only residents on the island. A half-dozen smaller islands surrounded them, all part of the Farne Islands, which were merely the tops or heads of a rocky mountain rising out of the deep sea. At daylight, it was safe to sail between these Farne Islands to the mainland, but at night, it was advised not only to sail outside them, but to keep a great distance. When the wind arose, it would wash with great violence between the small islands, where many vessels were wrecked.

"It's an ill night here, isn't it, father?" said Grace, a young woman of twenty-three. "Listen to the wind. I am glad you're not a sailor in such weather."

"It'll be an ill night for many a good ship out yonder," said Mr. Darling. "I trust there's no one between this and St. Abb's Head, or it's just like some will never see or know of it more." And the keeper wandered off restlessly to check if his light glowed its brightest to warn of its whereabouts, and to wonder how far its rays could pierce through such a thick sea fog.

But there was a large, handsome steamship beating and battling out yonder. It had started from Hull, and was sailing to Dundee, swiftly with wind and tide, until the blue sky had darkened suddenly. The wind had roused itself angrily, and just at the worst of the tempest, the unfortunate discovery was made that the steam-engine had failed and was no longer at the command of the helmsman, but at the mercy of the Almighty.

The Forfarshire drifted and tossed all night, till at the dawning rose the fearful cry of "Breakers!" The sailors saw the raging waves boiling and foaming and frothing over the stones; and yet, they could do nothing to hinder her headlong rush towards the dreaded Farne rocks, which lay in wait to waylay and destroy her. At length she came with a crash upon them. Then came another mighty roar and rush, and another wave struck her off the rocks, and down, down she went in very deep waters.

Many of the sailors managed to cram into a boat, which was later picked up by a ship. The passengers—fathers, mothers, and children—were left to save themselves. They clung to a cleft in the rock, shivering and begging for God's deliverance, while all the while the cruel rain beat, and the waves threatened to tear them away from their one poor chance of life.

More as a matter of habit than anything else, Mr. Darling, the keeper, went out and took a survey of the still rough waters. He noticed the rock and its load of human figures, but it was far over the seething waves, and in his boat he dared not venture.

He, with his daughter, rushed down to the beach, and looked at the crude boat. Mr. Darling shook his head despairingly. "Nay, lass; I could not row it alone, in such weather, much less get those miserable creatures aboard," he cried.

But, Grace would not despair. "Father, father, we must try," she urged. "We cannot let those poor souls yonder perish. Come! I can, I will, help you now. Let us try. Let us do our best; and the good Lord be with us, that we may save them."

Her father gave consent and while tying a little plaid shawl over her head to keep the wind from deafening her, Grace leaped into the boat, and seized an oar. They both bent to their work, sober and silent. It was a desperate task—an old man and a slight girl—to cross the rough frothing waves that lay between them and the trembling group clustered on the slippery weed-covered rocks beyond.

What an intense watch it must have been when once the poor creatures saw the approaching boat, and ascertained that those two rowers were coming to their aid! How those failing hearts must have revived; how those white lips must have muttered prayers and blessings on the noble pair.

In spite of tossing waves, and angry spattering foam, the old lighthouse keeper and his only daughter held their way. They were both drenched to the skin, and very, very weary, but they neither paused nor doubted. The chilly repellant wind blew fiercely into their pale faces, but with eyes and hearts fixed on the desperate group yonder, they rowed as for their own lives, on and on. They did not dwell on the thought that their return journey would be even more dangerous than this. For it was only at ebb-tide that the boat could pass between the islands, and the tide would soon be flowing. All this the lighthouse keeper and his daughter knew too well, but they never lingered or paused even to look back at the warmth of light flickering in the window of their home.

Their noble venture turned into a successful one, for the steamship's nine passengers were somehow dragged off the rock and stowed in the little boat. The peril was past, and there were some able to aid the rowers, or that laden boat could never have returned.

Once more Grace and her father were in Longstone Lighthouse, and with those they had saved from the very jaws of death. For some time yet the storm raged too fiercely for any one to be able to depart, but, without even a thought that her heroic deed would make her name a household word, the girl tended the rescued with bright smiles and sympathetic words. Brave, kind, womanly Grace Darling! When the world, heard of her doing, they praised and thanked her. Grace wondered and blushed at everyone's enthusiasm, saying she had only gone to the rescue because she could not bear to stay safe at home when poor folk were drowning.

The Life-saver Of Lime Rock Lighthouse
IDA LEWIS

Ida Lewis, "the Grace Darling of America," was born February 25, 1842. She was fifteen when her parents, Captain Hosea and Idawalley moved to Lime Rock Lighthouse. Ida had attended the public schools of Newport, Rhode Island, but her father became paralyzed, and she was obliged to use the oars to bring all the supplies to the lighthouse, and row her brothers and sister to and from school. Hence she became an expert rower, and was as fearless on the ocean as others on the land.

In the fall of 1858, the sixteen year-old won a place among the brave, by rescuing four young men from drowning, when their pleasure-boat had been upset through recklessness. Eight years after, when Ida had barely reached the age of Grace Darling, she rescued a drowning soldier from the neighboring fort.

In 1867 she rescued three Irishmen who were out in a boat after a sheep which was drifting out to sea. Their skill and courage failed them, and surrounded by the white-capped billows they were powerless to reach the shore. She took the men off their sinking boat and safely rowed them to shore. She then returned to rescued the sheep! Two weeks after, a man's boat had sunk, leaving him up to his neck in water, while the rising tide was threatening to engulf him. Once again, Ida came to the rescue.

On the evening of the twenty-ninth of March, 1869, at about five o'clock, Ida was sitting in her favorite seat beside the fire, finishing some work before the preparation of the family's supper. Her mother, looking out to sea, spied a sailboat suddenly capsize. One young man had already drowned, but the two remaining men were clinging desperately to the overturned boat. Mrs. Lewis rushed toward her daughter, and shrieked out the awful news.

Ida only caught the words, "drowning men," and was already upon her feet, prompt and eager for action. All thought of the warmth and safety within had vanished now. She had no shoes upon her feet, no hat upon her head, no outer garment to protect her slight figure from the storm. A towel was hastily seized, and knotted loosely about her neck. Her stocking-clad feet were bruised by the sharp rocks and stones, as she sped her way to the ever-ready boat. A younger brother, at her request, went with our heroine, to assist in dragging in the drowning men. But to Ida's practiced hand, and to Ida's willing arms, were trusted the plying of those oars, upon whose dexterous use depended, under Providence, the saving of the lives now so sorely threatened. Never before were those hands so tried, nor the strength of her woman's arm so tested.

As the green billows, crested with foam, flying over the open boat, drenching its occupants to the skin, and every instant threatening their destruction, Ida pulled bravely though. It is all Ida could do, and she did it well. The race for life was accomplished, the drifting wreck overtaken, and the two exhausted men, soldiers from Fort Adams, added new laurels to Ida's wreath of well-earned fame. Once in a place of safety, they speedily reached the lighthouse, where Sergeant Adams was barely able to totter up to the house, while his companion was so far gone that their united strength was required to remove him from the boat.

So ends the story of our heroine's exploits,— deeds worthy of emulation, which, in the grand old days of classic Greece and Rome, would have gained the applause of senates, and been perpetuated through the sculptor's marble, and upon the historian's tablet of brass, to ages yet unborn.

A silver medal and a check for one hundred dollars were awarded Ida from the Life-Saving Benevolent Association of New York. In the General Assembly of her native State, Rhode Island, resolutions in acknowledgment of her valuable services were passed, and communicated to her in due form by a document from the Secretary of State, and with the State seal affixed. The officers and soldiers of Fort Adams sent their thanks, and a purse of two hundred and eighteen dollars; and letters from all parts of the country, with various gifts, were forwarded to her, indicative of her fame as a heroine. Thousands came to the Lime Rock Lighthouse to see her; among them the vice-president of the nation, Mr. Colfax. And when President Grant visited Newport, he solicited an interview with her, with the same spirit of regard for her heroism. On the 4th of July, 1869, her fellow-townsmen presented to her a beautiful boat, to honor her for her self-sacrificing deeds of bravery.

Tragedy Turned To Triumph

ANNE HUGHES

Anne Hughes was born in a Welsh valley, and her father was an elder of the little church on the hillside close by. While tending her father's cattle as they grazed on the mountain-land, she would knit stockings, and create figurines out of the nature around her.

While visiting the pretty seaside town, Aberystwith, one day with her mother, the wonderful books in the bookseller's shop excited her admiration. How she longed to have money that she might be able to buy a book. At last, she really did possess a penny of her own, and then she walked ten miles to Aberystwith to buy a penny book. So she bought "Bob, the Cabin-boy," and with it walked all the way home again.

That sort of thing was repeated again and again, as pennies came into the little maiden's hand. She soon acquired a nice little library of her own. These books gave her much food for thought. As often as she could be spared from 'minding' the cows, Anne attended the village school, and was taught by the schoolmaster, who was proud of his best scholar; for, in spite of her interrupted attendance, Anne rose to the top of the school.

When she was fourteen years old an accident befell her, which might have spoiled her whole life if she had not had a truly brave spirit. There was a small woolen mill in the village; so small indeed that the master only employed one man and a few boys, amongst whom he worked himself. One day Anne was sent there with a parcel of wool from her father's own little mountain sheep, which was to be made into yarn for knitting. Unfortunately, the manager happened to have gone to tea, and the boys left in charge of the place, instead of minding their work, were having a game of play. Anne stood still and watched the machine, which was called the 'devil,' tear up and card the wool and fling it about. How strange it was! Deeply interested, she drew nearer to watch more closely. She never thought of danger; but, suddenly, her right hand was caught by the iron teeth of the terrible machine.

Poor Anne! Her arm was drawn in and crushed to pieces. She would have been killed, but just at that moment the strap which connected the machine with the water-wheel outside the building slipped off its place, making the machinery come to a sudden stop.

The boys coming back to their neglected work soon after, found the poor girl lying senseless on the floor. When she recovered consciousness, although she realized that she had lost her clever right hand and the greater part of her arm, Anne's first thought, was for her mother, a most tenderhearted woman in very delicate health.

Anne was carried home; doctors came and consulted over her sad case. The shock was indeed terrible for her mother. The arm, of course, had to be amputated. It was before the days of chloroform; but Anne bore the pain bravely. She was a true Christian, and her trust in Christ helped and comforted her in her time of trouble.

Then came long months of pain and helplessness. The village people were very kind and ready to help the brave, patient girl in any way in their power. But, as she lay there, Anne resolved that she would make the best of her life, even if she had only one arm. She, who had always taken such delight in helping all who needed assistance, had no wish to be now a burden on others. She must try and make her left hand do the work which the right had done.

So she learned to wash and dress herself and arrange her silky black hair, help her poor failing mother in her household duties, cook, and do almost all the work with her left hand. But more than that, after much patient practice, she found she could write very neatly indeed with her left hand. Her mother, however, never recovered the shock which Anne's accident had occasioned her. When Anne was nearly seventeen, after having been in a decline for two years, Mrs. Hughes fell ill of typhus fever. In her delirium, all her talk was about little girls who have but one arm, asking Jesus to feed them with enough bread.

Anne caught the fever and was ill, too; but just before her mother died, she called for Anne, and the poor girl came to her bedside. It was a touching meeting. The mother gave her crippled daughter a last blessing, and committed her to the care of her eldest brother. Then the mother died; and Anne slowly regained her strength. She found life dreary enough for a time without her best friend, but still she bravely set to work to train and educate her left arm to greater usefulness.

A short time after Mrs. Hughes death, Anne's father married again. Her eldest brother, mindful of his mother's charge, resolved that Anne should have a better education than the village could afford her, and so he paid for her to be a whole year at a school in Aberystwith. After that, Anne returned home, and remained there until she was twenty-one; but then returned to Aberystwith to open a school of her own. Was it not a great thing for a one-armed girl to do?

Pupils flocked to her; for there was quite an enthusiasm about the brave young villager who was so cheerily fighting the battle of life against what most would call such fearful odds. The villagers back home were proud of their Anne for her victories and accomplishments.

Anne found that she must take lessons herself in the higher branches of education, that she might more worthily fill her new position. And so, learning and teaching busily, her house was the home of an immense amount of true energy and life. Because of her perseverance and lack of self pity, Anne Hughes' life was a benefit to many.

Heroism On The Darkest Day

MARY McCANN

It was the fifteenth day of June, in 1904. A small sixteen-year-old girl sat gazing out a window in the convalescent ward of the hospital on North Brother Island, in New York harbor. With nothing else to do, she often would peer out onto the waters of East River, and watch the ships of all nations bring their cargoes to the great metropolis of the New World. As far as her eyes could see, everything and everyone was busily engaged in their various occupations—the great steamships hauled passengers and freight to and fro; tall sailing vessels leisurely cruised by; and an endless stream of vans and people bustled about on the bridge above.

This was all intensely interesting to the little immigrant girl in the great hospital, for she had but lately arrived in America from Ireland. She had come to this country a little more than a month before. Shortly after landing in the New World, she had been stricken with scarlet fever and taken to the hospital. She was now nearly recuperated, and was greatly enjoying the sight of the busy vessels on the river.

Suddenly, there was the clang of the fire-alarm. Again it sounded. Looking about to see the cause, she saw a great excursion steamship, the General Slocum, headed for the island. The boat was crowded with little children and their mothers. From all parts of the vessel flames were pouring and hissing. The panic-stricken passengers were rushing to and fro. Everything was in the utmost confusion. Mothers were rushing about, with their little ones clasped closely in their arms, seeking a means of escape from the burning steamship. The crew members were endeavoring to quiet the passengers, but their best efforts could not prevail against the frightened women and children. Just a short hour before, these passengers had embarked on the boat, anticipating a day of relief from the summer heat at a neighboring pleasure resort.

Young Mary McCann saw all this in a brief glance, and knowing that the stricken passengers would need the help of everyone, even of a sixteen-year-old girl, just risen from a sick-bed, she rushed to the beach. The first one she saw in need of assistance was a small boy struggling in the water, half drowned, and almost ready to give up the battle for life. Shouting a word of cheer, she rushed into the river, seized the child and turned to battle her way back to the shore. Reaching the beach, this heroic girl bundled her prize in a provided blanket, and giving the child to a bystander, she turned again to her duty. The top deck of the steamship had by this time given way and crashed down on the ill-fated passengers, throwing some of them into the water, while others were pinned down to be consumed by the angry flames.

The steamer was now a mass of roaring, hissing flames. The nearby waters were filled with shrieking and drowning men, women, and children, who had chosen a death by water rather than by fire.

Undaunted by the fearful sight, the brave girl-heroine again rushed into the debris-strewn water. Out in the stream, further away than the first little victim, another little boy was feebly struggling against the terrible odds. His strength was failing fast when she reached him. Grasping his arm, she turned to the shore. Impeded by her clothing, choked by the dense smoke of the burning wreck, she fought her way, inch by inch back to safety. Hands reached up from beneath the water in their last death struggles grasping for a hold. Drifting timbers from the wrecked steamer buffeted them, but shielding the little boy as best she could, she struggled on until she reached the shore. Leaving the boy to kindly hands there, she again started on her heroic work of rescue, though almost exhausted.

As Mary stepped into the water, the little lad called after her, "Please save my little brother. He is out there."

Utterly regardless of her weakened condition and of the terrible risk that she was taking, Mary rushed into the midst of the wreck-strewn river to another gasping boy, and brought him to the shore through the terrible mass of wood and blackened bodies. Again and again this heroic little Irish immigrant labored to snatch these endangered lives from the hands of Death.

The burning of the steamer General Slocum was the scene of innumerable deeds of heroism and self-sacrifice. Men released their hold on floating wreckage to give women a chance for their lives. Young girls calmed their frenzy of fright to tear from their own bodies the life-saving belts and bind them about babies whose cries touched their hearts in that awful hour—the young, unknown heroines sinking in sacrifice to the bottom.

The work of rescue was carried on for hours, until all the living were dragged from the water, or their bodies recovered. The General Slocum was a complete wreck, beached on the shore of North Brother Island.

The world stood aghast, horror-stricken, at this fearful accident that cost nearly one thousand lives, while the numerous deeds of daring and heroism thrilled the hearts of the nations. Heroes in every walk of life may be found on the roll, and the record of the darkest day in the history of New York harbor is brightened by golden letters which tell of high courage and self-sacrifice.

But none were nobler than those of the sick, little Irish immigrant girl. Mary McCann, was called to the House of Representatives where she was honored by the United States Government. They presented her with a gold medal as a mark of appreciation of her high courage and daring.

CHAPTER TEN

Daughters of Vision

"Her children arise up, and call her blessed; her husband also, and he praiseth her.

Many daughters have done virtuously, but thou excellest them all.

Favor is deceitful, and beauty is vain: but a woman that feareth the LORD, she shall be praised.

Give her the fruit of her hands; and let her own works praise her in the gates."

Proverbs 31:28-31

They Call Her Blessed

A woman is seen in her most sacred and dignified character as wife and mother. She has great influence over the character of individuals, over the condition of families, and over the destinies of empires. It is a fact that many of our noblest patriots, our most profound scholars, and our holiest ministers, were stimulated to their excellence and usefulness by those holy principles which they derived in early years from devoted mothers.

It is usual to affect some degree of astonishment when we read of men whose after fame presents a striking contrast to the humility of their origin; yet we must recollect that it is not ancestry and splendid descent, but education and circumstances, which form the man.

Our mothers are our earliest instructors, and they have an influence over us, the importance of which, for time and eternity, surpasses the power of language to describe.

It is the mother who first discerns the inborn gifts and talents of her child, and she too, is the quickest to encourage and draw them out. Many eminent and useful men have been able to trace their success to a mother's insight into their capabilities, as seen in the following examples:

ST. AUGUSTINE

"If I am Thy child, only God, it is because Thou gavest me such a mother."

THOMAS CARLYLE

"My dear mother, with the truthfulness of a mother's heart, ministered to all my wants, outward and inward; and even against hope, kept prophesying good . . . My kind mother did me one altogether invaluable service; she taught me, less indeed by word than by act and daily reverent look and habitude, her own simple version of the Christian faith . . . My mother, with a true woman's heart, and fine, though uncultivated sense, was in the strictest acceptation religious. The highest whom I knew on earth, I here saw bowed down with awe unspeakable before a Higher in heaven: such things especially in infancy, reach inwards to the very core of your being."

COLERIDGE

"A mother is a mother still, The holiest thing alive."

THOMAS EDISON

Thomas Edison, another inventor whose discoveries have contributed much to the efficiency of our times, likewise had a mother with a vision. After he had been at school for three months, his teacher sent him home, claiming he was too stupid to learn. His mother took over the task of teaching her son, and later in life he declared that his mother's faith in him and her patience in helping him to learn, were largely responsible for his achievements.

ROBERT FULTON

The mother of Robert Fulton, the inventor of the steamboat, early visualized what her boy's possibilities were. "I grew up under the care of my blessed mother. She developed my early talent for drawing, and encouraged me in my visits to the machine-shops of the town." Because Robert was a poor pupil at school, his teacher complained to the mother, who gave this far-sighted answer, "My boy's head, sir, is so full of original notions that there is no vacant chamber in which to store the contents of your musty books."

"I was only ten years old at that time," said Fulton. "My mother seemed to be the only human being who understood my natural bent for mechanics."

GLEANINGS

"If I were asked to name one principle that seemed to have an almost universal application, it would be this one—show me the mother and I will show you the man!"

GEORGE HERBERT

"The influence of a good mother is worth more than a thousand school-masters."

SAM HOUSTON

Sam Houston's mother was an extraordinary woman. She was distinguished by a rather tall and matronly form, a fine carriage, and an impressive and dignified countenance. She was gifted with intellectual and moral qualities, which elevated her, in a still more striking manner, above most women.

Her life shone with purity and benevolence, and yet she was nerved with a stern fortitude, which never gave way in the midst of the wild scenes that checkered the history of the frontier settlers. Her husband died, leaving Mrs. Houston with the heavy burden of caring for their six sons and three daughters on her own. But she was not a woman to succumb to misfortune. She made ample provision for their future care and education. To bring up a large family of children in a proper manner is, under the most favorable circumstances, a great work. There is no finer instance of heroism than that of one parent, especially a mother, laboring for that end alone. "The excellent woman," says Goethe, "is she who, if her husband dies, can be a father to her children."

WASHINGTON IRVING

"The happiest part of my happy life has been my mother."

ANDREW JACKSON

Incidents drawn from the early life of the seventh President of the United States, will prove with striking clearness the lasting influence of a mother's teachings.

The massacre at Warsaw by the blood thirsty Tarleton was one of the darkest periods of the Revolution. The British prison pens in South Carolina were crowded with wounded captive patriots. It was at that time that an elderly woman was seen moving among the hapless prisoners, relieving their wants and alleviating their sufferings. This woman with the strongly marked Scotch-Irish countenance, had come the great distance, alone and on foot, through swamps and forests, and across rivers, from a border settlement, on this errand of compassion.

After her work of charity and mercy had been finished, she set out alone and on foot, as before, upon her journey home. She sped on, thinking doubtless of her sons, and most of all of the youngest. He was a bright and manly little fellow whom she had watched over and trained with all of a mother's care and tenderness. The way was long and difficult. The unbridged streams were cold. The forest was dark and tangled. Wandering from her course, weary and worn with her labors of love and pity, she sank down at last and died.

That woman who gave her life to her country and humanity was the mother of Andrew Jackson, and that youngest son, her especial pupil, was the seventh president of the United States. He had lost his father when an infant. His early training devolved upon his patriot mother, from whom he also inherited some of those marked and high traits of character for which he was afterwards so, conspicuous. She was an earnest and devoted Christian woman, and strove, like the mother of Washington, to glorify God as much in the rearing of her children as in the performance of any other duty.

She taught Andrew the leading doctrines of the Bible, in the form of question and answer, from the Westminster catechism. These lessons he never forgot. In a conversation with him some years since, says a writer, "General Jackson spoke of his mother in a manner that convinced me that she never ceased to exert a secret power over him, until his heart was brought into reconciliation with God."

Just before his death, which occurred in June, 1855, he said to a clergyman, "My lamp is nearly out, and the last glimmer is come, I am ready to depart when called. The Bible is true. Upon that sacred volume I rest my hopes of eternal salvation, through the merits and blood of our blessed Lord and Savior, Jesus Christ."

If the saints in heaven are permitted to look from their high habitation, upon the scene of earth, with what holy transport must the mother of Andrew Jackson have beheld the deathbed triumph of her son. The lad whom she sent to an academy at the Warsaw meeting-house, hoping to fit him for the ministry, had become a man, had filled the highest elective office in the world. Now an old man, Jackson was able in his last earthly hour, by the grace of God providing his early pious instruction, to challenge death for his sting, and to shout "victory" over his opening grave.

AMOS LAWRENCE

Amos Lawrence, the 17th century American colonizer and Philanthropist, always spoke of his mother in the strongest terms of veneration and love, and in many letters to his children and grandchildren, are found messages of affectionate regard for his mother, such as could have emanated only from a heart overflowing with filial gratitude. Her form, bending over his bed in silent prayer, at the hour of twilight, when she was about leaving him for the night, was among the earliest and most cherished recollections of his early years and his childhood's home.

ABRAHAM LINCLON

"I remember my mother's prayers—and they have always followed me. They have clung to me all my life."

"All that I am or hope to be I owe to my mother."

FRANCIS MARION

General Marion was once a plodding young farmer, and in no way distinguished as superior to the young men of the neighborhood in which he lived, except for his devoted love and marked respect for his excellent mother, as well as his exemplary honor and truthfulness. These qualities marked his character through life.

DR. McLEOD

"There are no men or women, however poor they may be, but have it in their power by the grace of God to leave behind them the grandest thing on earth, character; and their children might rise up after them and thank God that their mother was a pious woman, or their father a pious man."

D. L. MOODY

"All that I have ever accomplished in my life I owe to my mother."

SERGEANT S. PRENTISS

From his mother Mr. Prentiss inherited those more gentle qualities that ever characterized his nature—qualities that shed over his eloquence such sweetness, and gave to his social intercourse such an indescribable charm. A remarkably characteristic anecdote illustrates his filial affection. When on a visit to the North, after his reputation had become wide-spread, a distinguished lady, of Portland, Maine, took pains to obtain an introduction. She visited a steamboat in which she learned he was to take his departure in a few moments.

"I have wished to see you," said she to Mr. Prentiss, "for my heart has often congratulated the mother who has such a son."

"Rather congratulate the son on having such a mother," was his instant and heartfelt reply.

This is but one of the many instances in which the most distinguished men of all ages have been proud to refer to the early culture of intellect, the promptings of virtue, or the aspirations of piety, and to the other's early training.

DEAN STANLEY

"Nothing can ever make my mother's memory, other than the greatest gift I ever received!"

DANIEL WEBSTER

Daniel Webster's childhood home was in a log-cabin on the banks of the Merrimac, in a sequestered portion of New Hampshire. Here he passed his boyhood and youth, and received from his admirable mother those lessons which formed his mind and character, and fitted him for that great part which he was to play in public life. She recognized the scope of his genius when she gave him the copy of the Constitution on a pocket handkerchief. She pinched every household resource that he might go to Exeter Academy and to Dartmouth College, as if she had had a prophetic vision that he would come to be called the defender of those institutions which his father fought to obtain. And when in after years he had grown gray in honors and usefulness, he was wont to refer with tears to the efforts and sacrifices of this mother who discerned his great capacity and was determined that he should enjoy the advantages of a college education.

It is the affectionate and noble ambition of many other pioneer mothers, besides Mrs. Webster, which has secured to their sons the benefits of a thorough academical training.

BENJAMIN WEST

In one of the forest homes on the skirts of civilization in Pennsylvania, Benjamin West, the greatest historical painter of the last century, first showed to his mother's eyes the efforts of his infant genius. On a summer's day when the little painter was but a child of seven, he made a picture of a smiling babe. This caught his mother's delighted eyes and she covered him with her kisses. Years after, when Benjamin West was the guest of kings and emperors, when praised for his work, he would recall his mother's caresses and say, "my mother's kiss made me a painter."

Mother's Empire

The queen that sits upon the throne of home, crowned and sceptered as none other ever can be, is mother. Her enthronement is complete, her reign unrivaled, and the moral issues of her empire are eternal. "Her children arise up, and call her blessed."

Unruly, at times, as the subjects of her government may be, she rules them with marvelous patience, winning tenderness and undying love. She so presents and exemplifies divine truth, that it reproduces itself in the happiest development of childhood—character and life.

Her memory is sacred while she lives, and becomes a perpetual inspiration, even when the bright flowers bloom above her sleeping dust. Scotland, with her well-known reverence for motherhood, insists that "An ounce of mother is worth more than a pound of clergy."

Napoleon cherished a high conception of a mother's power, and believed that the mothers of the land could shape the destinies of his beloved France. Hence he said in his laconic style: "The great need of France is mothers."

The ancient orator bestowed a flattering compliment upon the homes of Roman mothers when he said, "The empire is at the fireside." Who can think of the influence that a mother gives in the home, and not be impressed with its far-reaching results! What revolutions would take place in our families and communities if all mothers were fully consecrated to the welfare of the child and the glory of God.

There is one vision that never fades from the soul, and that is the vision of mother and home. No man in all his weary wanderings ever goes out beyond the overshadowing arch of home. Let him stand on the surf-beaten coast of the Atlantic, or roam over western wilds, and every dash of the wave and every murmur of the breeze will whisper, home, sweet home. Set him down amid the glaciers of the North, and even there thoughts of home, too warm to be chilled by the eternal frosts, will float in upon him. Let him rove through the green, waving groves, and over the sunny slopes of the South, and in the smile of the soft skies, and in the kiss of the balmy breeze, home will live again.

John Randolph was once heard to say that only one thing saved him from atheism, and that was the tender remembrance of the hour when a devout mother, kneeling by his side, took his little hand in hers, and taught him to say "Our Father, who art in Heaven."

Fathers, mothers, let the home go with your children to Jesus,— let it go with them at every step, to cheer them in every struggle, until from the very crest of the cold wave that bears them from you forever, they shout back their joy over a home on earth, that helped them rise to a home in Heaven.

The Controlled Mother

Be gentle. That does not mean to be spiritless. It means to be the opposite of violent, irritable, ill-tempered, and moody. Study to be so, for your own soul's sake, and as if you lived in God's presence, always keeping down every movement of anger, irritability, ill-temper, or moodiness. And be gentle,—precisely because you have much to do, much to bear, many cares to burden you, many things which continually try your temper.

Be low-voiced. It is wonderful what effect a mother's gentle manner and low voice—when she teaches, or corrects, or praises—will have on a band of children. Take a school-room filled with very young boys or girls. Let their teacher be nervous, fidgety, and irritable; you will see all these little ones thrown into a ferment and fever and agitation, which is nothing more than a kind of disorder which they catch from the teacher's manner. Let her be loud-voiced, teaching or speaking in loud, quick, nervous tones, and it is ten to one but you will see within a few minutes all these children becoming restless, talkative, inattentive, and ungovernable. Now, let some quiet, gentle, calm-mannered, and low-voiced person come in, and all these children will become quieted, will listen, and be ready to give their whole attention to what is said. And they will work steadily as long as the calm eye is on them and the gentle, low voice is directing them.

You will spare yourselves and your dear ones much trouble and much unhappiness by laying this lesson to heart. You can do what you like with them—if you are perfectly self-controlled. Besides, what a service you do them; and how they will bless their mother in afterlife for having taught them this gentleness!

Be patient—not only when you are suffering from aching limbs and head and heart, but when you do not succeed in making your dear ones all that you would wish. They will learn more than you think. They profit much more than you can see by your lessons, and especially by your example. Even should son or daughter of yours turn out to be every thing but what you trained them to be, the memory of their gentle, patient, loving mother will remain in their souls to their dying day, like a silent voice from the past bidding them return to God

and to the paths of their childhood.

Some say that steel beaten into its proper form and given a keen edge while cold, is more apt to preserve both form and edge forever. So is it with the temper your patient gentleness will impart to your children's souls. And this firmness, which is only one of the most precious dispositions of true manhood and womanhood, will be both of infinite value to them and of indispensable necessity.

A Mother's Opportunity

Mothers, you are the divinely-appointed teachers and guides of your children. And any attempt to free yourselves from your duty is in direct opposition to the will of God. If you neglect them, the consequences are swift and sure. Broken-hearted mothers bow in anguish over their lost sons; who, neglecting them in childhood, have at last seen them dead to every manly virtue.

Let me say to you who still have the opportunity to do so, train your children, whether boys or girls, to usefulness. Give them something to do. And as soon as they can walk, teach them to bring any little thing to you, and as they grow older, let them do all they can to help you. Spend most of your time with your young children. Sleep near them; attend to washing and dressing them; let them eat at the table with father and mother; read, talk, play, walk with them; be their companion and guide in all things and at all times. When the father can leave his work to take a little recreation, let him take it with the children, making it a special holiday. Don't be in haste to send them to school, but teach them at home. Oral instruction can be given while you are doing your work, and for a while will be of much more benefit than many hours of study.

As soon as they want playmates, see that they have those of their own age, who have been well cared for at home, and are truthful. Let them play in or near the house, that you may observe the character of their intercourse.

Always allow your children to tell you all that has happened to interest or annoy them while absent from home. Never think anything which affects the happiness of your children too small a matter to claim your attention. Use every means in your power to win and retain their confidence. Do not rest satisfied without some account of each day's joys or sorrows. It is a source of great comfort to the innocent child to tell all its troubles to mother who lends a willing ear.

For as soon as they cease to tell you all these things, they have chosen other confidants, and therein lies the danger. O mother! this is the rock on which your son may be wrecked at last. I charge you to set a watch upon it. Be jealous of the first sign that he is not opening all his heart to you.

Boys who are thus cared for and trained find more to please and amuse them at home than away. They are thus saved from temptation. But if they are neglected until they arrive at the age when they would wish to go out evenings, there is small hope that any but arbitrary measures will prevent or secure obedience, and then it hardly can be called obedience. It is much more pleasant to apply the "ounce of prevention" than the "pound of cure" in such cases. When boys know that their society is valued highly at home, and that all its pleasures are marred by their absence, they will willingly stay if they can have something to occupy their time.

Care And Affection

On the battlefield, in many terrible battles during our late horrible war, I always noticed that those boys who had been reared under the tenderest home culture always made the best soldiers. They were always brave, always endured the severe hardships of camp, the march, or on the bloody field most silently, and were most dutiful at every call. They resisted the frightful temptations that so often surrounded them, and seldom returned to their loved ones stained with the sins incident to war. They were always kind and polite to those whom they met in the enemy's country. Under their protection, women were always safe. How often I have heard one regiment compared with another, when the cause of the difference was not comprehended by those who drew the comparison! I knew the cause—it was, the home education.

The same is true every day in the busy life of the city. Gather one hundred young men in our city, and spend an evening with them, and you will know their home education. Watch them as they approach young ladies, and converse with them. You will know who has been trained under the influence of home affection and politeness, and who has not.

Affection does not beget weakness, nor is it effeminate for a brother to be tenderly attached to his sisters. That boy will make the noblest, the bravest man. That young man who was accustomed to kiss his sweet, innocent, loving sister night and morning as they met, shows its influence upon him, and he will never forget it. When he shall take some one to his heart as his wife, she shall reap the golden fruit thereof. The young man who was in the habit of giving his arm to his sister as they walked to and from church, will never leave his wife to find her way as best she can. The young man who has been taught to see that his sister had a seat before he sought his, will never mortify a neglected wife in the presence of strangers. And that young man who always handed his sister to her chair at the table, will never have cause to blush as he sees some gentleman extend to his wife the courtesy she knows is due from him.

Mothers and daughters, wives and sisters, remember that you have the making of the future of this great country, and rise at once to your high and holy duty. Remember that you must make that future, whether you will or not. We are all what you make us. Ah! throw away your weakening follies of fashion, and soul-famine, and rise to the level where God intended you should be, and make every one of your homes, from this day, schools of true politeness and tender affection. Take those little curly-headed boys, and teach them all you would have men to be. They will be just such men, and will go forth to bless the world, and crown you with a glory such as queens and empresses never dreamed of. Exercise your power now, and you shall reap the fruit in your ripe age.

They Who Mold The Men Of Story

Oh! these are they who mold the men of story,

These mothers, ofttimes shorn of grace and youth,

Who, worn and weary, ask no greater glory

Than making some young soul the home of truth;

Who sow in hearts all fallow for the sowing

The seeds of virtue and of scorn for sin,

And, patient, watch the beauteous harvest growing

And weed out tares which crafty hands cast in.

Women who do not hold the gift of beauty

As some rare treasure to be bought and sold,

But guard it as a precious aid to duty—

The outer framing of the inner gold;

Women who, low above their cradles bending,

Let flattery's voice go by, and give no heed,

While their pure prayers like incense are ascending

These are our country's pride, our country's need.

ELLA WHEELER WILCOX

The Hand That Rules The World

Infancy, the tender fountain,

Ever may with beauty flow;

Mother's first to guide the streamlets;

From them souls unresting grow—

Grow on for the good or evil,

Sunshine streamed or darkness hurled;

For the hand that rocks the cradle

Is the hand that rules the world.

Mother, how divine your mission

Here upon our natal sod!

Keep, oh, keep the young heart open

Always to the breath of God!

All true trophies of the ages

Are from mother-love impearled,

For the hand that rocks the cradle

Is the hand that rules the world.

Blessings on the hand of mother!

Fathers, sons and daughters cry,

And the sacred song is mingled

With the worship in the sky—

Mingled where no tempest darkens,

Rainbows ever gently curled;

For the hand that rocks the cradle

Is the hand that rules the world.

Mothers The World Needs

"Mothers with courage; mothers who pray,

These are the kind the world needs today.

Mothers who think, who study and plan;

Mothers who laugh as much as they can,

Having the gift that is better than money—

The habit of seeing that some things are funny.

Mothers whose faith never wavers or falters;

Mothers whose spirits the world never alters;

Loving the right and scorning the wrong;

Facing the problems of life with a song.

Mothers whose bravery transcends their fears;

Winning the battle with patience and tears;

Never submitting to weakness or sin—

Storming heaven's gates till the children are in.

Mothers heroic, not guilty of whining;

Hands graced with service and faces with shining.

Mothers of purity, virtue and faith,

Steadfast in life and triumphant in death;

Looking beyond the dark pathway of sorrow,

Seeking a home in God's joyous tomorrow,

Leading the children; pointing the way—

These are the mothers, the world needs today!"

KATHRYN BLAKBURN PECK

True Loveliness

My mother's face is wrinkled now,
And not so soft and fair,
And silvery threads are shining where
There once was jet black hair;
But when I see the love light shine
From out her dimming eyes,
It seems but a reflection from
The gates of paradise.

Her hands, once soft and lovely,
Are thin and aged now;
But oh, how many, many times
They've soothed some aching brow.
They might not seem so lovely if
Their shape alone you see,
But oh, I know their deeds of love—
They're beautiful to me.

Her steps are feeble, faltering,
That once were firm and light.
How many steps her feet have made
By day as well as night!
She may seem old to others—not
So beautiful to see;
But she'll always be the loveliest
Of all on earth to me.

ANONYMOUS

Mother's Elbows On My Bed

I was but a youth and thoughtless,
As all youths are apt to be;
Though I had a Christian mother
Who had taught me carefully,
But there came a time when pleasures
Of the world came to allure,
And I no more sought the guidance
Of her love so good and pure.
Her tender admonitions fell
But lightly on my ear,
And for the gentle warnings
I felt an inward sneer.
How could I prove my manhood
Were I not firm of will?
No threat of future evil
Should all my pleasure kill.
But mother would not yield her boy
To Satan's sinful sway,
And though I spurned her counsel
She knew a better way.
No more she tried to caution
Of ways she knew were vain,
And though I guessed her heartache
I could not know its pain.
She made my room an altar,
A place of secret prayer,
And there she took her burden
And left it in His care.
And morning, noon and evening
By that humble bedside low,
She sought the aid of Him who

Best can understand a mother's woe.
And I went my way unheeding,
Careless of the life I led,
Until one day I noticed
Prints of elbows on my bed.
Then I saw that she had been there
Praying for her wayward boy,
Who for love of worldly pleasure
Would her peace of mind destroy.
While I wrestled with my conscience,
Mother wrestled still in prayer,
Till that little room seemed hallowed
Because so oft she met Him there.
With her God she held the fortress,
And though not a word she said,
My stubborn heart was broken
By those imprints on my bed.
Long the conflict raged within me,
Sin against my mother's prayers.
Sin must yield for mother never
While she daily met Him there.
And her constant love and patience
Were like coals upon my head,
Together with the imprints
Of her elbows on my bed.
Mother-love and God-love
Are a combination rare,
And one that can't be beaten
When sealed by earnest prayer.
And so at last the fight was won,
And I to Christ was led,
And mother's prayers were answered
By her elbows on my bed.

UNKNOWN

My Mother's Hands

Such beautiful, beautiful hands!
They're neither white nor small,
And you, I know, would scarcely think
That they were fair at all.
I've looked on hands whose form and hue
A sculptor's dream might be,
Yet are these aged, wrinkled hands,
More beautiful to me.

Such beautiful, beautiful hands!
Though heart were weary and sad,
These patient hands kept toiling on
That children might be glad.
I almost weep, as looking back
To childhood's distant day,
I think how these hands rested not
When mine were at their play.

Such beautiful, beautiful hands!
They're growing feeble now;
For time and pain have left their work
On hand, and heart, and brow.
Alas! alas! the wearing time,
And the sad, sad day to me,
When 'neath the daisies, out of sight,
These hands will folded be.

But O, beyond this shadowy damp,
Where all is bright and fair,
I know full well these dear old hands
Will palms of victory bear;
Where crystal streams, thro' endless years,
Flow over golden sands,
And where the old grow young again,
I'll clasp my mother's hands.

ANONYMOUS

I'd Rather

I'd rather be a mother
Than anyone on earth,
Bringing up a child or two
Of unpretentious birth.

I'd rather tuck a little child
All safe and sound in bed—
Than twine a chain of diamonds
About my foolish head.

I'd rather wash a smudgy face
With round, bright baby eyes—
Than paint the pageantry of fame,
Or walk among the wise.

MEREDITH GRAY

Mother

Mid life's commotion—dismal fears—
Mid cares and woes, and floods of tears,
How sweetly breaks upon the ear
Some word of comfort or of cheer;
Yet of our friends there's not another
Who speaks as gently as our mother.

Here disappointments crowd each day,
Our brightest hopes soon fade away,
And friends long trusted oft deceive;
We scarcely know whom to believe,
Yet, though we fear to trust each other,
We are not afraid to trust our mother.

Yet here where there's so much deceit,
Some friends we have we love to meet;
There's love we know that will endure,
Not sordid, selfish, but all pure;
But though beloved by sister, brother,
There's none that love us like our mother.

Among the names to mortals given,
There's none like mother, home, and heaven;
For home's no home without her care;
And heaven, we know she will be there;
Then let us, while we love each other,
Remember and be kind to mother.

E. L. CASSANOVA

Mother! Mother!

"Mother! Mother! watch and pray,
Fling not golden hours away!
Now or never, plant and sow,
Catch the morning's earliest glow.

Mother! Mother! guard the dew,
While it sparkles clear and true.
No delay! the scorching noon
May thy treasures reach too soon.

Mother! point them to the sky,
Tell them of a loving eye,
That more tender is than thine,
And doth ever on them shine.

Mother! lead them soon and late
To behold the golden gate;
When they long to enter there,
Lead them to the Lamb by prayer.

Mother, seize the precious hours,
While the dew is on thy flowers!
Life is such a fleeting thing,
Mother! Mother! sow in spring."

SELECTED

Mother's Sacrifice

She gave the best of her life, with joy, for me;

She robbed herself with loving heart, unstintingly.

For me, with willing hands she toiled from day to day;

For me, she prayed, when headstrong youth would have its way.

Her loving arms, my cradle once, are weary now;

And time has set the seal of care upon her brow,

And though no other eyes than mine their meaning trace,

I read my history in the lines of her dear face.

'Mongst gems of Him who showers gifts on shining sands,

I count her days as pearls that fall from His kind hands.

ANONYMOUS

Benediction

May the blessings of thy God blow gently upon thee and the sun of glory shine around thy head; may the gates of plenty, honor, and happiness be always open to thee and thine.

May no strife disturb thy days, nor sorrow distress thy nights, and may the pillow of peace kiss thy cheek, and pleasures of imagination attend thy dreams; and when length of years consumes thee, and the curtains of death gently close round the scene of thy existence, may the angels of God attend thy bed, and take care that the expiring lamp of life shall not receive one rude blast to hasten its extinction; and, finally, may the Savior's blood wash thee from all impurities and prepare thee to enter into the land of everlasting felicity.

Bibliography

American History in Verse (1932)

Conquering the Wilderness (1883)

Girl Stories of Great Women (1930)

Hero Tales from American History and Home Life (1909)

Heroines Every Child Should Know (1908)

Historic Girls (1887)

Mother Home and Heaven (1878)

Noble Lives and Brave Deeds (1906)

Queenly Women Crowned and Uncrowned (1885)

Some Brave Boys and Girls (?)

Stories of Hymns We Love (1934)

Ten American Girls from History (1917)

The Mirror of True Womanhood (1877)

The Royal Path of Life (1876)

True Stories of Our Famous Men and Women (1898)

Women on the Frontier (1876)

Heartfelt Thanks to:

Daddy, for this whole idea,
and for motivating me to go through with it.

Josh Wheeler, Doug and Beall Phillips, Al Mendenhall,
and Mike McCoy, for your help and support in this project.

Abbe Riebel, Mark and Terri Fisher, Esther Class and
Sigbrit Bakke, for your expertise in proofreading.

Joshua Goforth.
Without your sacrificial time and dedication,
this book would never have been successfully completed.

My Lord and Savior Jesus Christ.
My entire existence I owe to You.

"It is of the LORD'S mercies that we are not consumed, because His compassions fail not. They are new every morning: great is Thy faithfulness."
-Lamentations 3:22-23